Stepping Further

A Comprehensive Guide to Applying to University in the U.K.

Previously published...

- Maths and Calculator skills for Science Students

  March 2016

- Maths (The Chemistry bits) for GCSE Science

  May 2016

- Science revision Guide   April 2017
- Maths Revision Guide   April 2017
- Summer Start for A-Level Chemistry   May 2017
- Atoms, Electrons, Structure and Bonding Workbook

  June 2017

- GCSE Maths Grade 7, 8 and 9 Revision Questions

  September 2017

- 75 Long answers questions for GCSE science

  March 2018

Coming soon...

- A-Level chemistry workbook
- A-Level biology workbook
- Organic Chemistry Workbook
- Maths for A-Level Chemistry
- Summer Start for A-Level Physics

Chances are if you want a maths/science book I've written it or I am writing it.

For full book listings visit www.PrimroseKitten.com and follow @primrose_kitten

Acknowledgements

Thank you to my husband for putting up with my spending every night writing this.
To my sons for being the inspiration behind Primrose Kitten.
To KG for being a very patient and dedicated editor.

To every single subscriber and follower, you are the reason this book exists.

A large amount of research has gone into checking the accuracy of the information in this book, the constantly changing nature of the application system means that some of this information may be out of date. You should check with UCAS and the individual universities for the most up to date information. The author cannot be held liable for any actions taken based on the information in this book.

Table of Contents

Introduction

Applying to university is a massive step. The decisions that you make now will determine your future and shape the direction that your life takes for the next three to four years.

I've been guiding students through the UCAS application process for years now, and with this comprehensive guide I intend to share with you as much information as I can.

The first step to this complicated puzzle is finding the right course at the right university. Do you need a bachelor's degree, an honours degree? Do you need a foundation course or a sandwich course? Are you looking for a city university or a campus university? Student finance is complicated, so you also need to consider the costs of living and tuition fees and ask yourself whether you can afford to go to university.

Over the course of this book, I will advise you on how to write successful personal statements. Along the way you'll learn what to write, what not to write, what admissions tutors are looking for (and what they hate), and what is going to guarantee that you end up in the reject pile straight away.

We'll go over what universities are looking for, so you will know the specific entry requirements for all the different degree subjects. We'll cover everything an aspiring university student needs to know, including: What are the application procedures for medicine? Do you need the BMAT or the UKCAT? What are UCAS points and how do they work? What are natural sciences and liberal arts? What are some university courses that you may not have considered? The list goes on, but worry not! I'm going to talk you through how to prepare for interviews and cover all the different routes you can take into university, including A-Level and non-A-Level routes. And then we'll cover the most important part: what to do on results day!

How Do U.K. Universities Work?

Universities here in the U.K. are different from those in America, in Europe, and in the rest of the world.

Unlike in the U.S. and mainland Europe, U.K. universities only infrequently offer liberal arts degrees. New students are required to pick one subject, or maybe two subjects in rare cases, and then study that one subject in depth for two, three, four, five or six years. Recently there has been a move to reduce the time that it takes to two years to reduce the cost. Alternatively, you can change a three-year course into a four-year course by adding on a work placement, starting with a foundation year. Alternatively, you can extend it even further if you want to add a master's year in the end. Degrees in medicine and law can be six years long, and you can start these at 18. There is no need to do a separate undergraduate course beforehand; you can do law or medical degrees straight after high school.

The applications are all made via a centralized system, known as the UCAS system. If you want to apply for medicine, veterinary science, or any course at Oxford or Cambridge, that needs to be done by mid-October for a September start the following year. If you are going to apply to other universities or subjects, then that needs to be done by January for starting in September the same year.

Tuition fees are paid yearly in the U.K. At the moment the fees for home students are up to £9,250 a year. For international students, they can range anywhere between £12,00 for a lecture-based course up to £20,000 a year for a practical or a lab-based course. The teaching is going to be a mixture of lectures, with class sizes ranging from a few students up to a couple of hundred students. Small tutorials with a professor will be smaller, and are going to be probably less than five students. In some cases, your degree will include practical work, where you are going to be in a large lab with students and a few post-graduate student supervisors. Some examples of practical work projects include lab time for a computer engineering project, a mechanical or civil engineering project, or an architecture project.

There is no extensive scholarship system in the U.K. The universities are very, very popular, so they do not need to use scholarships to entice people to come to them. Teaching is generally for thirty weeks of the year and usually Monday to Friday, but this does vary from university to university. Oxford and Cambridge, for example, teach on a Saturday but have long holidays. Conversely, some universities are having shorter holidays so that the overall length of the course is shorter, thus making it cheaper. Oxford, Cambridge, and Durham also have a collegiate system, where you apply to a specific college that you wish to attend, not the overall university. With this system, most of your time is spent in the college, not in the broader university environment.

The final grade you are going to get at the end is either going to be a 1st, a 2:1 (upper second), a 2:2 (lower second), or a 3rd. This is going to be based on a mixture of things, but mainly your end-of-year exams. Your first year will not count for too much, so only about 10% of your first-year exams will go to your final grade—but you will need to pass your first year so that you can progress on to the second year. Your second-year exams will count for between 20 and 40% of your overall grade, and then your final-year exams, whether that is your third or your fourth year, will count for anywhere from 50% to 70%. Universities will generally provide you with accommodation, but only for your first year. After that, you are expected to go and find lodging with friends.

Student Finance

Tuition Fees

Now that we've introduced them, it should be noted that tuition fees in the U.K. have become rather controversial. Working out how much you'll pay in tuition fees in the U.K. is a complicated mix of where you come from, what university you attend, what year you're in, and what type of course you are taking.

Home students are British and other European Union citizens, and the level of fees the university charges these home students is regulated by the government. These can change on a yearly basis according to the university rating in the Teaching Excellence Framework (TEF). The TEF gives grades of gold, silver and bronze to successful universities, which allows them to raise fees in line with inflation.

If you do a sandwich course—taking a year away from the university—then you'll probably be able to pay a reduced level of fees for that year even though you'll have very little to do with the university during your time away.

For international students, I'm afraid there are no guidelines or limits when it comes to fees. It is a free market, and the universities can charge whatever they think they can get away with charging. This ranges from £12,000 a year for a lecture-based course up to £25,000 a year for practical courses like science, computer science, architecture, or medicine.

If you're an international student, your fees may vary depending on what year you are currently enrolled in. For example, if your first year is lecture-based, your payment may be on the lower end of the spectrum; once your courses become more practical-based (for example, if your final year is completely lab-based), then your fees may be much higher in the last year than they were in the first year.

Home Students Fees

Home Location	University Location	Fees
England	Anywhere in U.K. or E.U.	£9,250
Scotland	Scotland or rest of E.U.	£0
Scotland	Rest of U.K.	£9,250
Wales	Anywhere in U.K. or E.U.	£9,000
Northern Ireland	Northern Ireland or rest of E.U.	£4,160
Northern Ireland	Rest of U.K.	£9,250

Can You Afford to Go to University?

Attending university is a massive investment. Not only is it three, four, or five years of your life, but it also costs tens of thousands of pounds. The other question, however, is whether you can afford *not* to go to university? You should also consider how much do you have to pay upfront, and what your options are if you can't get a job afterward.

Many students worry about tuition fees and whether or not they can afford university. I'm sure you've heard loads and loads of horror stories about the amount of debt you'll be in if you go to university, so I'm going to break things down and make things as transparent as possible for you.

While you're at university, there are going to be two main areas where your money will go: tuition fees and living costs. You can get a loan toward your tuition fees of up to £9,250, depending on where you live and what course you're taking. You can get a further loan to cover your living costs, as well. The tuition fee loan is paid straight to university, so you won't have to deal much with that, but the living cost loan is paid straight into your bank account, likely on a per-term basis.

The loan to cover your living costs will depend on what type of course you're taking; whether you're doing a teaching course or a medical course; what kind of background you come from; whether your parents are in employment; whether you have support from your parents or partner; how much your parents and partner are earning; whether you're going to university in London; whether you're going to university outside of London; whether you're going to be living at home or living on your own. These loans only have to be paid back once you've left university and once your income passes a certain threshold, currently set at £21,000. Then you only pay it back as a percentage of your income. Interest on the amount is charged right from the beginning, and you will have to pay that off as well.

You do not have to pay for university upfront, nor do you do not have to start saving money straight away. You'll get a loan, and then you'll pay it back years later once you're earning.

Let's consider an example. We have a student whose parents are both employed. They're each making £20,000 a year, so the combined household income is £40,000, a little bit below the national average. This student will go to university full time, paying £9,250 in tuition fees, and living away from home, outside of London. They will get £9,250 in tuition fee loans each year, and then on top of that, they will also get a £4,920 loan for living costs.

This student will get roughly £14,000 in loans a year. Over a four-year course, taking into account interest, by the time you have to start paying it back, this is going to be around £60,000. It sounds like a lot of money, and it is a lot of money, but it shouldn't be scary.

Somebody who has no parental help, living and studying in London, can get up to £11,000 pounds for living costs as well as £9,250 for tuition fees. They're going to have a loan of £20,000 per year, or £80,000 after four years.

You've got massive debt when we're coming out of university, but how much are you going to pay back?

Once you start earning over £25,000, you pay it back at nine per cent of your income over £25,000. The average starting salary for a graduate is £29,000, so you pay interest on the difference between £25,000 and £29,000, that's £4,000. At nine per cent of that £4,000, this works out as £30 a month from a take-home salary of £1,690, not very much at all. Not a massive impact on your daily life. That's a takeaway pizza or going out, or a pair of shoes. If you earn less than £21,000, you'll pay nothing. You don't have to worry about paying it back at all. You only pay it back once you pass £21,000, and then you just make payments for 30 years. After 30 years, it's entirely written off. If you have a starting salary of £25,000, in 30 years, you'll have paid off about 80% of your debt, and then the rest of it will just be forgotten. It is not the horror story that the newspaper headlines are trying to make it out to be. Yes, it's scary owing £50,000 or £60,000 pounds in your early 20s—it is a lot of money, but the repayments are very manageable. It's a small amount of your take-home pay, and that level of pay might not have been available to you if you hadn't gone to university and didn't get that degree.

Costs for International Students

There are lots and lots of things you need to consider when you decide to come to the U.K. to study as an international student. The biggest chunk of the cost for you is going to be tuition fees, which can range from £12,000 to £20,000, depending on the location of the degree, whether it's an academic subject, whether it's a lab-based subject, which year of your degree you're in, and exactly the subject that you are doing.

On top of that, you're going to have roughly £9,000 living costs; these costs rise to about £13,000 if you are studying in one of the big cities like London, Oxford, Cambridge, or Edinburgh.

You need to consider your costs of traveling home, as not all universities will let you stay there over the holidays; in other words, you might be forced to go home for Christmas as your accommodation may be used for tourists during that time, so you will need to factor in the cost of traveling home three or four times a year. Communications with home might require you to get a more expensive mobile phone contract than other students. You might need to get calling card, or you might need to consider accommodation that has Wi-Fi included, as not all of them do.

The Cost of Living at University

University can be really expensive, and in addition to those expensive, you will also have the added stress of managing your finances, perhaps for the very first time. So, can you afford to go to university?

In this chapter I'm going to talk you through estimated costs for each week at university, extrapolated across each year. We will compare this value to the loan you're going to get for your living fees, and then we'll talk about what you can do with the difference.

The first thing and most important thing to consider is your accommodation. At university, there is often a wide range of accommodation available, from self-catering shared rooms to en-suite rooms which are fully catered, as well as everything in between. These rooms can go for about £100 a week up to about £200 a week, but for this example I've gone for a middle range figure about £140 a week. You can expect to spend about £30 a week on food, about £10 a week on transport, and about £5 a week on your phone. Socializing at university is pretty cheap, often for about £30 a week. And then there are all the other things, like stationary, photocopying, pens, and other items that you will need for your coursework, all of which comes out to about £5 a week. All of this together is going to come to £225 a week of living costs while you're away at university.

Estimated cost each week:

Accommodation	£140
Food	£30
Transport	£10
Phone	£5
Social life	£30
School supplies	£5
Total	£225

While the actual length of courses varies, some terms are very short, some are very long, and holidays should be factored in as well. It's roughly 40 weeks that you'll be at university, so £225 pounds a week for 40 weeks brings us out at £9,000 a year.

There are some additional expenses that you should expect as well. For example, at the start of the course you're going to need to buy some books, which will cost a few hundred pounds. For lab-based courses, you might need to buy a lab coat or equipment. You might also want to buy yourself a computer to use in your room.

All of these estimates are going to vary by person. The food cost will range depending on whether you eat meals you've made yourself or whether you eat out. Socializing would depend on how much you drink, how often you go out, and whether you go to student bars or whether you go to ones that make fancy cocktails. The transport costs will depend on whether you're living on campus—which quite a few of you will be doing for your first year, so you'll be able to walk to lectures—or whether you have to get a bus or a train to your lectures. And if some of you are studying in London, the cost of the Tube is actually quite expensive.

A few of the universities have published their estimates for living costs while in attendance. Edinburgh's estimates are between £7,000 and £13,700 a year, while Manchester's estimates are about £9,000. The NUS estimate about £13,000 in London and about £12,000 for the rest of the U.K. Birmingham says just below £9,000, and Oxford says a year there will cost you between £12,000 and £18,000.

This money is not including tuition fees. The tuition fees are in addition to these living expenses, but remember, you're going to get your tuition fee loan up to £9,250 to cover your tuition fees. As we discussed earlier, you won't see that money in your bank account, as it just gets paid straight to the university.

The living cost loan, on the other hand, is paid straight to you. For the majority of students, the living cost loan will be about £4,920 per year. This is quite different from my estimate of £9,000 a year for you to live on, which leaves you with £4,080 short over the year, or just over £100 a week, for you to find so that you can afford to go to university. You have three main options for this: parental support, getting a job while you're at university, or saving up during the holidays.

The student loans company often assumes that your parents will be giving you some money. When you apply for your student loan, you tell student finance how much parental support you will be getting, including information such as how much your parents make or whether you're in contact with your parents. If you are not going to be getting any parental support, then the level of loan you will receive will be higher, up to £11,000.

Saving up is also a possibility. You have long summer, Christmas, and Easter breaks, so you have lots of time in there to work really hard and save up money for the term ahead. If you're going to be working during the term time, the minimum wage for 18-year-olds is £5.90 an hour. To make up that £100, this means you're going to have to work 17 hours a week. The advantage of any work that you do while you're at university is that it looks really good on your CV. The disadvantage is that you won't have as much time to study and you won't have as much time to socialize.

For the majority of you, it will be a combination of all three. There might be some parental support involved, you might get a job, and you might have some savings as well. I know that I worked 15 hours a week in the university library sorting out books. It certainly wasn't the most exciting job in the world, but I did love being in the library! And then on top of that, my parents helped me out a little bit as well.

Believe it or not, the other hard part will come for when the loan is paid out to you. Because the loan is paid on a termly basis, this means that at the beginning of the term, you will have loads of money and everyone will go out that night, and the next night, and the next night, and the next night. And then towards the end of term, you won't have any money, which is when frequently my friends and I would eat 'tuna surprise'—the surprise being that we couldn't afford tuna so it was literally just pasta and a tin of tomatoes!

Budgeting is tricky, and it's especially tricky if you don't have any help with it or it's something that you've never done before. There are lots of things you can do to influence how much money you spend a university, and if you budget wisely, you can do it.

Lucy's Story - What I Wish I Knew Now

Lucy is studying Creative Writing at Bath Spa University. Her A-Level were in English Literature (B) Drama (B) and French (D)

I love my university and the course I'm studying, but there are many things I've found out along the way that I wish I had known before starting. My first two weeks in university were spent running around like a headless chicken. Due to the size and amount of the rooms the university has, I was never on time for my lectures. It took me a few weeks to familiarise myself with the layout of the university. Had I been forward thinking I would have settled into uni before the studying started. Once I received my timetable, I could have visited each lecture room and made a mental map.

I also recall arriving to university with an absolute ridiculous amount of furniture. I really wanted to make my room as comfy and pretty as I could. Looking back that could have been achieved with half the stuff I brought along. Not only were some of my purchases a complete waste of money, they were also very impractical. I really did not need a £100 coffee machine for my room. The kettle in the kitchen worked just fine. I sold my coffee machine without even using it once.

I could have saved a lot of money by taking along with me pre-prepared snacks and lunch. I barely had time during the day to sit at the university cafe for a sit-down lunch. Not only would bringing my own food along with me have been a healthier option, I wouldn't have ended up spending extortionate prices on a chocolate bar and a ploughman's sandwich.

This brings me to budgeting. With student loans coming into my bank account as a huge lump sum, I tended to overspend on things that were unnecessary. I really didn't need the same bag in three different colours. Had I budgeted I could have had a fairly comfortable student life without looking for a part-time job.

One big lesson I also learnt was to make friends. I have a close-knit bunch of friends who I've known for years, and I've never felt the need to make more friends. Whilst at university, however, making friends is simply networking. It helps to make friends with those on the same course as you, especially when it comes time to creating study groups. These friends are useful in helping you to catch up on any work you may have missed out on due to illness.

Keeping on top of your work is probably one of the most important lessons I learnt. I now write up my lecture notes in an organised manner a few hours after the lecture has finished. The lecture is still fresh in my mind and the notes still make sense. It helps me to have a head start on exam preparation.

I have also learnt that I should enjoy every aspect of university. These few years are character-building years. The good and the bad have allowed me to transform into a somewhat responsible adult.

UCAS Applications – The First Things to Think About

The Application Process

The UCAS application process is tricky, and you need to make sure you get it right because this decision determines what you do with the next three or four years of your life.

The first that you need to do—and this is not a small thing in any way—is to pick five courses you want to apply for. This is complicated; you need to think about what you're going to enjoy; you need to think about entry requirements; and you need to think about where you want to live. After you've picked five courses, you need to write a personal statement. This is going to be a big part of deciding whether you get into university or not. This is the bit that the admissions tutors are going to look at when they are making their decision whether to accept you, whether to interview you, or whether to reject you. So if you get this bit wrong, you might end up with no offers. After you've picked your five courses and written your personal statement, you can then start to fill in your UCAS application form.

You're going to need to give them your essential details, as well as student finance information if you're from the U.K. or the European Union. You're going to add your course choice, your education level, your employment history, and then you're going to write your personal statement and add in your references at the end.

Your references will be significant. This is what helps the admissions tutor decide whether you're a yes, a maybe, or a no. Please note that these references have to be submitted at the same time as your application, so you shouldn't fill in your application at the deadline because you will need to have your references from previous teachers ready and waiting. If you want to apply for medicine, veterinary medicine, or dentistry, only four of your five choices can be for those courses. This is to give you a guaranteed insurance choice in case you don't meet the entry requirements for those courses because they are highly competitive. This is also true if you want to apply for Oxford or Cambridge, as only one of your five choices can be for either Oxford or Cambridge. For example, you can't apply for Oxford and Cambridge, and then three other things. For courses at Oxford, Cambridge, medicine, veterinary, or dentistry, your application needs to be in mid-October if you plan on starting your course the following September/October. The rest of your applications need in by the deadline of the middle of January for a course beginning September of that year.

It's important to note, however, that universities will not wait to hand out offers until after the deadline. Universities start reading applications and making decisions as soon as they receive them at the beginning of September. By the time January comes around, they might have already given away a large number of their places. Just because January is the last time you can submit your application, that doesn't mean that's when you should submit your application. Get your application in as soon as possible. University admissions tutors are going to have a massive pile of admissions to go through, so you need to make sure that yours stands out, and stands out in the right way.

This is where your personal statement, your references, and your predicted grades are going to play a major factor. These three components will determine whether you are accepted straight away, whether you get asked for an interview, whether you get rejected, and whether the offer they give you is conditional or unconditional. If you get a conditional offer, you'll have to get specific grades to go into the course— whereas an unconditional offer means that they thought you were so amazing that they have accepted you no matter what your results are. Once the university has made this decision, they will notify UCAS, and then UCAS will inform you. Once you've received all of your offers, that's when you can decide which university is the one for you.

You choose one firm choice (which is where you really want to go, assuming you get the grades) and one insurance choice (which is where you want to go if you don't get the grades for your firm choice). The objective is to make sure the required grades for your insurance choice are lower than the grades for your firm choice. Then, the rest is just hard work.

On results day, you're going to need three plans: A plan for what happens if you get better results than expected, as you might be able to apply for an Adjustment higher-tier university (more on this later); a plan for what happens if you get the results that you need; and a plan for what happens if you get worse results than expected.

The UCAS Application Timescale

Applying to university is a long and complicated process. You need to get it right so that you end up in the right place.

You need to start at least a year beforehand, but if you're thinking about applying somewhere really competitive—say, Oxford, Cambridge, or a course in medicine—you need to start much, much earlier so that your UCAS application and your personal statement look impressive. Let's assume that you've done that bit, and that you've got all the work experience and all the different bits you'll need for your personal statement.

It's summertime, and school has broken up, so what I want you to do is start thinking about your university choices. Start doing a bit of research into courses and universities, and start thinking about your personal statement. The best place to start is by making a big, broad list of things about you. Don't start writing it yet, but start thinking about what sort of things you could put in there. Loads of university open days happen in June/July, so it's a great idea to go and visit the places you're interested in to see what it feels like to be there. Do you get a good feeling when you're there, or is the feeling not so great? University applications open early September, but universities do not wait around until the deadlines to start handing out places.

Remember, the earlier you apply the better, so the more organized you are, the sooner you can get your application in. That's why it's terrific to have spent the summer thinking about what course you want to pursue and which university you want to attend. All of this will help you craft a polished personal statement. You also need to start nagging your referees—and I mean gently nagging, of course! You don't want to bother them too much, but your application can't be submitted until your referees have added their reference. So even if you're super organized, and you've written your personal statement, and you're ready to go at the beginning of September, your referee may not be. That's why it is a bad idea to leave your application until right before the deadline. If you tell your teacher the day before the deadline that you want to apply to Oxford, they will have to write a reference quickly, and they may not do an outstanding job if they don't have much time. They may not even get it done at all!

The deadline for Oxford, Cambridge, Medicine, Veterinary, Dentistry is mid-October. That's mid-October the year before you start. The deadline for the rest of the courses is going to be mid-January, which is the same year that you start. If you get rejected by all five places, you can add some more on in about mid-February. Art and Design courses have slightly different deadlines, which tend to be around mid-March.

After you've received all of your five decisions, you have roughly a month to decide which one you're going to accept as your firm and which one is going to be your insurance choice. For example, if you have them all by the end of March, then you have to make your decision by the beginning of May. If you have them all by the end of May, you have to make your decision by the beginning of July.

In July, **Clearing** is going to open. If you don't have any offers and you didn't want to put any more on, then you can apply through Clearing. If you didn't apply at all the first time around, then you can also apply through Clearing. This is where the universities open up any remaining unfilled slots they have in their courses. In mid-August, we get to A-Level results day, and this is when **Adjustment** places open. If you did better than expected, you could apply for an Adjustment place, or if you did worse than expected, you might have to go through the Clearing system.

Ana's Story - What I Wish I'd Known Back When I Was Applying

Ana has A-levels in Biology (B), Chemsitry (B) and German (C). She undertook a lot of work experience at a local science start up company.

My name is Ana and I'm a student at the University of Nottingham, currently finishing off my final year of Pharmacy. As well as having experienced the UCAS application process myself, I've helped friends and family with their applications, and volunteered for the University during interview and applicant days, which has left me with lots of experience with university applications on the whole.

Now that I've been through it all, the only thing I regret is not doing more reading around before submitting my application. This was vital, especially since, at first, I was on the fence about whether or not to go to University at all. Whilst I wouldn't change a thing about the past few years and ultimately I'm happy I ended up here, it would've been nice to know what other routes there were into my chosen career path. The one thing I did do in terms of research was attend a UCAS University Exhibition day, where representatives from different subjects and universities come along to sell their course to prospective students. These sorts of events are the best ways to gauge your interest in a course or a subject matter, and attending one definitely made me certain that University was where I wanted to be.

Another thing I'm glad I researched is the individual course breakdowns once I'd decided which course I wanted to go into. Whilst many people may tell you a degree is a degree, this is only true to an extent. Different universities can teach similar subjects in very different ways. I'm definitely more suited to coursework, and it was important to me that I didn't end up doing a course where the majority of my grade was based on performance during exams. Nowadays course breakdowns are available on the University's website, but when I applied a few years ago, the information wasn't as readily available – so I phoned up and asked. While it did take a while for some departments to get back to me, it was definitely worth it.

Another thing I wish I'd done is spend a little bit more time in the cities I was considering studying in, just to see what living here would be like. At the end of the day, University isn't just about the course – essentially you're moving home, so the city around it is just as important. My course has about 30 timetabled hours per week, and during term I spend all of the rest of my time in libraries, cafes, restaurants, the gym, or out in the evenings. When I was making my choice, I focused solely on the university itself, not its surroundings, and whilst I've finally learned the ins and outs of the city, I wish I'd factored it in when I was picking between courses. Having said this, if you end up really falling in love with a university even if the city it's in doesn't quite appeal to you, you could always take public transport or taxis to neighbouring cities.

The last thing I wish I had done was pay more attention during my interview day. The people who interviewed me were the same people teaching me when I returned in September, and the building where I was interviewed was the exact same building I found myself back in during first year. Getting to know the campus a little bit better during my *interview would've made settling in during first year much less daunting*

University Courses

What Types of Courses are Available at U.K. Universities?

There is a diverse and dizzying range of courses that you can study at U.K. universities.

I'm going to take you through what they all mean. Before you pick the university to apply for, you'll need to select the type of course you're going to apply for. The most common type is going to be a Bachelor's. This can be a BA, a Bachelor's of Art, or a BSc, Bachelor's of Science. If it is a three-year course, it's going to be Bachelor's; if it's a four-year course, it's going to be a Bachelor's with Honours. This is an undergraduate course, generally three or four years, and it can be taken straight after high school.

Master's degrees come after your undergraduates. Typically they are an extra year which is added onto the end of your course; alternatively, sometimes you can take an integrated course that already has the additional year added onto the end. If you're doing a combined course, you'll probably just continue from your undergraduate Bachelor's straight onto your Master's without even noticing it. Or you can choose to switch universities for your Master's year and try somewhere new, or try something different.

Some courses also have foundation years, which is a year before the course starts. These are going to be aimed at people that want to do challenging courses like Medicine, but haven't quite got the intro requirements from their A-Levels. Foundation courses are also for international students who wish to spend their time familiarizing themselves with the country and the language before they start their studies.

Foundation degrees are much more than vocational degrees, because they will include a significant element of work experience. They can be offered through employers, and they are often two years long, but some university's offer the opportunity to add a third year onto that and turn it into a Bachelor's.

Dian's Story - What made me decide on a course to study at the university

Dian has A-Levels in maths (B), Business (D) and Art (D).

People opt to go to university for different reasons: some go because of family worth, some go simply for the fun of studying a course that they are really interested in. But if you are like me, you went to university to study for a specific career area.

I spent a very long time pondering on the 'what to study' question. I swept across from film to law, marketing to science, until I finally found Education Studies. I had spoken to my parents and friends in various occupations, as well as my teachers at school, and they offered me some really helpful insights. I also visited several lectures and discussed careers related to the various departments. Once I put all of this together, I did some research behind it, and I settled on Education Studies.

I found the Education Studies course at university because I realized that I needed a career anywhere in the realms of education. When choosing my course, I was adamant that I would be a school teacher, so I thought my course was perfect. It was a mixed course and covered a variety of topics, and it also involved practical experience in a work area of my choosing. It sounded great and it would suit me right down to a T.

I also chose it because I realized that by the end, I'd have far more career opportunities than if I had opted for the BEd course, which was my original idea. For me personally, that was a great choice because what I've been learning on my course has sparked a pastime in the areas of education and dealing with young people.

Nearly every year at university, I've met some very nice people and made good friends with people on my course. I've gotten to analyse subject areas and gain experiences that I wouldn't have had otherwise. I feel that learning education studies is a good groundwork for studying over a PGCE course to become qualified teacher.

If there's any advice that I possibly could give to someone choosing a university level course, it's think long and carefully, and make you know that you will want to be doing a similar thing by the end of those three years.

How to Pick a Course

One of the first things you need to do when thinking about attending university is picking what course you want to study. It is very important to recognize, however, that the types of courses at university can be wildly different from those you studied in school.

Even if the title of the course is familiar, there is no longer a set curriculum for universities. When you're at school, maths A-Level in one school is going to be identical to maths A-Level in another school, because there's a curriculum set up by the exam boards. This doesn't happen at university. At university, the courses are determined by the lecturers, and they're going to lecture in what they're interested in. So, a history degree at one university could be very different to a history degree at another university.

The first thing you need to do is decide what you're interested in, because you're going to be studying this for two, three, four, five, potentially even six years. That is a long time to be doing something that you're not interested in! Take a look at the subjects that you're studying at the moment, and even if the whole subject doesn't interest you, ask yourself whether or not there is one module, or one topic, or a specific part of a subject that interests you? Is there part of this subject and part of that subject that interests you? Two half-subjects that you like? Sit down and think about this. Even if it's something outside of school, or outside of the scope of what you've been taught in class that interests you, put that on your list as well. If there's anything you're doing that's extracurricular—such as setting up a business, leadership in a youth organization, or a hobby of visiting bridges all over the world—these interests may lead you to a degree subject that works for you. With the full range of degree subjects out there, chances are you're going to find a degree in it.

The next thing you need to do is think far ahead into the future. Do you have any idea what you want to be doing in five, ten, or twenty years? If the answer is no, that's fine; most people don't. But some of you do, and the courses related to those paths will provide you with a degree that will lead straight into a career. Conversely, some of you may have a particular job in mind, but there is no specific degree that feeds into that career, so we need to start thinking skills. Physics, chemistry, history, geography—these are all great degrees because of the skills they teach you. All of them involve writing reports, collecting data, analysing data, looking for patterns. The skills that these types of degrees can teach you are highly valued by employers. For example, if you want to be a spy, you can't do a degree in that, but you can do a physics degree, or a computer engineering degree, or a law degree. All of these courses teach you valuable, essential skills that employers love. People who come out with a physics degree are snapped up by employers quickly because of the fantastic things they've learned to do on the course, not necessarily because of the physics that they've learned.

After you've thought about what you enjoy, and thought about possible careers and the skills you'll need, the next step is to start compiling a long list of potential courses that can get you where you want to go. Anything that catches your eye should go on that list. There are two ways to go about this: on the Internet, or hard copy prospectuses. Believe it or not, the Internet may not be the best place to start. This is because in order to search for something on the Internet, you have to know what you're searching for—and at this stage, you might have no clue at all what you want to do. So, I'm going to suggest something a little bit old-fashioned, which is getting a hard copy of the prospectus.

Flip through the prospectus, have a look at all the course titles and the course descriptions, and see what catches your eye. It might be something surprising. It might be something you've not thought of before. It might be something you didn't know existed. Don't limit yourself too much at this stage. I want you to make a broad, long list. It doesn't matter if you've got some humanities subjects on there, some science, and then some maths. At this stage, we're just coming up with a broad list of what interests you.

Then we need to start thinking about the nitty gritty a little bit. Look at sandwich courses, placement courses, or anything that has work experience associated with it. Leaving university with work experience is going to be useful, because the job market is very competitive and anything you can do to give yourself a bit of an edge once you get out there is worth the effort. For example, I did a year's work experience between years two and four at university. I spent a year working in London, then went back and did my fourth year, and that gave me a year's work experience. It gave me that little bit of an edge when I eventually went to get a job after university.

If you can't narrow down your long list at all, think about combination courses. Bizarre combinations do exist. If you want to study sciences but you don't want to narrow yourself too much, you can consider a natural science degree. There are a few universities that offer liberal arts degrees, which are just combinations of different things. These are quite rare, but they're becoming more and more popular.

Once you've started to narrow down a course, start looking at the details. Look at the syllabus to see if there is something you love. Say you want to do English to study this particular author, or do history to explore this particular time period, or you want to do biochemistry because you love epigenetics, then look at the syllabi. They are going to tell you exactly what is taught year by year. Make sure that the things you're interested in are taught at the university, because there is no point in going to a university to study a particular topic if they don't cover it. Some universities will have an element of professional exams in there as well. For example, some universities will do the professional accountancy exams as part of the university course.

The most valuable resource that you have in deciding whether a course is going to be right for you are the people currently doing the course. Be gutsy, be brave, and go and talk to other students! If they like the university, they are going to give you their honest opinion. If they don't enjoy the university, they are also going to give you their honest opinion—believe me! Of course there's a chance that they might be rude and tell you to go away, but there's just as much of a chance that they'll be really friendly, and it is worth trying to get as much information as you can. Obviously, there are loads and loads of university YouTube vloggers, and they're going to tell you all about their university, their course, their accommodation, their UCAS experience, and so on. Do your research and get as much information as you can from many different people.

Next, we need to start thinking about matching a course with a university. If you have your ideal course and your ideal university in mind, hopefully they match up. If you have your perfect course in mind, but you hate the university, then that's bad luck. But there are so many different courses and so many various universities that I'm sure you will find something that you like.

Then we need to think about entrance requirements. When you make your five choices, you need to have a range of entrance requirements. You cannot put five options down that all have B's, because that's not very sensible. You need to have a range of conditions. Some with high entry requirements (what you're predicted to get) and some with low entry requirements (just in case it all goes a little bit wrong on results day).

Hamz's Story - Why Did I Pick the University Course I'm Doing?

Hamz is 19 and studying medicine at Cardiff University. He has A-Levels in Chemistry (A*), Biology (A), Maths (A*), and Urdu (A).

Principally, picking a university course is narrowing down the path towards what you want to do for the rest of your life and what you've dreamed of since childhood.

Like all children, I have always been inquisitive. Looking up at the sky, or observing the environment around me, I have always wondered about the correct order of things and how it all works. This drive to learn more and understand complexity has always been a part of me. However, the more I learnt, the more I realised how little I know, thus increasing my determination to learn and pick a course where learning never ends.

Growing up and witnessing people suffering and struggling around me, a part of me always wanted to help them, but I felt powerless. At the same time, watching my dad relieve the suffering of his patients and being available for people to save lives at all costs was inspiring. Looking at my dad gave me a vague abstraction about how my career choice can be beneficial for me, as well as a source to help the unfortunate and sick people around me.

What turned my vague abstraction into a much more clear and definite choice was an incident when I went to meet my grandparents in Pakistan during A-Levels. The detailed memory of the life-changing day is engraved in my brain. That day, I accompanied my grandmother for her routine check-up from her family doctor. Having been born and brought up in a developed country like the UK, I had never imagined how difficult life—or to be precise, healthcare—could be in underdeveloped countries like Pakistan. During my visit to my grandmother's family doctor, I got a chance to witness the conditions of the unprivileged people who had been waiting in the queues to see a doctor. When I enquired about it to the doctor, he explained that because of lack of resources and a low number of doctors, these people fail to receive proper medical help. This experience made me more adamant than ever to be capable enough and help these people.

After analysing and scrutinizing my interests and goals at an individual level, I decided that medicine is the perfect career for me. It quenches my thirst to keep learning and understanding the unknown along with using this knowledge in helping those less fortunate.

Accelerated Degrees

For a traditional degree, teaching terms at university take close to ten weeks. When you take into account exam weeks, reading weeks, freshers weeks, and short holidays, you'll be spending between 30 and 40 weeks a year at university. This leaves a lot of time for holiday and relaxing.

Accelerated degrees, however, skip out the long holidays and teach three years' worth of content in two years. It's exactly the same content, just taught over two years instead of three, with teaching extending into the summer holidays.

The advantage of accelerated degrees is the timespan. You can spend less time studying and get on with your career sooner, and instead of paying for three years of tuition fees, you only pay two years of tuition fees. Longer degrees, like Law, can be completed in much fewer years.

The disadvantage of accelerated degrees is their newness. The government announced them in December 2017 and the first students will start in September 2018. This means that only a few universities will be offering courses in a limited number of subjects. It is also unknown how employers will react to these accelerated degrees and how long they will be around for.

Current courses and providers:

University of Aberdeen; Law.

Anglia Ruskin University; International Business Management.

Coventry University; Digital Design Consultancy; Global Business Management; International Finance and Accounting.

University of Dundee; Law

Edinburgh Napier University; Law

University of Greenwich; Primary Education

University of Hertfordshire; Law

Leeds Beckett University; Primary Education

Leeds Trinity University; Secondary Education, Physical Education and Sport

London Metropolitan University; Early Years Education; Medical Sciences; Primary Education

Newcastle University; Medicine

University of Northampton; Management

Royal Veterinary College, University of London; Accelerated Veterinary Medicine

University of Salford; Building Surveying

University of South Wales; Law

University of Southampton; Law

Staffordshire University; English; Law; Accounting and Finance

University of Wales Trinity Saint David; Digital Marketing

University of York; Law

Foundation Years

Foundation years are fantastic things, but how do you know if they're right for you?

Foundation years are offered by a wide range of universities, and they've got two target groups in mind. The first is students who want to get on a course but don't quite reach the requirements. For example, if your A-Levels weren't quite good enough to get onto Medicine, then Medicine with a foundation year is going to have slightly lower entry requirements at some (but not all) universities. Or if you've got a BTEC or an NVQ, and things that aren't quite right on your application for a specific course at a specific university, then you can do a foundation year to boost your chances. For Medicine, getting on the foundation course generally, but not always, has lower entry requirements. For example, doing Medicine with a foundation year at Nottingham, the offer is B-B-C, compared to going straight into Medicine, which is three A's. At Manchester, however, the requirement for both the foundation course and straight Medicine is three A's. At Leicester, you need three A's to go straight into Medicine, but three B's to go into the foundation course. So getting on to foundation courses, especially for competitive subjects, is still tricky.

The other group of students who benefit from foundation courses are international students. These are students who don't have the same routes into university as students from the U.K. who have A-Levels. The teaching in the foundation year will bridge the gap between what they've done in their home country and what the university expects of them here in the UK. It gives international students a bit more time to settle in, get accustomed to the culture, and get used to being taught in a different language. For international students, it's a welcome chance to get comfortable, whereas for home students, it's an alternative route into challenging courses. Foundation years are fantastic things, but only if they're right for you.

Lofti's Story – How I Found the Right Course

Lofti has A-Levels in Art (B), RS (C) and English language (D)

The essence of the course was one of the main reasons for me to make Coventry University my first choice. Its first major advantage was how broad and open-minded the course is. Although the title is Graphic Design, the course does not end there. It allows students to give a chance to a whole range of other Industrial Design subjects such as Product Design, Illustration and even Architecture. The tutors are open to realizing common projects between the disciplines and will give you amazing help from their experience in the fields.

Its second major advantage is the chance of choosing to get in rolled on a four year Master's degree, instead of a three year Bachelor's degree. This allows students with financial difficulties to graduate with a Master's degree in the selected field, since they get a student loan for all their years, and also gives one year of work experience. In this day and age, when almost everyone graduates with a diploma, one of the most required aspects in the battle to find a job is relevant experience, which made this program a perfect choice for me. Another benefit for choosing this course is that the students are obliged to take an "Add + Vantage Class", which can be something related to the subject you are studying or it can be something you've always wanted to try. My choice for this year was studying a foreign language.

I am extremely happy with the support the tutors and lectures have provided me during the whole year. The teaching methods allow a lot of freedom, which I believe is really important when it comes to subjects of a creative nature. Also the environment turned out to be quite competitive, which motivated and gave me an additional stimulus.

The application for University is simple, simply requiring a form on the website and an English test. After they have checked the information provided, I had to go for an interview. I also submitted a portfolio including some areas from Graphic Design and Illustration and I had to write an essay about it.

Liberal Arts Degrees

Liberal arts degrees are rare and beautiful things. They are the unicorns of degrees, but not many people know about them, and not many people can find them, but they are brilliant.

Despite the name, it doesn't involve any painting or drawing. It's a mixture course; it's a make-your-own course that allows you to pick modules and units from loads of different subjects, put them all together, and make a degree that is specific to you.

You can pick from science, philosophy, history, international politics, philosophy, law, arts, languages, global development—loads of different things. You have to do a certain number of credits each year; you can't just do one module one year and then ten modules in another. There are also a certain number of modules or credits you have to do each year, but you can add in a foundation year to this. Or you can add a year abroad, where you go and study, work or volunteer in a foreign country. You can bump it up and add in a Master's year as well. It's going to be rare to find somebody else who's doing the same combinations of units, or who has added in the Master's degree or the year abroad in the same way as you, so this could give you a real edge after university because it's going to be unique.

Not a lot of universities are offering liberal arts degrees at the moment, but a few are, including:

Aberystwyth University
University of Birmingham
University of Bristol
University of Central Lancashire
University of Dundee
Durham University
University of Essex
University of Exeter
Keele University
University of Kent
King's College London, University of London
University of Leeds
University of Nottingham
Queen's University Belfast
Regent's University London
Royal Holloway, University of London
SOAS University of London
University of Wales Trinity Saint David
University of Warwick
University of Winchester

The nature of the course means that it is broad and varied, which also means that it's going to vary widely between universities. If you want to follow a liberal arts education, you're going to have to sit and go through every single university on that list. Look at precisely what modules they offer and decide which one is going to best suit you, because a liberal arts degree from one university could be entirely different to a liberal arts degree from another university. There is no set structure or set units that have to be included in this. Just because you pick a university because it has a specific set of courses, that doesn't guarantee that it's still going to have that particular set of classes and modules by the time you get there or by the time you get to the third or fourth year.

Max's Story - What Made Me Decide on a Course

Max has A-Levels in Economics (C), French (D) and PE (D).

When choosing a course to study, I took the advice of my sister, who is a third year student and is very content with her course choice. Her advice was to collect prospectuses from as many universities as I could. I picked up a bunch from college and ordered more online. With an unbelievable amount of prospectuses in front of me, I admit I was feeling over-whelmed. My sister advised me to keep it simple and go through each prospectus and jot down on a list the courses that really stood out for me. This would be my long-list, which I would then shortlist.

I realised that there are many different types of courses to study at university. There are Bachelor's degrees, Diplomas of Higher Education, NVQs, amongst many others. After reading about the differences between each type, I was certain that I wanted to complete a Bachelor's degree. This narrowed down my list quite significantly.

I sifted through the module and course content of each course on the list. This was to see whether I would enjoy studying the course content. One discovery I made whilst doing this was that, unlike A-Levels where course content is usually identical no matter where you study, undergraduate degrees vary a whole lot. Two separate universities that have a course of the same name do not necessarily share the same course content. This was an important discovery as it could potentially mean I would enjoy one course of the same name in one university but not in another.

Once I had my shortlist, I looked back on all the courses I had studied so farm, which included my GCSEs, a BTEC I had completed, and currently my A-Levels. I wanted to see if the courses I had particularly enjoyed so far shared similarities with the courses on my short-list, as a few did I paid more attention to these.

Another aspect that really helped to choose a course was the end-line. Would this course help me to achieve the career I wanted in the future? I'm one of those people who isn't completely settled on one career choice. I had a few in mind and they were pretty similar. Luckily a few courses were very flexible in that they would allow me to work towards the different careers I could see for myself. This would take the pressure off of me having to make a career decision right away.

To help me further narrow down my search to five courses (this is the maximum number of courses you can apply to), I used online course statistics. These websites are great for telling you about other peoples' general experience and opinion of each course. I was able to look at the rate of student satisfaction, academic resources given, and even things like how much of a voice students are able to express whilst completing the course. These methods in choosing a course have helped me to find a course I'm beyond happy with!

Natural Sciences

Natural science degrees are fantastic things. In my opinion, they are one of the best hybrid degrees out there. If you're considering doing science at university, then before you apply, you should definitely at least consider applying in natural sciences.

These courses are a perfect fit if you like physics and chemistry but want a bit of experience in management to help your work prospects outside of school; or if you love maths and working in the lab but also want to learn a bit about behavioural psychology; or if you can't specify which bits of science you like, but you know you just like science. They work by giving you a choice of modules for you to build your degree. With natural sciences, you can pick from biology, chemistry, physics, maths, pharmacy, psychology, and then you can add in other bits such as management, languages, and education. This enables you to build a degree around what you find interesting, not what the university has designated. You pick which modules you want to do. It is not a complete free for all. Each module is going to have its own set of intro requirements, either based on A-Level or on previous years' modules. For example, if you want to do a fourth year module that is going to be very physics heavy, but you haven't done any physics in the first, second, or third years, you're probably not going to be allowed to do that. These degrees could also come with a year abroad, and they could also have a Master's degree added at the end.

You'll end up with a degree with a major subject and a possibly a minor subject, which makes it a little bit easier to explain your specific degree to employers. If the majority of your years were in chemistry, your major will be chemistry, but then you might have enough units to have a biology minor and a physics minor. You could have chemistry with education, or chemistry with maths, or biology with physics and management—the choice is yours!

The downside to these courses is the competition. With each module, there is going to be a limited amount of space, whether that's lecture space or lab space or computer space.

It is not guaranteed that you're going to get the modules or the units that you need or want. If everyone wants to do loads of physics, some students will miss out because universities only have limited resources. So if you're going to university knowing that you want to do natural sciences, but you want it to be all physics, then it may not happen.

While natural science degrees aren't offered everywhere, they are currently offered at:

Aberystwyth University
University of Bath
University of Birmingham
University of Bolton
University of Derby
Durham University
University of East Anglia (UEA)
University of Exeter
University of Greenwich
Keele University
Lancaster University
University of Leeds
University of Leicester
Liverpool Hope University
Liverpool John Moores University
Loughborough University
Newcastle University
University of Nottingham
Open University
University of Oxford
University of Portsmouth
University of South Wales
University of Southampton
UCL (University College London)

University of Warwick
University of Winchester
University of York

Rachel's Story - How I Decided Which Course to Do

I tutored Rachel in in GCSE and A-Level Chemistry, and we talked extensively about university choices. She has A-Levels in English (B), Chemistry (A), and History of Art (C).

I made my A-Level choices based on the subjects I enjoyed, but I didn't have any idea about what I wanted to do at uni or after. I picked chemistry and maths because I enjoyed those at GCSE and did well in them. I chose history of art because I wanted to do something different and I liked the look of the units. This wasn't the best idea, because it wasn't good for getting into uni and the other people on the course were just using it as a doss subject.

When the school started talking about UCAS applications I started to panic. I had NO IDEA what I wanted to do. Jen talked to me and helped me realise a few things. I enjoyed my chemistry the most, but didn't want to study chemistry at uni, I didn't enjoy all the inorganic bits. I was good at maths but didn't think it was that interesting. Jen suggested liberal arts and it seemed like a great idea. I didn't have to decide what I was interested in now, I could wait and do that at uni. Pick units as my interests developed. I'm studying it Warwick and I'm loving all the new things I'm learning.

Vocational Courses

Vocational degrees are strongly linked to the career that you are pursuing, such as a medical degree. You cannot be a doctor unless you have a medical degree, and your medical degree trains you specifically for that one job: being a doctor. There are loads of other degrees that are vocational, including teaching, accountancy, landscape design, nutrition or game design. There's a broad and wide spectrum of vocational degrees, and if you're absolutely certain of the career that you want in the future, then this could be a very good choice for you.

Specific universities may have strong links with companies that might come in and do special recruitment at that university, or you might get to attend lectures or talks from experts within that field of work. You might also get the opportunity to shadow them on the job and get some much needed work experience. There could also be a large amount of specific training within the course.

For example, some of the accountancy degrees also incorporate your professional qualifications within the degree structure. This means that when you come out of your degree, you don't have to do the extra exams because they're all bundled in within your degree. If it is a vocational course you are thinking of following, look closely at the modules. Check that they match up with what you actually want to be doing in the future. For example, there is no point in doing a course on game design if you really want to learn a certain part of animation, and the university you're applying to doesn't teach that certain part of animation. Go and find a different university that it does teach it!

Before you pick a vocational degree, try and get as much work experience as you can. It is very important to get a real, honest feel for the profession before you start. If you change your mind partway into a vocational degree and decide that you want to do something different, it can be quite difficult to complete a vocational degree and then switch into doing something completely different. But don't worry, if you do end up changing your mind halfway through your degree, it is not the end of the world. You don't have to leave the course and start something else (which is of course an option, as any degree in itself is going to be valuable), but completing any sort of vocational degree is going to be attractive to employers. If you find yourself at the end of three, four, five, six years with a vocational degree, and you've then decided that you don't want to follow that career path, don't despair.

It is not all going to be over. There are still some very attractive skills that your degree course has taught you. You may face future questions about why you spent so long studying this one topic and then decided to go do something else. Maybe it's related, or maybe it's completely different, but as long as you can come up with sensible, logical, truthful answers for your reasoning, then you shouldn't have any problems.

The other problem with following a vocational degree and changing your mind halfway through that you might lose your motivation. You might not have the enthusiasm to study for the final exams as much as you would have if you were studying something you were passionate about.

If you are unsure about what career path you want to follow, then you should consider following a more academic career path. I know lots and lots of you are really concerned about the worth of academic degrees in today's economic climate, but you cannot assume that doing a vocational degree course will automatically get you into a job at the end. You still have to go through the application process; you still have to find jobs that are available that suit your skill sets; you still have to go through and actually get the job. There is no guarantee you'll get a job at the end of a vocational course, just as there is no guarantee that you'll be better suited to it than somebody who did an academic subject in their degree.

Anna's Story - How I Decided Which Course I Wanted to Do

Anna work very hard during year 12 and year 13, she managed to get A-Levels in Chemsitry (A), Art (B) and Spanish (B).

The one thing anyone knows about me is that I love lists. During the summer of year 12, the walls of my bedroom were covered in lists – pros and cons about the different courses and lists of qualities I have and how they lend themselves to each prospective course. When I was reflecting on what I wanted to do, I spent a week writing an A4 pages listing my strengths and weaknesses, and next to each quality I wrote which courses I thought each one was suited to. From this I figured out that I ultimately wanted a job where I was directly involved in healthcare, which led to several more lists and some difficult self-reflection—but through this process, years later I've ended up doing something I truly enjoy. Even if lists aren't your style, writing things down is a great way to sort through your thoughts and help you come to a conclusion.

Even after this process, I was still between choices for a long time—for a period of at least a few months. What helped me decide was speaking to people who had done the course and who were now working in the field. I spoke to lots of people involved in pharmacy one way or another—whether they were currently studying the subject or working in a related position. I even spoke to those who had studied it and dropped out or were now working in an unrelated career entirely. Each of their experiences helped guide me all the way from the application to the enrolment stage.

The other thing to look into is career prospects. Whilst there's nothing wrong with studying for the sake of learning, I definitely chose my degree based off prospective salary and career opportunities. If you enjoy a subject matter but couldn't see yourself doing it (or a related job) for the rest of your life, then it might be worth reconsidering your choices. University is a big step but it does have its downfalls—I couldn't possibly have worked full time whilst studying, and I didn't have help from my parents, so it proved to be very financially straining. I currently have 4 years' worth of student loans putting a dent in any future earnings as well. I tried to make a decision based on long-term benefits, so that the difficulty during my student years would be worth it.

I do want to add that if you don't want to commit yourself to just one course, or you're between very similar courses, you could always apply to more than one. The downfall is that you can only submit one UCAS application to all of your choices. I didn't do this because I was set on the course I wanted to do, and also because it's very risky. Most of the time admissions boards can tell that you're not applying directly for their course, but I know of others who have successfully done this and got it right. The key is to apply to courses that are very similar to begin with, and make sure that you write something that is applicable to all. This way, once you get to your interviews and visit the universities in question, you can make a better-educated decision on what feels right for you.

Is a Non-Vocational Course a Waste of Money?

I know lots of you are concerned that, in today's economic climate, doing a non-vocational course is a waste of time, effort and money, but that's not actually true.

Vocational training provides strong suitability for a specific job, but it can be really hard to know whether you're *actually* suitable until you start doing the job. And you can't start doing the job until you have a degree in it, and you can't apply for the degree until you've decided that you have a strong suitability for the job—which is a loop in the wrong direction!

I know some of you are potentially feeling stressed about what you're going to do in the future and you don't know what job you want, but don't worry—this is completely normal! It is completely fine at your age to not know what you are going to be doing in five years' time. It can be really hard to know what you love doing because you haven't tried everything yet. It can be really hard to say whether you have a vocation or not whether at this stage.

You may be concerned about spending time and money on a degree course that isn't linked specifically to a career, or a degree that might make it harder for you to get a job afterwards, but a degree is so much more than just something that's going to get you a job.

Any degree that you do, whether it's a vocational degree or non-vocational degree, will give you a large amount of skills that are very attractive to employers.

Take physics, for example. Physics is an academic course, not a vocational degree. If you want to go on and be a physicist in the future, then you have to do another degree, and a PhD afterwards. And then, hopefully, maybe, you can get a job as a physicist. You have to specialize even further. Physics as an undergraduate is an academic not a vocational course, but it is a very attractive course to employers because of the skills that it teaches you. For a physics degree you have to look at chaos (say, looking at a map of stars) and then be able to pick out meaningful patterns from all that jumbled data.

This is something that is attractive to lots of employers, no matter the industry. You have to be able to follow standard procedures, you have to be able to work in a large group and follow instructions. You have to be able to write analytical reports based upon evidence that you have collected. These types of skills are really attractive to places like the Home Office or MI6. Lots of lawyers come from a physics background because the same skills are involved: Writing reports based on evidence and seeing patterns within the chaos.

History and religious studies are more essay-based subjects that involve large amounts of evidence, large amounts of opinions, and making up your opinion and writing arguments based on that evidence. From many different bits of evidence (some contradictory, some missing), you have to delve deeply into your sources and do thorough research, and then you have to craft long essays where you present your argument in the most convincing fashion possible. These are great skills if you're thinking about going into journalism, or if you're thinking about going into politics or business consulting. Any degree will give you a wide number of transferrable skills.

It is very rare these days that you'll stay in one job the rest of your life. People often switch career paths, and sometimes a vocational degree can be rather limiting in the opportunities that it gives you. If you know that you want to go into business but you're not exactly sure what type of business, then you should consider undertaking a course with a major and a minor, or a liberal arts degree, as both will cover lots of topics.

Weirdest Degree Courses

Baking Science and Technology Management is a 2-year course offered at London South Bank University, Southwark Campus. Some of the aspects that are covered in the course include bakery food science, bread theory, and analysis of production management product design, packaging and flow processes, among many others. To undertake this course, one is required to have either an A-Levels at D,E,E, BTEC National Diploma MPP, and hold 5 GCSE A-C in Maths and English or an equivalent.

Brewing and Distilling is a Master's level course offered on a full-time or part-time basis at Heriot-Watt University, Edinburgh. Some of the aspects that are covered during the course study include alcohol beverage technology, distilled spirit production, and maturation, filtration and packaging of alcohol beverages and fermentation and beer maturation. To undertake this course, one must have a First or Second Class Honours Degree or an equivalent qualification in a science or engineering subject such as biological science or chemistry.

Equestrian Psychology and Sport Science is a 3- or 4-year course offered at Nottingham Trent University, at their Brackenhurst Campus. It teaches knowledge of equine behaviour, rider performance, equine-assisted therapies, equitation science and equine welfare. To undertake this course, one is required to either has A-Level at B,C,C including a science subject, 104 UCAS Tariff points from three A-Levels or BTEC Extended Diploma.

Horology is a 3-year course offered at Birmingham City University, looking at the theories behind clocks and watches, as well as new designs and materials. Aspects covered in the coursework include production techniques, specialist horological skills, introduction to horology and introduction to gemology, among others. To undertake this course, one is required to have B,B,C at A-Level, 112 UCAS tariff points from A/AS-Level.

Contemporary Circus with Physical Theatre is a 3-year course from Bath Spa University taught at Circomedia's Kingswood site in Bristol. The various aspects covered during the course study include body training, physical theatre movement, voice and creative movement, practice and evaluations and acrobatics, among many others. Tutorial, practical sessions, and formal lectures are some of the methods used while teaching the course.

Hand Embroidery for Fashion, Interiors and Textile Art is a course from the University for the Creative Arts, Canterbury, that equips students with skills necessary to do hand embroidery. Some aspects covered in this course include the introduction to technical stitches, textiles, and application in fashion, interiors and textile art. To undertake this course, a portfolio of your work is required. Additionally, 112 new UCAS tariff points, pass at Foundation Diploma in Art and Design and distinction Merit at BTEC Extended Diploma.

Surf Science and Technology is a 2-year course by the University of Plymouth at Cornwall College, Newquay. To undertake this course, the requirements are either UCAS Tariff of 48 points is required or Pearson BTEC Level 3 in an appropriate subject. Some of the aspects covered in the coursework include development, surf practices, scientific techniques and application of Computer Aided Design (CAD) in the surf industry, among others.

Cruise Management is a 3-year course, with placement opportunities, from the University of Plymouth. It teaches students with the knowledge and skills that they require for professional hospitality in cruise operations. Some aspects covered during the course study include hospitality management, cruise and maritime services, facilities and resource management and food safety for hospitality industry, among others. The following are some of the requirements for undertaking this course: UCAS Tariff of 96 points, a minimum of two A-Levels (excluding general studies), or at least 33 credits at merit/distinction for a HE diploma in any subject.

Ethical Hacking is a 4-year course from The University of Abertay, Dundee, that looks at curbing cybercrime and preventing the penetration of unauthorized people into a computer or network system. Some of the aspects that are covered in the coursework include computer networking, programming, software design, and computer hardware architecture and operating systems. To undertake this course, one should have a pass in National 5 grade c/4 or B,B,C at A-Level, including any Computer Science, Engineering, Geology, Physics, Maths or ICT is required.

Viking and Old Norse Studies is a course from UCL that focuses on the study of medieval and modern Scandinavian languages, Old Norse Literature, and medieval history to bring understanding on the Viking age. The course is offered at UCL and it takes four years when being administered on a full-time basis. To undertake the course, applicants should have A,B,B at A-Level in English Literature or History, and a language is preferred. Some of the aspects covered in the coursework include Viking and material culture, introduction to Old Norse, Nordic storytelling, and many others.

Applied Golf Management Studies at the University of Birmingham is a 3-year course that aims to equip students with the professional practices to be applied in golfing. To undertake this course, a minimum of three A-Levels which might be PE, Sports Studies, Maths, Science, or Design and technology are required. Various aspects that are covered in the coursework include equipment technology, coaching theories, and applied sports science, among others.

Fire Engineering from the University of Central Lancashire is a course that focuses on studying how fire works and the effects it has on the environment and society at large. The requirements for undertaking this course is 96 UCAS points including Maths, Physics, Chemistry, Environmental Science or Applied Science. Some of the aspects covered in the coursework include safety and fire law, energy transfer and thermodynamics, fire investigation and probabilistic risk analysis among others.

Sandwich Courses and Work Placements

This is an odd term for something that is not edible, but nevertheless useful! In fact, it could be the difference in determining whether you get a job after university or not.

I did a 'thick' sandwich course at University, but I had friends who did a 'thin' sandwich. A thick sandwich means that I spent two years at university, then I spent one year working in London, and then I came back to university for another year of study in my fourth year. My friends that did a thin sandwich course spent the first year at university, six months of their second year at university, and then six months on work placement. In their third year, they did the same: six months at university, six months on work placement, and then back to university for a whole year in the fourth year. I did one long placement, whereas other people at the same university (and doing the same course) did two six month placements. The silly term 'sandwich course' just means that your degree has an element of work experience or working somewhere else, working abroad, studying abroad or volunteering abroad already built-in to it.

The advantage to doing a sandwich course is that you get hands-on work experience. As soon as you come out of university, you have that bit of experience that you can talk about in your CV. Your placement employer might offer you a job after university, and you might get paid for your work experience. You may get to travel and live somewhere completely different. You may get to be involved in entirely new and fascinating research that you wouldn't have done if you hadn't done placement. These types of courses are frequently offered in science, engineering, business, and languages.

One of the downsides is that if you're doing a four-year course and all of your friends just doing a three year course, by the time you get back to university in the fourth year, you may find you don't know a lot of people. Now, this wasn't a problem for me because 90% of my friends were also doing four-year courses, so when we all came back to university for the fourth year, it was just like our first year. So if you know you want to do a work placement or work abroad for a bit, look for a course that has that beforehand. Remember that you can always apply to do work experience after you've started your course, but they're not always guaranteed.

Spending a Year Abroad

Spending a year of your degree working, studying, and volunteering overseas is a fantastic way to travel, get some experience, and make sure your CV stands out from the crowd.

A large number of degrees come with the chance for you to study overseas, and you can apply for a degree with a year abroad already integrated into the coursework. This opportunity gives you a fantastic experience and gives you the chance to have that little bit of an edge over people when you leave university and start to think about applying for jobs. The opportunity to spend a year abroad can be something that's integrated into your degree from the start, or it can be something that you apply for later once you start at university. If you apply for a course where it's integrated, the majority of universities will let you change your mind if you decide that you do not want to go. They are not going to *force* you to go abroad for a year!

Study abroad opportunities can be much more varied than a sandwich course where you just go on work experience. Studying abroad provides you with the chance to go and study at a university in another country, studying the same subject that you went to university to study. You can go and volunteer in a different country, or you can go and work in a different country. Language degrees offer the most obvious example of this, but it is not just limited to languages. Business, sciences, medicine, law; all of these have undeniable opportunities for you to go abroad for a year to work, volunteer, or study. There are loads of advantages to this, the main one being that in today's global economy, you are showing people straight out of university that you are a world traveller. You demonstrate that you can work with people from other cultures; that you have the experience of living and working in different places; and that you can successfully integrate yourself into a new business in modern culture. These days it is rare that a company is just going to operate locally or within one country, so they are looking for people who can work with people from a wide range of different countries.

Erasmus

This scheme has a really fancy name, and hiding behind that little name is a long name—and also a fantastic opportunity to work, travel, live abroad as part of your degree!

Erasmus stands for, get ready, the European Region Action Scheme for the Mobility of University Students. If you decide you want to work, study, or volunteer overseas during the time that you are doing your degree, and it's not integrated into your course already, then the Erasmus Scheme will let you do just that. If you're confident that you want to work abroad or study abroad, then you might want to consider *not* using the Erasmus Scheme, but rather apply instead for a course that has a year overseas already integrated into it. The reason for this is because with the Erasmus Scheme, you apply to when you're already at university on a degree course. You apply to it during your first year, but there's no guarantee that you're going to be accepted. You apply via your university Erasmus or international office, and you have to apply for something that is relevant to your course. You can't be studying architecture and apply to spend a year in Italy studying creative writing.

If you get accepted to an Erasmus course, your university will help you find accommodation while you're there. It will also help you fill in the forms, which might be in a completely different language or structured in a way you're not familiar with. Lastly, your university will help you through the process of picking modules and courses of study while you're there. An Erasmus placement can last anywhere between three and twelve months, and you can go on more than one Erasmus placement during your time. The total time that you're on placement cannot be more than 12 months, however. The exceptions for this would be extended courses like medicine or architecture, where you can spend up to 24 months on placement. If you want to apply to a school, both the university where you're currently enrolled and the college you're applying to need to be part of the scheme. You'll need to be doing your placement in your second, third, fourth, or fifth year; you cannot do it during your first year.

There is some financial support available via the Erasmus grant scheme, but the grants are competitive and not everyone will receive them. While you're on your Erasmus placement, your host university won't be charging you tuition fees, but you may still have some other associated expenses, like lab fees that you have to pay.

Even though it is called the European scheme, there are loads of countries outside the European area that are involved in this project.

Countries that can participate fully are:

Austria
Belgium
Bulgaria
Croatia
Cyprus
Czech Republic
Denmark
Estonia
Finland
France
Germany

Greece
Hungary
Iceland
Ireland
Italy
Latvia
Liechtenstein
Lithuania
Luxembourg
Malta
Northern Macedonia
Netherlands
Norway
Poland
Portugal
Romania
Slovakia
Slovenia
Spain
Sweden
Turkey
United Kingdom

Countries that have limited participation are:

Albania
Algeria
Azerbaijan
Belarus
Bosnia and Herzegovina
Egypt
Georgia
Israel
Jordan

Kosovo
Lebanon
Libya
Moldova
Montenegro
Morocco
Palestine
Russia
Serbia Armenia
Syria
Tunisia
Ukraine

For the moment, Brexit is not going to impact the U.K.'s involvement in the Erasmus scheme. The advantages are wide-ranging. This is going to be a fantastic opportunity for you to go and live, study, volunteer, work, or just deeply experience the culture in a completely different country. It is also going to look amazing on your CV after university. You're showing that you can work independently, that you are open to experiencing new things, that you can travel, and that you can work well with a wide range of people.

Ellie's Story - Choosing my Course

Ellie moved to the U.K. form Bulgaria as a small child, she struggled to adapt at first but alter excelled at school, getting A-Levels in Economics (A*), Maths (A) and Chemsitry (B).

For a lot of people, going to university is about studying something you're passionate about or looking to get into a career with, but for me that wasn't the case. I wasn't sure about what I wanted to do career-wise after finishing my studies, and I didn't really have any passions that I could take further. So I picked a subject I enjoyed and was good at and looked to see what different courses were on offer around it. In the end I settled on Business Economics (which I am thoroughly enjoying and doing well in).

This wasn't actually my first idea. Initially I wanted to go into architecture, however it required certain qualifications which at the time were not my forte and that demotivated my interest in perusing it any further (not that this affected my interest in architecture in general). Through my time in 6th form, I developed an interest in business studies and psychology (which lead to a possible study/career interest in criminology). However, when it came down to my exams, out of the two I did far better in business, which helped sway my final course choice. I think the thing that students need to remember is that you don't need to feel pressured to have your life planned out already. It's great if you do, but it's also fine if you don't. So long as you end up doing something you enjoy, that's all that matters. (I was lucky to find that fairly quickly, but it can take trying several different things.)

Apprenticeships or University

University can be a costly few years, and you may think it's a necessity to get your dream job straight away, but this is not always the case.

Apprenticeships are a viable, realistic, and valuable alternative to doing a university degree. There are loads of jobs where you might assume you need a degree, but you don't. You can go into them straight after school by doing an apprenticeship. For example, apprenticeships are a viable route for accountancy, banking, insurance, HR, public relation, veterinary, nursing, loads of science careers, construction, surveying, IT, or even teaching. You will get the same professional qualification, just without the degree. You'll get the same whether you start your apprenticeship straight after school or whether you go and do a degree first. The same qualifications will still apply, but with an apprenticeship, you'll be getting specific job-related work experience from day one.

You'll also be getting paid a little bit—not as much as a fully qualified person, but you will be getting paid nonetheless—and then you won't have the massive student loans at the end of your degree course. The average wage of an apprentice is about £170 a week, and you'll be learning to apply what you know straightaway right from the beginning, instead of reading it from a textbook and just thinking how to implement it. You'll be learning something and learning how to apply it straight away. People who take an apprenticeship are going to get a higher starting salary. They might also find it easier to get a job because they have the work experience, and they might be offered a job with the company they did their apprenticeship with.

However, university is fantastic. There's the social side being in an academic environment for years. Besides the long holidays, it is lots of fun and degrees still have this particular level of kudos. Both pathways have advantages and disadvantages, and you need to work out which route is right for you.

Degree Apprenticeships

Degree apprenticeships are a relatively new thing in the U.K., but they're a fantastic combination of on-the-job experience and getting a degree at the same time.

These are apprenticeships where you come out with a degree at the end. You have the job, you're earning the money, you're getting the experience, and at the same time you are working towards your degree. The majority of apprenticeships are going to include some study, but the level of study will vary, as will how much time is actually devoted to that study. Like all apprenticeships, this is going to be a joint venture between the place where you're actually working and the university where you're doing your studying. The university is going to be delivering courses that are very relevant to what you are doing in your day-to-day job. For example, Thames Valley Police and the University of Wales have developed a degree apprenticeship in Protective Services. This is a straight path to becoming a Police Constable, so they're not going to teach you things at the university that you don't need to know in your day-to-day job. Your employer is going to say to your university, "We need our people to know this, this, this, and this," and the university is going to develop a way to teach it to you. All the modules, lectures, and tests will feed back to your employer so they can assess how you're doing in university. It's a two-way relationship, and everything is built upon the needs from the other side.

There are loads of jobs that offer degree apprenticeships, like podiatry, civil engineering, aerospace engineering, tailoring, conveyancing, or actuaries. This is a very specific combination of a vocational degree and on-the-job experience. One of the massive advantages about degree apprenticeships is that your tuition fees are going to be paid by either the government or the employer, so you're not going to come out of university with massive debts. And because you're being paid for your apprenticeship, you also don't need to take out a loan for your living fees as well. So if you're not in a financial position to go to university—or if you have a caring responsibility, or if you have dependents, or if you don't have parental support—then this could be a real viable chance for you to get a degree, earn money at the same time, and increase your chances that your employer will keep you on after you've completed your apprenticeship.

The way that your study and your work time will be divided up is going to vary between your employer, your university, and the type of course that you're doing. You may find that you have one or two off from your job where you will be expected to study at university. It may be blocked, so this month you're at work, next month you're studying. Your employers may even give you time off to study for your exams. There are a wide range of firms across a broad spectrum of different industries that have signed up for degree apprenticeships. For example, Rolls-Royce and loads of other car firms; HSBC and loads of other banking firms; GSK and loads of other science firms; EDF and things like the RAF also offer something similar. These programs are a very viable, very sensible alternative to vocational degrees and apprenticeships, since they offer a combination of both.

The following sectors have degree apprenticeships in place, or are currently developing them:

Accounting
Agriculture
Animal Care
Business and Administration
Childcare and Education
Construction
Design
Digital Technology
Education
Engineering and Manufacturing
Environmental Services
Finance
Health and Science
HR
Legal
Marketing
Protective Services (e.g. Police)
Sales
Social Care

Course Summaries

Accounting/Finance

Accounting is a discipline that aims to equip you with skills that will enhance your ability to deal with accounts-related tasks and also skills of decision-making, communication, problem-solving, business focus, and numeracy. Additionally, it will help you gain proficiency in working in industries such as marketing, management of public finances, and banking, among others. There are no specific A-Level subjects that are required to undertake the course, but it is important to have a good foundation in Economics and Mathematics. This is a lecture-only course and lessons can be conducted by use of tutorials in small groups.

Aerospace Engineering

Aerospace Engineering is a course that provides students with skills that aid in the design, manufacture, and operation of equipment that are able to defy gravity. The various A-Level subjects that are required include Mathematics and Physics. This is solely because the course involves the combination of knowledge from mathematics, computer science, physics, engineering, and design. The course is not a lecture-only course, since it also involves lab work where students are required to practically display their understanding of the theories that they have learned. Graduates of aerospace engineering can comfortably work as maintenance engineers, aerospace engineers, manufacturing systems engineers, and automotive engineers, among others.

Agriculture

An agricultural course equips students with the necessary knowledge and skills to achieve optimum production for both animal and plant production. Additionally, it provides farm management skills that are environmentally friendly. An A-Level in either Chemistry, Biology or Physics is required when undertaking the course. Other subjects that have proved to be useful for this course include Geography, Environmental Science, and Business Studies. It is not a lecture-only course, since there is some lab work that is normally conducted as one progresses with the course.

American Studies

American Studies is a degree course that aims to equip students with the knowledge of American history, culture, literature, ethnicity, and politics. The interested student is only required to have English literature or history as the A-Level subject to qualify for this course. Moreover, it is an advantage to have studied Politics, since it is a crucial area throughout the course. The student is not required to have any work experience. This interdisciplinary degree is a lecture-based course since it does not need the use of lab to do any practical activity. Students can organize themselves into groups where they can share online tutorials and discuss the coursework.

Anatomy/Physiology

Anatomy is a degree course which mainly focuses on human cells, tissue, skeleton, and organs, whereas Physiology focuses on how the internal body structure works. Anatomy combined with Physiology focuses on the body structure of a living thing. The A-Level subjects required are Chemistry and Biology. Also, there are subjects which have proved to be advantageous, including Psychology, Physics, and

Mathematics. It is not a lecture-only course, since students have to use a lab for practical lessons which involve dissection and observation of the internal structures. This course is ideal for students who have an interest in studying medicine and body functions without studying a medicine course.

Animal Science

Animal Science is a course where students are provided with knowledge of animal biology. Additionally, they learn how human beings relate and depend on animals for food and leisure. The various A-Level subjects required are Chemistry and Biology. It is proven that a student who has studied Psychology, Physical Education, Physics, Geography, and Mathematics will have an edge on this course. Animal science is a lecture- and lab-based course since the students have to practice what they have learned in labs or fields. Graduates from this course can apply their knowledge and skills in bio-ethics, livestock production, and agriculture.

Anthropology

Anthropology course equips a student with knowledge and skills to study similarities and differences between cultures and societies around the world. The student can additionally understand positive and negative issues affecting society, such as religion. There are no A-Level subjects required, but it is useful to be good in Sociology and Biology. It is a lecture-based course, and the students can have field trips to enhance their understanding. Graduates have an opportunity to study for Ph.D. in Public Health Studies and International Development. Also, job opportunities available are such as humanitarian aid worker, social worker, archaeologist, and public health worker.

Archaeology

Archaeology is an inter-disciplinary course which involves the study of human artefacts, prehistory, and any other physical evidence which was used and left by ancient human beings. It usually conducted through digging and excavating. The student can have an interaction with the past and can study the adaptive behaviour of animals in prehistoric times. There are no specific A-Levels subjects required to take the course, but it is advantageous for someone to have some knowledge in History. This course is not lecture-only, as students are required to do laboratory experiments that include the handling and studying of artefacts. A graduate of this course can get jobs such as an archaeologist, government officer, or lecturer.

Architecture

Architecture is a degree course that trains students with the art and science of planning and designing buildings of different types. The student also gets to appreciate and understand the megastructures that are built using current technology. There are no A-Level subjects required to undertake this course, but it is resourceful to have learned Art, Physics, and Mathematics. Not only is the course lecture-based, but students also get to do practical work and practical placements. Graduates of this course can become a lecturer, building surveyor, draftsperson, town planner, conservation officer, structural engineer, or proceed to do a Master's in Architecture.

Art and Design

Art and Design is a course that equips students with skills that enable them to work as professional designers and artists in various capacities. In this course, there are no specific A-Level subjects required for a person to have learned, but subjects such as Art, Modern Foreign Languages, History, and English Literature are all an added advantage. Art and design is both lecture and lab-based. This is because the students carry out projects that involve extensive hands-on designing. This course is an extremely competitive industry, but graduates can become artists, graphic designers, advertising executives, textile manufacturers, multimedia designers and fashion designers.

Art History

Art History is a course that equips the student with the skills of analysing and writing about art. The course teaches students transferable skills such as IT literacy, teamwork skills, and flexibility. There are no specific A-Levels required to study this course. Experience with subjects such as History, Art, English Literature, Religious Studies, and Modern Foreign Language will provide a considerable advantage in undertaking this course. Art history is a lecture-based course where students are required to do a research-intensive study. Also, they do field studies at various galleries and museum where later on they carry out practical projects. Graduate get to have an opportunity to become an artist, illustrator, or museum curator.

Asian Studies (East & South Asian Studies)

East and South Asian Studies are courses that involve students in the geography, language, and history of Asian peoples. Countries included in this region of study include Thailand, Malaysia, Cambodia, Singapore, Laos, and Vietnam. In this course, there are no specific A-Level subjects required. This is a lecture-only course, and no laboratory work is needed. Use of tutorials in small groups can help with lessons. Visiting these countries to study more deeply may exclusively be organized by the university. Graduates can get various jobs such as translating and interpreting, tourism, business, marketing and international banking.

Astronomy

Astronomy is an interdisciplinary course that equips one with knowledge and skills in studying the physical universe, celestial objects, and outer space. Students learn technical skills such as how to operate a telescope to observe and analyse celestial objects. The required A-Level subjects are Maths and Physics, but it is also useful to have Chemistry and Further Maths. The course is not lecture-only since it also involves some lab work where students are required to practically display their understanding of the theories that they have learned by using equipment such as a telescope.

Biology

Biology is a course that takes students through the study of living organisms that may range from the tiniest organisms to animals, plants and human beings. An A-Level in Biology is required when enrolling in this course, while other beneficial subjects include Physics, Chemistry, and Mathematics. Some of the areas that the course covers include Genetics, Physiology, Zoology, Biomolecules and Ecology, among others. The course is not all lecture-based, but also involves some laboratory work that aims to equip students with good laboratory practice skills. Graduates of this course may fit perfectly into careers like scientific analysts, environmental scientists, and hospital staff, among others.

Building and Surveying

Building and Surveying is a very technical course that requires A-Level in Mathematics. Other subjects that are of importance include Chemistry, Physics, and Biology. Students undertaking this course will be equipped with skills that will enable them to design and appropriately plan for building projects and the conservation of historic buildings. This is not a lecture-only course, as it involves some field work where the students are expected to display their understanding of the knowledge they have learned in class. Graduates from this course may get employed in the construction industry as construction managers, surveyors, and civil engineers, among related careers.

Business and Management Studies

Business Management Studies is a course which aims at equipping students with skills that will enable them to organize and control the functions of any company or business. Some of the various activities that a graduate of this course can undertake may include finance, marketing, human resource, and accounting. To undertake this course, no specific A-Level subject is required, but it is resourceful to have some subjects such as Business Studies, Mathematics, and Economics. No lab work is undertaken during the course study, but the students are required to carry out presentations, work in groups, and attend seminars. There is some work experience that students are expected to undertake to broaden their knowledge.

Celtic Studies

Celtic Studies is a subject that aims to create a better understanding of the historical culture of not only Britain, but also Europe as a whole. Understanding various cultures among the European peoples will help the students develop skills that will enable them to articulate information vividly and in a concise manner. To undertake this course, it is necessary to that a student has an A-Level in either Humanities or a language. Graduates from this course may work in museums or teach and publish historical books, among other related tasks. Work experience is not part of the course, and no lab work is undertaken when studying the course.

Chemical Engineering

Chemical Engineering refers to a course that is focused towards equipping students with skills that will help them combine physical sciences and life sciences to develop and convert raw materials into useful finished products to be used for various purposes such as pharmaceuticals. A-Levels in Mathematics, Physics, and Chemistry are necessary for one to undertake the course. Additionally, having Further Mathematics and Design Technology can be useful. A graduate of the course can work as an energy engineer, petroleum engineer and chemical engineer, to name only a few. Lab work is usually undertaken at the final stages of the course to put into practice the various knowledge learned in class.

Chemistry

Chemistry is a physical science that focuses on studying the makeup of physical matter. The properties, structure, and composition of matter are broadly examined when undertaking the course. It requires an A-Level in Chemistry to undertake this course, but it is useful to have Biology, Physics, and Mathematics. Some aspects that are usually covered include Physical, Inorganic, Organic and Biological Chemistry. There is lab work that is generally involved in the course study to enhance one's skills of working with laboratory equipment. A graduate from the course can work as a forensic scientist, as a healthcare researcher, and as an analytical chemist.

Civil Engineering

Civil Engineering is a course that focuses on equipping

students with skills to enable them to design, construct and look after infrastructure within a country. Some of the structures that a civil engineer is assigned to take care of include roads, bridges, pipelines, railways and nuclear plants, among others. One wishing to undertake this course is required to have A-Level in Mathematics and Physics. Moreover, it is resourceful to have Design Technology and Further Mathematics while undertaking the course. The coursework is administered not only through lectures but also through constant lab work that is aimed to put student's knowledge to the test while at the same time expanding it. A graduate from this course can work as a civil engineer, contractor, structural engineer, and quantity surveyor among others.

Classics

Classics is a course that actively engages students to analyse and understand the history, art, and culture of Ancient Greece and Rome. As it combines the languages of Latin and Greek to enhance the translation process, a student is required to have an A-Level in Latin or Ancient Greek to undertake the course. English Literature, History, Classical Civilization and Modern Foreign Language are among other subjects that are useful when undertaking this course. No lab work is involved when studying this course, but students are required to participate in group works, oral presentations, and to attend lectures. Work experience is not part of the course study.

Communication and Media Studies

Communications and Media Studies is a course that provides students with an understanding of how the modern world works through study of media in order to interpret the culture and personality of a society. There are no specific subjects that are required to undertake this course, but it is useful to have subjects such as History, Modern Foreign Language, and Sociology. No lab work is involved in the course study, but students are required to come up with projects, attend seminars, and make presentations. Graduates from this course can serve as producers, multimedia planners, and TV runners among others. Work experience is not part of the coursework.

Computer Games Design and Programming

The **Computer Games Design and Programming** course focus on equipping students with the design, production, game analysis and testing skills that are needed in game production. An A-Level in Mathematics is required to undertake this course, but it is also useful to have ICT, Physics, Philosophy, Further Mathematics, and Computing. Students are required to come up with projects which are aimed at putting the students' programming skills to the test. A significant portion of the coursework is practical, and lecture sessions are accompanied with presentations. A graduate from this course may work as a game developer or a game analyst, among other related tasks.

Computer Science

A Computer Science course is focused on equipping students with skills that enable them to get a clear understanding of computer programs and how a user interacts with a computer. Besides that, the course exposes students to computer programming, which is the backbone of creating new designs and computer applications. A-Level Mathematics is required to undertake this course, but other subjects that may be of significance, include ICT, Philosophy, Physics, Computing and Further Mathematics. Laboratory sessions on programming are usually undertaken, and they are reinforced with lectures and tutorials that help get students gain a better understanding of the industry. Work experience is not part of the coursework that students should undertake. Graduates from this course are fit for tasks in the IT industry.

Counselling

Counselling is a course that focuses on producing students who are capable of offering therapy to persons who might be undergoing emotional and psychological problems. It equips students with the knowledge that they require to approach a disturbed person with empathy and understanding that will create confidence in the patient. In general, an A-Level Psychology is necessary to undertake this course, but the entry requirements vary from one institution to another. No lab work is conducted during the course study, but presentations are usually conducted. Work experience is not part of the coursework to be undertaken. Graduates from this course may work as psychologists, career advisers, and as social workers.

Creative Writing

Creative Writing is a course that focuses on the different aspects of writing that vary from non-fiction to fiction writing. The course helps in cultivating the written and spoken communication skills that may be helpful for people in the journalism and advertising industries. There are no specific A-Level subjects that are required, but it is resourceful to have English. No laboratory work is undertaken, but the lectures are accompanied with group discussions and presentations. Graduates from the course can work as journalists, authors, brand consultants and marketers, among other related careers. Work experience is not typically part of the course study.

Criminology

Criminology is a discipline that focuses on studying criminal behaviour among individuals. It helps the students to understand what pushes individuals to commit a crime. Strategies include coming up with ways of dealing with criminals while at the same time preventing crime. The entry requirements vary from one institution to another, but in general, A-Levels in Sociology and Psychology are required. Additionally, it is useful to have Psychiatry and Social Anthropology. No lab work is undertaken during the study, but students are expected to actively participate in group discussions and presentations. Graduates from this course can work as police, probation systems staff, and in community and charity organizations.

Dance

Dance is a course of art that familiarizes students with the various categories of dance that range from street dance to ballet. Undertaking such a course enables a student to gain exposure that will make one competitive and competent as a professional dancer or choreographer. There are no specific A-Level subjects that are necessary to undertake this course, but it is useful to have Performing Arts and English Literature. No lab work is undertaken, but most of the classes are practical so that the students are given a chance to improve their art. It is also important to note that work experience is not part of the coursework.

Dentistry

Dentistry is a course that provides a path to becoming a dentist. A-Level in Chemistry and Biology are necessary to undertake the course. The course equips students with the knowledge that is required to diagnose, prevent and treat any illnesses that occur within the mouth. Other subjects that are of importance when undertaking the course include Physics, Mathematics, and English. Different aspects that are usually covered in the course study include Physiology, Microbiology, and Genetics among others. There is laboratory work that is undertaken in the course of study to enable students to demonstrate their understanding. Furthermore, practice exams are usually administered after a given interval of time.

Design
Design is a course that is focused on proving ideas and visual images. Design is a broad subject and students have several choices that they can choose to specialize in, namely: Fashion Design, Product Design, Graphic Design, Animation, and Interior Design among others. An A-Level in Art or any other design related subject is necessary. Additionally, a Diploma in Foundation Art and Design are required for students to undertake this course. Besides that, it is useful to have Photography, History of Art and Design Technology. No lab work is undertaken during the study, but studio sessions are held to broaden the skills of students. Work experience is not part of the course study.

Drama and Theatre Studies
Drama and Theatre Studies is a course that combines the study of the history of theatres with reading and analysing performance skills in the theatre. Practicals take up a considerable portion of the study and students are required to hold group discussions and presentations. To undertake this course, there are no specific subjects that are, but it is useful to have English, English Literature and Language, and Drama Studies. Graduates from this course can work as actors, film and television directors, presenters and stage managers. Work experience is not part of the course, and no lab work is usually undertaken.

Economics

Economics is a course that focuses on wealth production and management. It also equips students with communication skills, accountancy skills, and presentation skills that are necessary for wealth creation and management. It is a lecture-only course that does not include laboratory work, although tutorials may also be used during the study. The course equips students with skills that are necessary to analyse economic and financial data to come up with solutions to universal problems. Work experience is not part of the coursework. Graduates from this course can work as economists, accountants, and investment advisers, among others.

Electronic and Electrical Engineering

Electronic and electrical engineering is a course that aims at equipping students with skills that will enable them to overcome electricity-related challenges. The course also enhances student knowledge on matters of electronic systems that may be used in the transport, manufacturing, and communication industry. A-Level subjects that are required to undertake this course include Mathematics and Physics. Other useful subjects to have to include Further Mathematics and Design Technology. Laboratory work is involved, allowing students to practice what they have learned in theory. Work experience is not part of the coursework that is undertaken by students. Graduates from this course may work as electrical engineers, aerospace engineers, and also in the IT industry.

English Language and Literature

English and literature is a course that requires students to analyse books, plays, and poems to gain an understanding of what the author intended to put across. Through the study of such books, students can improve their skills in writing and communication. An A-Level in English and Language is required to undertake this course. Some aspects that are usually covered in the course of study include poetry, grammar, novels, and films. No laboratory work is conducted during the study, but students are expected to hold group discussions and give oral presentations. Graduates from this course may work as journalists, literature teachers, and also do other literature-related tasks.

Environmental Science

Environmental Science is a course that provides the necessary skills to create solutions for climate change, sustainable development, environmental pollution, and an ever-growing population. Two A-Levels in either Biology, Mathematics, Physics, Geography, or Chemistry are required to undertake the course. The students are required to conduct laboratory work at the various stages of the course of study. Work experience is not part of the coursework. Graduates from this course can work as environmental analysts, nature reserve wardens, recycling officers, and scientific advisers among other careers.

Fashion

Fashion is a course that deals with the outward appearance of people ranging from contemporary clothes, shoe accessories, make up and body piercings, among other aspects. The requirements for this course vary from one institution to another, but it is useful to have a portfolio of work. No lab work is conducted during the study, but there are a lot of practicals and workshops that students are expected to participate in. This course equips students with skills that foster creativity, helping them remain relevant in this competitive industry. A graduate from this course may work as a fashion journalist, fashion designer, or as an event manager.

Film

Film is a course that aims to train students to not only professionally produce films, but also edit and write scripts. Art, Media Studies, and Drama are required A-Level subjects to undertake this course. The course involves practicals as students engage in various aspects of film production, such as editing, directing and scripting. Work experience is not part of the course study, and no lab work is conducted. It is important to note that workshops and seminars are usually offered in addition to lectures to broaden students' knowledge. Graduates from this course may work as producers, film editors, and camera operators.

Finance

Finance is a course that offers knowledge on the relevant ways of conducting finance-related tasks such as accounting, trading, banking, and investment. There are no specific A-Level subjects that are required to undertake this course, but it is resourceful to have Economics, Business Studies, and Mathematics. Various aspects that are usually covered in this course include accounting, principles of economics, financial markets, quantitative methods for economics, and banking, among others. No lab work is involved during the course study, but students will be actively engaged in group discussions and oral presentations. Important to note is that work experience is not part of the coursework.

Fine Art

Fine Art is focused on developing skills in Printmaking, Performance Art, Sculpture, and Photography to enhance the expression of one's creativity. A-Level subjects in Art and a diploma in Foundation Art and Design are necessary to undertake this course. Furthermore, it is useful to have History of Art, Design Technology and Photography. Additionally, having a portfolio of artwork is an added advantage. No lab work is conducted, but students are actively involved in studio-based work which is meant to reinforce the lectures that they undertake. Graduates from this course may work as designers, photographers, or as lectures for administering art.

Food and Beverage Studies

Food and Beverage Studies is a course that prepares students with skills that are necessary to enable them to safely handle foods and drinks. The various aspects that are normally covered in the course study include cooking techniques, management of facilities, and styles of serving. These skills prepare students to preserve, prepare, and serve foods and drinks professionally. Laboratory work is involved in the course of study and work experience is not part of the coursework. Two A-Level core sciences are required to undertake this course, and they may be Mathematics, Biology, Chemistry, and Physics. Graduates from this course may work as dieticians, restaurant managers, and caterers, among other related careers.

Forensic Science

Forensics Science is a course that aims at equipping students with the necessary skills to examine any piece of evidence that might be at a crime scene. A-Level Chemistry and Biology are required to undertake this course. Various aspects that are covered in the coursework include crime scene procedures, report writing, examining evidence, and fingerprinting. Laboratory work is usually conducted to equip students with the analytical skills that they need to undertake various investigations on pieces of evidence. Lectures are reinforced with tutorials that broaden students' knowledge on the subject. Graduates from this course may work as forensic scientists, analytical chemists, and data analysts.

Forestry

Forestry focuses on equipping students with skills of forest and woodland management with respect their function as water catchment areas, a source of timber, and wildlife habitat. Any of the Sciences (Chemistry, Physics, and Biology) is required to undertake this course, but it is useful to have Geography, Environmental Science, and Business Studies. No laboratory work is involved in the course study, but a lot of field work is undertaken to help familiarize students with the nature of forests. The aspects covered in the coursework include management of commercial plantations, protection of hedgerows and woodlands, among others. A graduate of this course may work as a farm manager, agricultural manager, and conservation worker.

General Engineering

General Engineering is a broad course that deals with engineering in general and covers the different principles of engineering design. It equips students with the skills that they need so that they can construct and create machines and structures. There are no specific subjects that are required to undertake this course, but it is useful to have Mathematics and Physics. No laboratory work is required, but students are expected to actively participate in workshops, group discussions, and presentations. Work experience is not part of the course study. Graduates from this course can work as industrial engineers, broadcast engineers, automotive engineers, and other engineering-related tasks.

Geography

Geography is a course that is focused on equipping students with knowledge that is related to the physical world that surrounds us. An A-Level in Geography is required to undertake this course. Additionally, it is useful to have Chemistry, Physics, Biology, and Mathematics. The courseworks include Physical Geography and Human Geography that are covered through lectures, group discussions, and fieldwork. Graduates can work as landscape architects, cartographers, surveyors, social researchers, Geographical Information System officers, and teachers in this field. Laboratory work is not usually involved in the coursework. It is also important to note that work experience is not part of the coursework.

Geology

Geology is a course that equips students with the knowledge of the formation of the earth and the changes that have taken place ever since. One A-Level subject in either Physics, Mathematics, Chemistry, or Biology are required to undertake this course. Having Geography and Geology is an added advantage for this course. No laboratory work is conducted, but fieldwork and practicals are conducted to reinforce the knowledge learned in the lectures. Work experience is not part of the coursework that is to be undertaken. Graduates from this course may work as geologists, quarry managers, geophysicists and land surveyors.

History

History is a course that aims at providing insights across various societies, politics, cultures, and beliefs. It equips one with the necessary skills that will enable them to get an understanding of past events and how these events have shaped the lives of different peoples. A-Level in History is required to undertake the course, and it is useful to have subjects such as Politics, Economics, Philosophy, English Literature, Sociology and Religious Studies. No laboratory work is undertaken during the course study, but students are expected to actively take part in oral presentations, group discussion, and the creation of critical reports. Graduates may work as curators, heritage officers, and subject teachers.

Information Management

Information Management involves appropriately managing the storage and use of public information that may be have been submitted to a company. The skills acquired in the course study enhance one's ability to collect and professionally conserve the essential public data that a company requires for a specific given purpose. There are no specific A-Level subjects that are required to undertake the course, but it is useful to have English and History. No laboratory work is involved in the course study, but seminars and group discussion are essential activities that students will engage in. Graduates from this course can work as librarians, information managers, and records managers at different institutions.

Information Systems

Information Systems focuses on equipping students with skills that are necessary to interpret and analyse computer systems within an applied business setting. There are no specific subjects that are required to undertake this course, but it is useful to have Mathematics. No lab work is involved in the course study, but students are expected to actively take part in fieldwork to give them exposure of what is expected from them. It is also important to note that work experience is not part of the coursework. Graduates may work as application developers, systems analysts, network administrators, and IT Technical Support officers.

Journalism
Journalism equips students with skills to help them in gathering, scripting, and presenting information across different media platforms. Various aspects that are covered in the coursework include handling the production equipment, video editing, and working with different industry-related software. There are no specific A-Level subjects required, but it is useful to have Media Studies and English. No laboratory work is involved, but students are required to do studio-based work and attend seminars. Other modules that may be covered under this course include online journalism, broadcast journalism, and media law. Graduates from this cause may work as video editors, journalists, web content managers, and advertising executives.

Land and Property Management
Land and Property Management is a course that enables students to manage different properties, ranging from shops and houses, to industrial facilities, to equipment estates. A-Level subjects that are required include Mathematics and English. No laboratory work is involved, but fieldwork and group discussions are an essential part of the course. It is important to note that work experience is not part of the coursework. Different aspects that are usually in the coursework include Economics, Law, Property Evaluation, Management, and Construction. Graduates may work as residential estate agents and surveyors, among other related careers.

Law
Law is a subject that deals with the study of legal theory to

enhance the application of law to real-life scenarios. There are no specific requirements for undertaking this course, but it is useful to have English and History. One is required to specialize in different categories of law that range from finance law, intellectual property law, media law, child law, family law, and many others. It provides a thorough overview of the legal systems and how they work to maintain law and order within a society. Laboratory work is not usually involved in the course study, but students are expected to take part in group discussions and join tutorials that broaden their knowledge. Graduates may work in the law industry and serve in the justice systems.

Linguistics

Linguistics focuses on creating an understanding of the various languages that exist among people in a given social setting. Other aspects of the course include conveying the meaning of language, understanding speech sounds, and the structure of a language in general. There are no specific A-Level subjects that are required to undertake this course, but it is useful to have Mathematics, English Language, Modern Foreign Language, and English Literature and Language. No laboratory work is normally undertaken in the coursework and work experience is also not part of the coursework to be undertaken. Graduates from this course may work as translators, English teachers, advertising consultants, and publications editors.

Marine and Ocean Sciences

Marine and Ocean Sciences is a course that focuses on creating an understanding of the various forms ocean life both at sea and along the coastline. Two A-Level subjects are required, and they may be any of the following subjects: Chemistry, Physics, Mathematics, and Biology. Geography and

Geology are other useful subjects. Laboratory work is undertaken at different stages of the course study to broaden students' experiences. Work experience is not part of the coursework that is covered within the study. Graduates from this course may work as marine surveyors, environmental officers, geophysicists, and oceanographers.

Marketing

Marketing is a course that equips students with skills that enable them to promote a product or service that is being offered by a company. This course is closely related to advertising, market research, public relations, consumer behaviours, and event organizations. There are no specific A-Level subjects that are required to undertake this course, but it is useful to have Business Studies and Media Studies. No laboratory work is usually conducted during the, but students are actively engaged in group presentations. Work experience is not part of the coursework that is to be undertaken. A graduate from this course may work as an event manager, media planner, retail manager, and an advertising executive.

Materials Science

Materials Science, also referred to as Materials Engineering, is a course that equips students with skills that they require to manufacture and develop new materials and products relevant to our modern age. A-Level in Mathematics and Physics are required to undertake this course, but it is also useful to have Chemistry. Workshops and laboratory work is usually involved during the course study. Work experience is not part of the coursework that is to be undertaken. Graduates from this course may work as product developers, quality control officers, materials engineers, and metallurgists.

Mathematics

Mathematics is a course that teaches students how to solve mathematical problems and develop analytical skills. A-Level in Mathematics and Further Maths are required to undertake this course, and it is useful to have Physics. No laboratory work is undertaken during this course study, but students are presented with tutorials to provide insights on how to go about mathematical problems. Aspects that are usually covered in the coursework include Probability, Differential Equations, Algebra, Calculus, and Regression ANOVA, among others. Graduates from this course may work as mathematics teachers, accountants, and analysts, among other related professions.

Mechanical Engineering

Mechanical Engineering is a course of study that focuses on the design and manufacture of various mechanical products, including satellites, mobile phones, and medical equipment, among many others. The course combines knowledge from Physics, Mathematics, and Computing to enable students to come up with these products. An A-Level in Mathematics is required to undertake this course, and it is useful to have Design Technology and Further Mathematics. Laboratory work is conducted during the course study and students are engaged in lectures, seminars, and practical workshops. Graduates from this course may work as mechanical engineers, aeronautical engineers, and design engineers, among many other careers.

Media Studies

Media Studies is a course that focuses on skills that are necessary to present information across various media platforms. Editing films, presenting programs over the radio, and reporting techniques are some of the skills that a student can acquire from this course. A-Levels in Media Studies and English Language and Literature are required to undertake this course. It is also useful to have Psychology and Sociology. No laboratory work is undertaken, but students are actively engaged in practicals and workshops. Some of the aspects that are covered in the course include cultures of consumption, power, and resistance, elements of visual media and screen media, and many others. Graduates from this course may work as video editors, sound recordists, public relations officers, and multimedia designers among many others.

Medicine

Medicine is a course that provides an understanding of the many functions of the human body. It focuses on the diagnosis, treatment, and prevention of diseases that may affect humans. To undertake this course, one must have A-Levels in Biology and Chemistry, but it is also useful to have Critical Thinking. Some of the aspects that are covered in the coursework include biochemistry, body systems, human reproduction, diseases, and epidemiology, among others. Laboratory work is usually undertaken in the course of study and students are also actively engaged in practicals and tutorials. Work experience is part of the coursework that should be undertaken. Graduates from this course may work as doctors, aid workers, health service managers, and medical specialists.

Microbiology

Microbiology refers to a course that deals with the study of micro-organisms. Some of the aspects that are covered in the coursework include virology, bacterial genetics, metabolism and molecular biology and microbial functions among others. To undertake this course, an A-Level in Biology is required, and it is useful to have Mathematics, Physics, and Chemistry. Laboratory work is usually included in the coursework and students are also engaged in fieldworks. Graduates of this course may work as toxicologists, quality assurance officers, microbiologists and as medical laboratory scientific officers.

Midwifery

Midwifery is a course that aims at producing graduates who can support pregnant women before, during, and after the birth of a child. Some of the aspects that are covered in this course include responding to needs during the antenatal period, foundations of postnatal care, and preparation of autonomous midwifery practice. A-Levels in Biology or another science is required, and it is useful to have Psychology, Sociology, and Chemistry. A lot of lab work is undertaken in the course of study, and there are numerous practicals and tutorials that are administered to broaden students' knowledge. Graduates from this course may work as adult nurses, midwife tutors, and delivery suite managers.

Music

Music is a course that equips students with skills needed in the composition, recording, reviewing, administrating, marketing and archiving music in general. Some aspects that are covered in the coursework include techniques of tonal music, composition and theory, musicianship, instrumentation, and harmonizing, among many others. A-Level in Music is required as well as grade 7 or 8 for any main instrument. It is also useful to have English and History. No laboratory work is conducted, but students are engaged in studio work and workshops. Graduates from this course may work as music tutors, art officers, and sound technicians among many others.

Nursing

Nursing is a course that focuses on studying the needs of patients, which may include physical, psychological, and social needs and how to meet them. Some of the aspects that are covered in the course study include personal development, health issues and ethics, therapeutic approaches and practice, epidemiology, and managing complexities in care delivery, and many others. The course involves laboratory work and practicals that help broaden students' knowledge. To undertake this course, an A-Level in Biology or another science is required, and it is useful to have Sociology, Chemistry, and Psychology. Graduates from this course may work as paramedics, care home managers, and as nurses in general.

Nutrition

Nutrition is a course that deals with the chemistry and biology of food and maintaining healthy nutrition. Some of the aspects that are covered in the course include the development of new foods, food production, food safety and hygiene, diet and efficient exercising, and public health promotion. A-Level subjects that are required include Chemistry and Biology, and it is useful to have Physics. Dietary-based workshops are involved in the course, but work experience is not part of the coursework. Graduates from this course may work as nutritionists, dieticians, and health information officers among other related careers.

Optometry

Optometry is a course that prepares students to examine eyes, determine the problems of a patient, and offer the most professional solution. Chemistry and Biology are some of the A-Level subjects that are required to undertake this course, and it is useful to have Physics. Various aspects that are covered in the course study include optics of the eye, foundation biology, practice management, low vision management and assessment, and many others. Laboratory work is involved in the course study and students are also engaged in practicals. Graduates of this course may work as optometrists, opticians, and orthoptists.

Pharmacy
Pharmacy is a course that equips students with the necessary skills to prepare and dispense drugs depending on the needs of a patient. Chemistry and Biology A-Levels are required to undertake this course, and it is useful to have Physics and Mathematics. Some of the aspects covered in the coursework include pharmaceutical chemistry, drugs discovery and delivery, responding to symptoms, dispensing competence, and pharmaceuticals, among others. Laboratory work is usually covered in the course study and students are engaged in group discussions and presentations. Graduates of this course may work as pharmacologists, retail pharmacists, packaging engineers, and quality assurance officers.

Philosophy
Philosophy is a course that focuses on creating an understanding of the ideas that have been expressed by great thinkers. Students also share their opinions on these ideas and critically analyse the ideas to determine the motive behind the thinkers. To undertake this course, there are no specific A-Level subjects that are required, but it is useful to have English, Mathematics, Religious Studies, Classical Civilizations, and Philosophy. Some of the aspects that are usually covered in the coursework include metaphysics, philosophical problems, and philosophy of films and literature. No laboratory work is undertaken in the course study, and work experience is not part of the coursework. Graduates of this

course may work as marketing executives, information analysts, and management information officers.

Physics

Physics is a course that focuses on the study of nature and some of the properties of matter. Additionally, it also creates an understanding of the energy from sub-atomic particles up to galaxies. To undertake this course, one is required to have A-Levels in Mathematics and Physics, and it is useful to have Chemistry and Further Mathematics. Some laboratory work is involved in the course, but work experience is not part of the coursework. Various aspects that are covered in the course of study include plasma and fluids, fabric physics, contemporary physics and stellar physics. Graduates of this course may work as instrumentation designers, medical physicists, and in other related jobs.

Physiology

Physiology is a course that focuses on the structure of living things and how they function to achieve various processes. This course enhances understanding of the anatomy and physiology of the human body. Chemistry and Biology A-Levels are required to undertake this course, and it is useful to have Mathematics, Psychology, and Physics. Laboratory work is involved in the coursework and students are engaged in group discussions. Tutorials and practicals are also essential activities that are carried out to enhance understanding. Some aspects that are covered in the coursework include epithelial physiology, neurobiology, integrative neuroscience, cell biolody and inherited disorders, among others. Graduates of this course may work as medical researchers, exercise specialists, perfusionists, and retail pharmacists.

Physiotherapy

Physiotherapy is a course that equips students with the skills that are necessary to provide solutions for patients with skeletal injuries, neurological problems, and breathing issues. A-Level in Biology is required to undertake this course, and it is useful to have Chemistry, English, Mathematics and Physical Education. Various aspects covered in the coursework include clinical skills, neurological physiotherapy, cardiovascular health, foundations in health and social care, among many others. Laboratory work is involved in the course study and tutorials may be offered to enhance student's knowledge. Graduates of this course may work as physiotherapists, sports coaches, and rehabilitation therapists.

Plant Science

Plant Science focuses on understanding the biology of plants and how they are related to the environment. Chemistry and Biology are the A-Level subjects required to undertake the course, but it is also useful to have physics, mathematics, and psychology. Various aspects covered in the coursework include plant diversity, whole organism biology, field crops, plant-microbe interactions, and ecosystems and environmental change. Laboratory work is undertaken during the course study and practicals are also conducted to broaden students' knowledge. Work experience is not part of the coursework that is undertaken. A graduate of this course may work as a biologist, conservation officer, and field trials officer.

Politics

Politics is a course that enhances understanding of how governments work and how public policies are developed. No specific A-Level subjects are required to undertake this course, but it is useful to have Sociology, Politics, Philosophy,

Law, History, and Sociology. Skills on how to collect, analyse and present political data are imparted to the students. Some of the aspects that are covered in the course study include international politics, the political economy of development, modern British politics, and the making of the modern world. This is a lecture-only course that does not involve laboratory work. Graduates of this course may work as political advisers, political analysts, and industrial relations officers.

Psychology

Psychology is a course that focuses on studying the mind. Psychology helps to create an understanding of what drives people's motives in every action that they take. No specific A-Level subjects are required to undertake this course, but it is useful to have Sociology, Mathematics, Biology, and Psychology. No laboratory work is conducted in the course study, but students are actively engaged in seminars and group discussions. Some of the aspects that are covered in this course include mind and behaviour, social psychology, evolution and behaviour, brain and cognition among others. Graduates of this course may work as counsellors, youth and community workers, HR officers, psychologists, and other related careers.

Public Relations

Public Relations is a course that equips students with the necessary skills to maintain the good image of an organization. There are no specific A-Level subjects that are required to undertake this course, but it is useful to have English. Some of the aspects that are covered in the course study include business strategy, transition to work, design in marketing, business fundamentals, human behaviour and public relations. No laboratory work is conducted in the coursework. Graduates of this course may work as public relations officers, web designers, conference managers, recruitment consultants and marketing executives.

Radiography and Medical Technology
Radiography and Medical Technology is a course that aims at equipping students with the necessary skills to use medical imaging for diagnosis through techniques such as ultrasound, X-ray, and MRI. At least one A-Level subject is required, and it may be Physics, Biology or Chemistry, and it is useful to have Mathematics. Laboratory work is involved in the course study, and work experience is part of the coursework. Aspects such as ethical and legal issues, imaging in care pathways, complementary imaging system, radiotherapy in practice, oncology, and cancer studies are covered in the course study. A graduate of this course may work as a clinical photographer, radiographer, or sonographer.

Social Policy
Social Policy is a course that exposes students to policies and how they work to address issues within a society, such as gender inequality, crime prevention, and poverty management. To undertake this course, there are no specific requirements, but it is useful to have Politics and Sociology. Some of the aspects covered in the coursework include policy processes, social engagement, comparative politics and policies and ideology into practice and many others. No laboratory work is conducted during the course, but students are expected to take part in group discussions. Graduates of this course may work as probation officers, paralegals, social policy advisers, education support officers and housing officers.

Social Work
Social Work is a course that equips students with skills that

will help them positively impact people's lives within society. There are no specific A-Level subjects that are required to undertake this course, but it is useful to have Sociology, Psychology, BTEC Health, and Social Care. Aspects such as social work in society, child and family social work, substance use and misuse, social policy and social work ethics and values are covered. No laboratory work is conducted in the study, but students are actively engaged in group discussions and presentations. A graduate of this course may work as a social worker, guidance officer, probation officer and adoption officer among others.

Sociology

Sociology is a course that studies and analyses human behaviours within a given society. The course helps students gain a better understanding of the average person in society. There are no specific A-Level subjects for undertaking the course, but it is useful to have Geography, Media Studies, Psychology, and Sociology. Some of the aspects covered in the coursework include urban sociology, sexuality and social control, applied ethics, media, crime, multiculturalism, and many others. No laboratory work is involved in the course study, but students are engaged in presentations. A graduate of this course may work as an HR officer, welfare adviser, and social researcher.

Software Engineering

Software Engineering aims at equipping students with the necessary skills for the development and management of computer software applications. An A-Level in Mathematics is required to undertake this course, and it is useful to have Computing. Computer laboratory work is involved in the coursework since it helps students develop and improve their programming skills. Various aspects covered in the coursework include system environments, information systems, programming languages paradigms, database and UML modelling, computer algorithms and modelling, among others. Graduates of this course may work as software consultants, technical consultants, website developers and IT project managers.

Speech Therapy and Audiology

Speech Therapy and Audiology is a course that focuses on not only people's hearing but also diagnosing, assessing and providing treatment for communication disorders. To undertake this course, students are required to have A-Levels in English Language and Biology, and it is useful to have Chemistry, Modern Foreign Language, Chemistry, and Physics. Aspects such as grammar, meaning, communications, science and technology, phonetic transcription, perception, cognition, and learning are covered in the coursework. Laboratory work and practicals are undertaken during the course study. A graduate of this course may work as an audiologist, medical technician, or speech therapist.

Sports Science

Sport Science is a course that provides insights on how the human body functions during exercise, and also focuses on how to develop strategies to maximize athlete potential. An A-Level in Biology or another science or Mathematics is required to undertake this course, and it is useful to have Physical Education and Psychology. No laboratory work is conducted, but students are engaged in workshops. Some of the aspects covered in the coursework include the coaching process, applying teaching and coaching, managing community sport, nutrition and physical activity and applied anatomy and biomechanics. Graduates of this course may work as sports officials, sports coaches, and gym/ leisure managers.

Statistics

Statistics is a course that equips students with the ability to analyse different statistics for use in fields such as medicine, finance, and management. An A-Level in Mathematics is required to undertake this course, and it is useful to have Statistics, English, and Economics. Aspects such as linear algebra, decision modelling, complex analysis, calculus, matrix methods, probability and operational research are covered in the coursework. No laboratory work is usually involved in the, but tutorials and presentations are offered. A graduate from this course may work as a management consultant, economic forecaster and as a statistical manager.

Teacher Training

Teacher Training is a course that trains students in methods to develop social skills, not only among young children but also among adults. An A-Level subject is required to undertake this course, and it may be IT, Mathematics, Music, Design and Technology, Modern Language, Religious Studies, or Art. It is useful to have CACHE (early years' primary teaching/ primary education teacher training). Some aspects covered in the coursework include excellence in English, lifestyles and society, learning how to learn, education, and values and society, among others. No laboratory work is involved in this course, and work experience is not part of the coursework. A graduate from this course may work as a private tutor, learning mentor, primary school teacher, and as a special needs teacher.

Theology and Religious Studies

Theology and Religious Studies is a course that focuses on

exploring the religious context while at the same time discussing global politics. There are no specific A-Level subjects required to undertake this course, but it is useful to have Philosophy, Religious Studies, English Literature, and History. Aspects such as living religions, theology, Hinduism, global Christianity, introduction to Islam and women in Islam are covered in the coursework. No laboratory work is involved, but students are engaged in group discussions and presentations. Graduates of this course may work in the clergy, or as community workers and teachers.

Tourism and Travel
Tourism and Travel is a course that gives insight into the principles of hospitality, world travel, and tourism. No specific A-Level subjects are required to undertake this course. Some of the aspects that are covered in the coursework include an introduction to tourism, sustainable tourism, and economics of tourism, passenger transport management, special interest tourism, and marketing for tourism among many others. No laboratory work is undertaken during the course study, but students are engaged in fieldworks, group discussion, and presentations. A graduate of this course may work as a tour manager, tourism officer, events manager, or as a hotel manager.

Veterinary Medicine
Veterinary Medicine is a course that offers understanding of the structure and functions of healthy animals and equips students with the necessary skills to address illness in animals. A-Levels in Chemistry and Biology are required to undertake the course, and it is useful to have Physics and Mathematics. Laboratory work is involved in the course, and it aims to broaden students' knowledge of the discipline. Aspects of animal disease, animal health science, veterinary practical

techniques, animal health handling and clinical management are covered in the coursework. A graduate of this course can work as a research veterinarian, veterinary surgeon, and veterinary investigation officer.

Zoology

Zoology is a course that deals with the study of animals and their behaviour within a specific habitat. Chemistry and Biology are the A-Level subjects that are required to undertake this course, and it is useful to have Psychology, Physics, and Mathematics. Laboratory work and practicals are undertaken during the course study. Aspects of animal behaviour, diversity in life, plant science, science and success, the animal kingdom, and gene and cellular control are some of the aspects that are covered in the coursework. Graduates of this course may work as animal welfare officers, environmental consultants, nature reserve wardens, and as zoological field surveyors.

Aine's Story - A Day in the Life of an Accounting Student

Aine has Irish Leaving Certificate grades H23333, this is equvalne to to ABB.

I know what you're thinking—all we do is maths all day long, right? Adding things up? Wrong! See my account what a 'typical day' is about. This is merely a snippet, just one day in my life as an accounting student.

8 a.m. – The start to my day typically involves an inner fight with myself to get out of bed (I'm not much of a morning person). Along with that fight is a ton of alarms and 15 minutes of getting ready, and I'm on my way.

8:30 a.m. – I've time to essentially wake myself up with a short walk into the campus.

8:45 a.m. – First things first, a cup of tea to start the day before heading to class.

Tea – I know you're probably thinking, tea? Yes, we've got a Starbucks on campus!

9 a.m. – Then straight on to an Audit seminar. These are nice and interactive, especially in the morning to wake us up. Seminars frequently have fewer students, typically between 10 and 15, and are far more relaxed than simply hearing the teacher in a lecture. Audit will involve very little mathematics/numbers; it's more centered on the idea and delves into scams. You 'must' have an extremely sceptical head for an Audit class.

10 a.m. – Directly into a Financial Reporting Lecture. Now this is focused on the quantities, BUT it isn't as frightening as it appears. The lecturer undergoes theory then provides examples to the class until you are able to do the work by yourself. It can be a lot of information to take in, so my best advice is to read, read, read before class, so you have an idea beforehand.

11 a.m. – We then have a financial reporting seminar, again a LOT fewer people so you can practice the work from the lecture and ask for tons of help. It really helps to go through it straight after a lecture while it's fresh to understand the work in your own terms.

12 p.m. – Lunch break! Time for a meet up with friends and a bite to eat. Sometimes I'll decide on a jacket potato from the student union, sometimes a good toasty from the management stop.

2 p.m. – A financial management lecture. This does indeed involve quantities, but not nearly as much as financial reporting. It's a good mixture of theory plus some equations.

3 p.m. – Home time! Yes, that early on, but some days it's even sooner! BUT this doesn't mean that it's over for your day...

5 p.m. – I visit a class at the gym (don't assume every day!). I like to complete my day with a good workout. It's a good way to take a rest from work before doing any at home.

6 p.m. – I take a period of time until 6 p.m. after visiting the gym. Then I can do my reading, printing, practice questions ready for the very next day. Staying together with things is really the key!

My day usually finishes once I've done all my printing, completed a section, and done a few practice questions.

I believe learning is all about believing in yourself.

Applying as an International Student

Deciding to apply to university in a different country can be a daunting prospect, but there are some fantastic opportunities out there if you're willing to strive for them. Nearly 15% of students studying at U.K. universities are international, so there are plenty of opportunities for foreign students.

For the majority of foreign applicants, the process is exactly the same as home students. You decide on your course, and then you decide on your university. You think about your personal statement, and you apply via UCAS. You can use the other sections of this book to see how to pick a course, how to pick a university, how to write your personal statement, how to get references if your school isn't used to applying through UCAS, and what you can do if you've been out of school for a while.

You'll still need to abide by the deadlines: the October deadline for medicine, veterinary, Oxford, and Cambridge, and the January deadline for everything else. However, because you are an international student, you are very welcome by universities because they can charge you more, which means they are much more likely to be lenient on deadlines than they are to home students.

You are going to need to think carefully about funding. There are going to be some funding requirements. You need to think about whether you're going to qualify for a visa, and also whether you're going to be able to show that you're proficient in the English language. There are some health considerations that the government takes into account as well, but universities really want international students, so your chosen university's international students' office will be more than happy to help you. If you need a bit of help, the universities that you're applying to are going to be a brilliant place to reach out to.

Chao's Story - Applying as an International Student

Studying abroad isn't just an extraordinary chance to gain from a number of the best educators—it is a chance to live in another country and learn more about it by taking an interest in regular activities. Having the opportunity to apply and study as an international student is an opportunity I would always take, because it's an experience I would never forget. In any case, before applying as an international student, all students going to U.K. need to get a student visa through the U.K. home office.

As an international student, the application process can be overwhelming. Foreign students face extra challenges and stress factors beyond that of our U.K. associates. This is because the majority of us might come from countries where mail services are costly, unreliable and slow. Application charges might need to be paid in this style which may be inaccessible to us and our relatives in our nations. Also, coming from a different educational system as an international candidate, we regularly need to independently explore school sites, deal with unfamiliar vocabulary and terms on applications, and manage different admissions materials. With this, we need to improve our English language and demonstrate it.

We can only exhibit our English language capacity by completing an English language course. However, if you are a citizen of a country that is amongst the English Speaking Commonwealth, for example, Jamaica, it is easier for you to do your own ESOL or IELTS at a private college if you wish to study in the U.K. in certain immigration classifications. IELTS level 7 is the Standard English Language section is required for most advanced education courses in the UK.

But for me, through my research, I found some ways which helped me improve my language skills while applying as an international student, and these might be useful for you too. They are:

(1)   Signup for online courses equipped towards not only English, but your basic coursework, too.

(2)   Ask some brilliant students, lecturers or professors to suggest great learning materials that you could work with freely.

(3)   If you have no one to ask, do not feel disappointed! There are books that deal particularly with language for academic settings. Check the Internet for a list of them, as they may really be of value.

(4)   Watch English language TV programs and movies to improve your familiarity with the language. It really helps!

(5)   Lastly, I made the Internet my best friend by making use of free resources online, specifically magazines, newspapers, and articles. These truly helped me Increase my language skills without costing a penny.

There is one thing most of us forget to do, which I almost forgot too, and this is contacting the university or college of our choice. Contacting them will make them inform you about whatever they require from you to determine if you are academically qualified to learn at their university or college. Among other necessities, you also have to show your school that you have sufficient money to support yourself while learning at their school, and you likewise need to have medical insurance in U.K. as the charge of health care with no insurance can be a heavy bill. Applying as an international student might be a bit stressful due to all the processes we have to follow, but at the end of it all, it is worth the stress.

SELT

If you want to apply to study in the U.K., you're going to need a Tier 4 (General) student visa. And as part of this process, you're going to need to show that you're proficient in the English language.

This proficiency testing is known as the SELT, or the Secure English Language Test. It is a requirement for your Tier 4 (General) student visa, and it is conducted by Trinity College, London, if you're in the U.K., or by the IELTS if you are outside the U.K.

Trinity College has several locations across the U.K., and you need to book your test online. The test will include a speaking and listening component, a conversation component, and a reading and writing component.

The IELTS needs to be conducted at an academic level, and there is quite a long test for this. There are four components to the IELTS. The listening section, which is 30 minutes long. The reading section, which is 60 minutes long. The writing section, which is 60 minutes long. You do all four components in a row, and you're not allowed a break in between them. The speaking, the listening, the conversation part is between 10 and 15 minutes, and you can do this a week either side of your written test. You will need to show your passport or your identity badge when you arrive to take the test, and the proctors will also use other methods to confirm your identity.

Visas

Getting a visa is an important part of coming to the U.K. to study. If you want to come for less than six months, then you can get a short-term visa. But if you want to study for an undergraduate degree, which is more than six months, then you're going to need a Tier 4 (General) student visa.

Your university will be your Tier 4 sponsor, and when they accept you in the course, then they'll give you all of the details that you need to fill in your visa application form, including your Confirmation of Acceptance of Studies, or CAS. For degree-level courses, student visas can be up to five years. There are some exceptions on the time limit if your courses are over five years, such as Medicine, Veterinary Medicine, Architecture, some Law courses, and some post-graduate courses.

The Home Office has fixed values to show how much money they expect you to have to be able to support yourself. You're expected to be able to pay all of your fees, and then you're expected to be able to provide yourself with £1,265 each month while you're studying in the U.K. Your course may not be for the entire year—for example, it may only be nine months—so you'd have to have that £1,265 for each of the nine months you were studying in the U.K. You would then have to return home for the other three months of the year.

You're going to need to prove that you're proficient in the English language by completing a SELT course at a certified centre (see previous section), and any criminal convictions are going to have to be disclosed on your visa application form.

There is a charge for applying for your visa, and there is no guarantee that the home office will actually grant you a Tier 4 visa. Be prepared: you're going to have to provide lots and lots of documentation to support all of the things that you've stated in your application. However, if you do manage to get your hands on one of those visas, it is going to be a fantastic opportunity for you to come and study in the U.K.

Immigration Healthcare Surcharge (IHS)

When you are applying for your visa, you'll be required to pay the Immigration Healthcare Surcharge, or the HIS. Once you have paid this fee, and once your visa has been granted, you'll be legal entitled to use the healthcare provided by the NHS. This means healthcare will be free at the point of use, but be aware that there are a few services that still required a minimal payment, such as medical prescriptions, dental treatments, and eye tests.

TB Testing

Tuberculosis (TB) is a bacterial infection that predominately affects the lungs and is spread by coughs and sneezes. TB can be fatal, but it is easily treated by a course of antibiotics. Due an extensive vaccination program today, there are very few causes of TB in the U.K. To prevent a resurgence of infection by students from countries with high infection rates, incoming students need to prove they are free from infection. TB tests require a phlegm sample and a chest x-ray.

Students from the following countries will need to take a TB test at a Home Office-approved centre:

Afghanistan; Algeria; Angola; Armenia; Azerbaijan; Bangladesh; Belarus; Benin; Bhutan; Bolivia; Botswana; Brunei; Burma; Burkina Faso; Burundi; Cambodia; Cape Verde; Central African Republic; Chad; Cameroon; China; Congo; Côte d'Ivoire; Democratic Republic of the Congo; Djibouti; Dominican Republic; East Timor; Ecuador; Equatorial Guinea; Eritrea; Ethiopia; Gabon; Gambia; Georgia; Ghana; Guatemala; Guinea; Guinea Bissau ; Guyana; Haiti; Hong Kong; India; Indonesia; Iraq; Kazakhstan; Kenya; Kiribati; Kyrgyzstan; Laos; Lesotho; Liberia; Macau; Madagascar; Malawi; Malaysia; Mali; Marshall Islands; Mauritania; Micronesia; Moldova; Mongolia; Morocco; Mozambique; Namibia; Nepal; Niger; Nigeria; North Korea; Pakistan; Palau; Papua New Guinea; Panama; Paraguay; Peru; Philippines; Russia; Rwanda; São Tomé and Principe; Senegal; Sierra Leone; Solomon Islands; Somalia; South Africa; South Korea; South Sudan; Sri Lanka; Sudan; Suriname; Swaziland; Tajikistan; Tanzania; Togo; Thailand; Turkmenistan; Tuvalu; Uganda; Ukraine; Uzbekistan; Vanuatu; Vietnam; Zambia; Zimbabwe

Student Loans

Students from the EU can apply for a student loan as if they were U.K. students. Students from outside the European Union and the U.K. will have to show they can the finances to self-fund for the duration of their studies.

Brexit

At the moment, Brexit will have no impact on the status of international students. The U.K. will leave Europe on the 29th March, 2019, and the negotiations regarding the status of international students has yet to be resolved.

Applying as a Mature Student

In many ways, mature students have lots of advantages over younger 18-year-olds, but they also face some extra challenges.

When you are 18, you don't have a lot of life experience. You may not know what you want to do, and you may not know what your future path holds. Some 18-year-olds just end up applying for university because that's what they think they should do. However, the advantage of being a mature student (anyone who is over 21) is that you have that extra bit of experience. Hopefully, you're applying to university because you're certain about what you want to do, about why you want to do it, and where it's going to lead you in the future.

The application process is exactly the same for mature students. There is no separate system, and you apply through UCAS just as you would straight out of school. You write your personal statement, you get it in by the deadlines, you pick your university, and your courses. However, the advantage for a mature student is that writing a personal statement should hopefully be a little bit easier, simply because you have more to write about. You likely have already been working, or you have some travel experience. If you have children, then you have the extra skills that come along with being a student parent. You should have a lot more experience to draw upon in your personal statements and in your interviews.

If your A-Levels were a while ago, then there are lots of other paths into university. You can consider doing an Access course or a Foundation course. These year-long courses help provide a transition between A-Levels and the degree coursework. Many of these Access and Foundation courses are offered at the same universities as the actual degree courses, and some of them will continue on into your degree coursework.

If your offer is based on UCAS points, then there are lots of different ways you can get UCAS points. I'm not going to talk about them all here, because the UCAS Guide to this runs to 130 pages long. But even things like life experience can count towards UCAS points. There are some universities that catered more towards mature students; for example, Birkbeck College in London isn't specifically for mature students, but the majority of its lectures are in the evening, which could make it easier if you want to combine working and doing your degree at the same time. There are also some colleges, such as at Oxford and Cambridge, that are specifically intended for mature student. And even though these provisions are in place, you will not be the only mature student no matter which university you attend. There are lots and lots of them out there! Maybe they won't be going as crazy as the 18-year-olds, but you will find a large number of mature students at any university across the U.K. There will be societies, there will be networking events, and there will be socializing events set up so you can meet other people your age.

If this is your first degree, then you can still apply for a student loan. There's no age restriction applying for a student loan, it's just it has to be your first degree.

The advantage that you have over those 18-year-olds is that, by now, you've hopefully had some experience with budgeting and managing your life. You experience with setting priorities means that you should be better equipped for handling the stresses of university. You will likely be more motivated because you've had time to think about your career path and your decision to attend university.

If you need a little bit more flexibility, then the Open University is also a brilliant place for you to consider. It has flexible online courses that you can fit in around the rest of your life. This is especially valuable for individuals with care responsibilities or those who don't live close to any universities. The best part is if you don't want to do your whole degree through the Open University, then it can provide a short course which will put you in a position to actually apply to university.

It can seem quite indulgent to leave jobs, or to step back from looking after your children to go back and study for a degree. But this is a massive investment in your future, and hopefully it will all pay off!

Applying as a Part-Time Student

Different universities and different courses are better equipped for students who wish to study part time. Not all courses and universities will allow part time students, however, so it's best to do your research before your get your heart set on a particular course.

The Open University has a wide range of flexible learning facilities, and Birkbeck University has a large number of lectures in the evening, both allowing you to fit in study around work, family, or other commitments.

Applying as a Student Parent

If you have a child or children when you apply to university, you are going to face some extra challenges. But along with these challenges, you will also find that there is a massive level of support for student parents.

Whether you are 18 applying to university with a young child, or whether you are a mature student applying with a few school-age children, you already have some fantastic parenting skills that will help you succeed at university. Trust me, I know that being a parent is hard! But without even realizing it, you have already done some amazing things. Because you are a parent, you are better at time management. You are better at prioritizing tasks. You are better at multitasking, and you're better at seeing through tasks to completion. And this is all because a small person's life depends upon you. These are skills that you've acquired in your day to life, but they will also help you succeed at university.

Thankfully, many universities provide extra support to student parents. Many universities have halls geared towards student families, and most campuses have nurseries and childcare facilities on site. There are limits to the number of places that are available, however, so don't apply to a university and assume that you're going to get suitable accommodation. You may have to decide upon a university that's closer to your support network so that you can get extra help while getting your degree.

Every university in the U.K. has student parents enrolled, so you are not going to be the only person in this situation. There are going to be support networks. There are going to be clubs. There are going to be student societies, and they're going to be geared towards helping student parents like you. No university will withhold an offer just because you are a parent. They recognize the extra skills that come with being a parent, and they want the best students that they can possibly get, irrespective of personal circumstances.

When applying for student loans, you will be automatically considered as an independent student, which means your parents' income will not be considered. The result is that you will likely get a higher level of loan to cover your living expenses. The government's childcare grant will pay up to 85% of your childcare costs, and this is paid in a lump sum at the same time as your student loan. You can also get the parents' living allowance, which is paid as a lump sum that you don't have to pay back. If you're a lone parent, or both parents are students, then you can qualify for extra benefits, such as income support and housing benefit.

If you're a parent and you're considering applying to university, then it is an absolutely fantastic step. By making this choice, you are going to be improving your future job prospects, and you're going to be setting a great example for your children.

Applications for Medicine

A-Levels for Medicine

For all medical schools, Chemistry is the core requirement, and this may come as a surprise to those who think Biology is the most crucial A-Level. Some schools do require Biology as well, but Chemistry is the most important. When you're thinking about some of your other A-Levels, you need to make sensible choices that will help you work towards your medical degree. If you've picked Biology, Chemistry, and Dance, then you had better be prepared explain in your interview how dance will help you become a better doctor. If you can't answer that question sensibly, then maybe you shouldn't pick Dance as an A-Level—or French, or Music, or Art, or History, or Politics, or Economics, or anything that doesn't directly relate to being a doctor. Anything that just looks a little bit weird may well put you at a disadvantage, since you're going to be competing against people who are doing four A-Levels: Biology, Chemistry, Physics, and Maths.

The other thing you need to be careful of when you're picking your A-Levels is that some universities will require you to have three sciences and Maths, but won't allow you to have Maths and Further Maths as two of your A-Levels. Or you can't have Biology and Human Biology, because they're too similar. The other thing is that Psychology doesn't count as a science in this instance. I know it's generally taught by science teachers, but it's not going to count as science as far as medical courses are concerned.

Typical Requirements and Offers for Medicine

University of Aberdeen – A-Level Chemistry is essential and then either Biology, Physics or Maths and one other. Typically offers AAA.

Queens' University Belfast – A-Level Chemistry is essential and another two from Biology, Physics, or Maths, as well as a fourth. Typically offers AAA and AS-A.

University of Bristol – A-Level chemistry is essential, plus another science. Typically offers AAA.

Brighton and Sussex Medical School – A-Levels in Chemistry and Biology are essential. Typically offers AAA.

University of Birmingham – A-Level in Chemistry and Biology is essential. Typically offers A*AA.

University of Buckingham – A-Level in Chemistry is essential, and either Biology, Physics, or Maths and one other. Typically offers AAB.

University of Cambridge – A-Level in Chemistry is essential, then either Biology, Physics, or Maths and one other. Typically offers A*A*A*.

UCL (University College London) – A-Levels in Biology and Chemistry are essential. Typically offers A*AA.

Cardiff University – A-Levels in Biology and Chemistry are essential. Typically offers AAA.

University of Dundee; A-Level in Chemistry is essential plus another science. Typically offers.

University of Exeter – A-Levels in Chemistry and Biology are essential. Typically offers AAA.

University of Edinburgh – A-Level in Chemistry is essential and either Biology, Physics or Maths plus one other. Typically offers AAA.

University of East Anglia – Typically offers AAA.

University of Glasgow – A-Level in Chemistry is essential and either Biology, Physics or Maths and one other. Typically offers AAA.

Hull York Medical School – A-Level in Biology and Chemistry are essential. Typically offers AAA.

Imperial College London – A-Level in Biology and Chemistry are essential. Typically offers A*AA.

King's College London, University of London – A-Level in Biology and Chemistry are essential. Typically offers AAA and AS-B.

Keele University – A-Level in Chemistry or Biology plus another science. Typically offers A*AA.

Lancaster University – A-Level in Chemistry and Biology are essential. Typically offers AAA.

University of Leeds – A-Level in Chemistry is essential. Typically offers AAA.

University of Leicester – A-Level in Chemistry and Biology is essential. Typically offers AAA.

University of Liverpool – A-Level in Chemistry and Biology are essential. Typically offers AAA.

The University of Manchester – A-Level in Chemistry is essential, and then either Biology, Physics or Maths, plus one other. Typically offers AAA.

University of Nottingham – A-Level in Chemistry and Biology are essential. Typically offers AAA.

University of Oxford – A-Level in Chemistry is essential and then either Biology, Physics, or Maths plus one other. Typically offers A*AA.

Queen Mary University of London – A-Level in Chemistry and Biology is essential plus another science. Typically offers A*AA.

University of St Andrews – A-Level in Chemistry is essential and then either Biology, Physics, or Maths, plus one other. Typically offers AAA.

St George's, University of London – A-Level in Chemistry and Biology is essential. Typically offers AAA.

Plymouth University – A-Level in Chemistry and Biology is essential. Typically offers AAA.

Applying for Medicine – The First Steps

If you are thinking about applying for medicine, there is quite a bit more to think about than other degrees.

The first thing you need to know is that only four of your five choices on your UCAS application form can be for medicine. The reason behind this is to protect you, simply because the entry requirements for medicine are so high. If you apply and don't get any offers, you still have that fifth choice to fall back on—or if you apply, get your offer, but then don't get your grades, you still have that fifth choice as your 'insurance' option.

When you're picking this non-medicine fifth choice, it is sensible to make it something medical-related. If you don't get onto your medical course and you decide that don't want to be a doctor anymore, then you don't have to take up your insurance option and can pursue whatever you like.

The other important thing that you need to know is that the entry deadline for medicine is much earlier than for other courses. You have until the 15th of October to get everything in, so things happen very quickly after you get back from the summer break. This typically means that you only have a month to get your personal statements and references sorted out. It is not a good idea to decide to apply for medicine when you go back to school in year 13—you need to have started sorting things out much earlier than this.

Less than 10 per cent of applications for medicine actually get offered a place. If you want to be one of this 10 percent, then you need to make sure that your application, your personal statement, your predicted grades, and your references really stand out.

You need to be thinking about your work experience. You should be asking yourself how you can be getting work experience, what type of work experience is important, and how to structure your extended project (EPQ) or extended essay. This is going to give you some fantastic things to write about in your application and in your interviews, and it's a really good way to show off your passion.

You need to look at the university entrance requirements and decide whether you're going to sit for the U.K. Clinical Aptitude Test (UKCAT) or the BioMedical Admissions Test (BMAT), or both. Universities will ask for either the UKCAT or the BMAT, so if you pick only universities that accept UKCAT, then you won't need to take the BMAT; however, chances are you're going to need to take both. Apply early for your tests so that you can have your choice of dates. Do not leave it until you are applying for your UCAS place, because there will not be enough time.

As early as possible, start getting ready for interviews. Think about potential questions that could come up and start thinking about strong answers. Think about ways that you can talk about your work experience, and be sure to demonstrate how much you've got out of it. Think about how you can prove that you are passionate about medicine, that being a doctor is your life. Think about ways you can impress the person interviewing you.

You should also start prepping for the UKCAT and the BMAT as soon as possible. These tests are very content-heavy, and you will have to demonstrate a lot of critical thinking, logic, and outside-the-box approaches to solving problems. These tests are not solely based on your knowledge from school.

The other thing you need to do before we even start thinking about filling out the UCAS application form is visiting universities and deciding where you want to apply. You should be looking at which course structure fits you, which module structure fits you, whether you're going to be happy at the university, city, campus, how far away it is from home, etc. There are lots and lots of things for you to consider. You have already made the difficult decision that you want to apply for medicine, but I'm afraid there is a lot of work for you to do!

The Fifth Choice

Only four of your five choices on your UCAS application form can be for medicine. This is to protect you from ending up with no offers at the end, but what should you put as your fifth choice?

You have four options when it comes to your fifth choice on your UCAS application form. The most common choice is to select a fifth medical-related subject. You could choose biomedical sciences, biochemistry, molecular biology, or anything that could potentially lead to medicine in the end. You have lots of options, but please make sure that your fifth choice has lower grade requirements than your medical school applications. This is because if you don't get your desired grades on results day, your fifth choice is going to be your insurance choice. Please remember that your personal statement likely isn't going to be tailored towards this fifth choice, so be prepared in an interview to answer questions about this, such as, "Why would you be a good student on this course even though you really want to be a doctor?"

There are lots of other medical-related jobs, and there are always other paths into medicine. I've covered all of those in different chapter. There are other vocational courses that you could put down, Dentistry and Ophthalmology for example, but those courses generally want people who really want to be dentists and ophthalmologists, so they don't always accept people who put it down as a fifth choice.

Your second option is to put down an Access course. An Access course is a year-long course which is either done at college or at university and is aimed to prepare you for a medical degree. It's basically a year-long course in-between A-Levels and a degree course, designed to get you ready for university. It also bumps up your A-Level grades if you didn't quite get them. These Access courses are often designed in conjunction with the medical schools, and the medical schools have a lot of impact into what is taught on that Access course. Some of them even guarantee you an interview at the end of the year.

Your third option is the rather risky choice of not selecting any insurance choice at all. If you are absolutely certain that the only thing you want to do is medicine, and you do not want to do anything else, then you could leave this fifth-choice blank. This is quite risky, because if you change your mind and decide you do want to do biomedical sciences, you'll then have to apply through Clearing.

Lastly, you could select something completely random. The universities do not see what your other choices are. Your medical school choices will not see, for example, that you put dance down as your fifth choice. The dance school might be slightly confused, however, because you will likely send them a personal statement which is all about how much you want to be a doctor. This isn't a very popular option, but it is something you could do if you wanted.

Your fifth choice is there to protect you. It's there to give you a safety net in case you don't get into any medical schools, so use it wisely.

Work Experience

When you're considering applying for medicine, getting the right work experience is absolutely vital for your personal statement and your interviews. But what is the right work experience, and how can you get it?

The aim of work experience is twofold. It's for you to see whether you are suited to life as a doctor before you commit all the time and effort into studying for it for years. Work experience also allows the admissions tutors at medical schools to see whether you are the right kind of person, whether you're going to be committed, and whether you're going to put the effort it takes to become a doctor.

I'm going to take you through how you can get a placement. We'll look at the different types of placements, what you're going to get out of placement, and how you can talk about it so that you really shine in your interviews.

All medical schools recognize that finding suitable work experience is going to be easier for some people than for others. No university will require you to have two weeks working experience within a hospital, because that's not always going to be possible for every student. It will be much easier for someone whose parents are both doctors working in London as opposed to someone whose parents are both unemployed and living in the countryside. Each student will have different experiences when it comes to finding work experience, so if you can't find work experience within hospital, there are lots of other things that you can do. Medical schools are simply looking for someone who is committed, who is dedicated, and who is caring. They want to know that you're going to be there and do the best for patients.

That being said, a placement within a hospital should always be your first choice because it will be a goldmine of opportunities. You may get to round with a junior doctor, you may get to sit in on meetings, or you may get to watch small procedures taking place. If you know someone who is a doctor, they should be your first port of call for trying to get this placement. Then talk to your teachers, as they quite likely have many contacts that can help get you a placement. They may know former students who are currently studying to be doctors, or who are already doctors, and they can put you in touch. They are quite likely your best source of finding a placement within hospital.

If that doesn't provide anything, then I suggest you get in contact with your local hospital trust. They may have a formal program in place which you can apply to; do this as early as possible because you don't want to miss out on the places and you don't want to miss any application deadlines. They can put you in touch with the right people. And don't just think about hospitals within your local area or within the same country. There are loads of hospitals across the world, and there may be better formal programs if you go abroad.

If you've never been to your local hospital, then I'm sure you've seen your local GP on a semi-regular basis. There are a lot more GPs around than there are hospitals, so this might give you a better shot of getting a placement, such as doing a week's worth of work shadowing. The first thing you can do is to email or call in to the reception and see if they have something in place. They may say yes; they may say no. The advantage of there being a lot more GPs around than hospitals is that you can apply at a lot more places, and hopefully one of them will say yes!

Volunteering is also an excellent idea. Even if you have a hospital placement or a placement with a GP, there's no reason why you can't add volunteering as well. It shows a different dimension, and it gives you more things to talk about in your interview and personal statements. Volunteering in a care home every Saturday morning for a year shows dedication, it shows commitment, and it shows that you're willing to turn up and do the hard work. Bear in mind that volunteering isn't something you can start right before your application, or something that you can promise to start after you've been accepted—you have to go into your application showing that you've already been volunteering for a sustained period of time and that you plan to continue doing it after you've been accepted to medical school.

St John's Ambulance is a fantastic place to start volunteering, because they are going to give you first-aid training and you're going to be treating real patients out in the field on a regular basis. The Red Cross has emergency volunteers who help during large emergency situations, such as distributing food bags or clothing to people affected by flooding, fires, or large storms. All of these volunteering experiences will expose you to a different side of medical care.

It is absolutely pointless, however, to do any work experience if you cannot reflect on it properly at the end. If you can't work out what you've seen, what you've learned, and what you could do about it, then work experience won't help your application. If you want to get the most out of your medical work experience, then you're going to need to get involved, not just stand back passively. Ask questions. Ask the doctor, why did they do this? Offer to help in any small way you can. Find out what's going on. At the end of each day, spend some time making notes on what you've seen. Follow up on anything that you found interesting. If there was an interesting condition or an interesting procedure, read some papers about it, or watch some YouTube videos about it. Follow up on what you've learned in any way that you can, and make sure that you write all of this down. This is actually the biggest piece of advice I can give. Because your medical work experience might be some time away from your interview, you want to be able to go back and read your notes about your work experience so that they're fresh on your mind when you sit for your interview.

Finding work experience can be a bit tricky, but you just need to keep going. You need to be determined, and show your passion for being a doctor.

Katie's Story – Getting Rejected from Medical School, and Not Giving Up!

Katie is a true inspiration. I asked her to write about how initially failing to get into medical school made her more determined to become a doctor. The alternate title for her response was, "How getting rejected twice taught me some valuable lessons about finding strength through failure!" Here is her story...

Medical school is renowned for its competitiveness. Those who become doctors are seen as successful and accomplished, so what do you do when they reject you? My message to you: find strength in your failures and use them to grow.

My first mistake when applying to medical school was my poor academic record. The A-Levels I achieved were far from the string of As most candidates possess. Medicine requires you to demonstrate your academic ability, and on paper, I did not look like the ideal candidate. So there are two choices: resit your A-Levels or do another degree to prove you are capable. I decided a degree was more appropriate as fewer schools accepted resit candidates.

My second mistake was not looking at my application objectively. I wanted to be a doctor so much that I poured my heart out in my personal statement, but I quickly received rejections as I didn't meet the basic requirements. Each medical school essentially has a tick-box list of what they are looking for. However much you would love to do medicine, however passionate you sound, it will all be for nothing if you do not meet the basic requirements. The key areas are academics, work experience, the personal statement, and entrance exams.

Whilst working on my academic record, I had a lot of time to dedicate to other endeavours. Volunteering and caring for patients, organising events, and taking on an additional job allowed me to build my experience in the care environment. Firstly, this made me absolutely sure I wanted to do medicine. Many people like the idea of being a doctor, but I have met many students who really didn't know what the work would entail and then realised too late that medicine wasn't for them. Secondly, it gave me the experiences to write about in my personal statement, so that I could demonstrate that I was the candidate they were looking for.

The personal statement is your chance to stand out and validate your claim for that all-important place. Reading Tomorrow's Doctors and the General Medical Councils' guidelines will give you a good overview of the qualities they are looking for. You should also look at your chosen universities – perhaps they have a specific goal in mind for their graduates, such as becoming a champion for mental health. Think of how you can look like their perfect candidate. How can you link what you have learnt and experienced to the university's mission statement?

Finally, there are entrance exams, my third mistake. There is a common misconception that you cannot revise for these, but it is not true! Practice makes perfect. Use well-reviewed resources such as books and online programs so you are prepared. I didn't revise the first time and my results were average. The following year with practice, I increased my score to a competitive one.

Those who have tried and failed have at least tried. By learning from my mistakes, I finally gained a place at medical school and I learnt so much more in the process. I hope this small insight inspires you to not be disheartened by failure but to embrace it, to grow as a person and become your best self.

Katie, aged 28.
Studies: Medicine at King's College London, Year 2.
A-Levels: A Psychology, C Biology
AS-Levels: D Maths, E Chemistry
Degree: 2.i Applied Biomedical Sciences

UKCAT

As well as your A-Level results, if you want to get into the majority of medical schools, then you will need to sit another exam as well. This is the UKCAT, or the U.K. Clinical Aptitude Test. The UKCAT may be in a format that you're not necessarily very familiar with, because it's a two hour exam that you sit on the computer. It's quite unlike the handwritten ones for your A-Levels.

The UKCAT has five different sections, and each section is strictly timed. You don't get the chance to spend as much time reading and answering the questions as you want, and it will automatically move on from one section to the next section when the time runs out.

The test starts with Verbal Reasoning, which has 44 questions to answer in 21 minutes—that's a lot of questions in not a lot of time. There are going to be 11 different blocks of text and 11 different scenarios, so you're going to need to read everything and then answer four multiple choice questions on each set. Your options will be 'True', 'False', 'Can't tell,' or you will have to finish an incomplete sentence by picking which of the options is the best match. This is really time-pressured because you have a lot of reading to do, a lot of comprehending to do, and then a lot choices to make, only 21 minutes.

The Decision Making section gives you 31 minutes to answer 29 questions. Again, these are going to be multiple choice, and you will have to use logic to solve puzzles, work out which of the statements is correct, or find the best argument to match a situation.

Quantitative Reasoning gives you 24 minutes to answer 36 questions. These are going to be maths questions, but they are not always purely maths-based. There will be logic and puzzle-solving in there as well.

Abstract Reasoning is a very short section, even though it has a large number of questions. In this section, you have 13 minutes to answer 55 questions. This section will challenge you to quickly match shapes and identify patterns. It is designed to force you into making quick decisions, so you can't spend a lot of time reasoning about things.

The final section is the Situational Judgment Test. You have 26 minutes to answer 69 questions about what you would do in a given situation. You're given a hypothetical situation where something has occurred and then you have to decide what your response would be. You will also be asked what the most appropriate response would be in this situation, and what the least appropriate would be.

None of the content will be based on your A-Levels. There is no science or maths in the UKCAT—it is all about reasoning, logic, and situational decision-making. It is unlikely you will have come across anything like this before in school.

It is possible to prepare for this test before you sit, however. There are lots of free questions available on the Internet, but there are also plenty of books and courses that you have to pay quite a lot to access. There is no negative marking on the UKCAT, so it is definitely worth going in prepared and putting an answer down for every single question.

The UKCAT test is sat online at specific test centres which are located all around the U.K., and also around the world. You can book them from May until September. The first test is taken in July, and the last test is early October. You have a couple of weeks after the last test date to get you a UCAS application in.

You cannot do this test within school; it has to be done at a registered test centre. Depending on where you sit the test or how early you sit, it's going to cost you between £65 and £115. There is a bursary scheme available, and students who are eligible for free school meals (or are in a few other situations) can apply for this bursary so that they don't have to pay to sit the test.

One of the great things about the UKCAT is that you get your results straight away. You can then take your results and compare them with what the universities are looking for. You can also assess how much the universities take the UKCAT into account when they're doing admissions. So if you got a high score, fantastic, but if your score's slightly on the lower side, then you should avoid the universities require a really high UKCAT score and you can adjust your applications accordingly. You're going to have two weeks after the last test date before your UCAS form needs to be submitted.

Each section is going to be scaled to between 300 and 900 marks. There are four sections that will be scaled this way (Verbal Reasoning, Decision Making, Quantitative Reasoning, and Abstract Reasoning), so the total score you will get at the end will be between 1200 and 3600. Last year's the mean result was 2540. They are then sorted into deciles, or groups of 10%, which means that both you and the university will know if you are in the top 10%, the bottom 10%, or anywhere in between.

The Situational Judgment Test, the last section, is going to be banded into four sections. Band one indicates that all of your responses were appropriate and you were doing the right things, whereas band four indicates that you weren't doing the right things or you weren't taking appropriate actions in that situation. Not all of the universities take the situational judgment test into account.

You can only sit the UKCAT once per year, and your test results are only valid for a year. Unfortunately, you don't really get a choice about whether you have to sit the UKCAT, because it is a requirement for almost every university. It isn't like any other exam you've sat before, so it is definitely worth trying to do as much preparation as you can.

Universities That Require the UKCAT
University of Aberdeen
Aston University
University of Bristol
University of Birmingham
Cardiff University
University of Dundee
University of Exeter
University of Edinburgh
University of East Anglia UEA
University of Glasgow
Hull York Medical School
King's College London, University of London
Keele University
University of Leicester
University of Liverpool

University of Manchester
University of Newcastle
University of Nottingham
Plymouth University
Queen Mary University of London
Queen's University Belfast
University of Southampton
University of St Andrews
St George's, University of London

UKCAT Bursaries
A range of students will qualify for a bursary to cover the cost of sitting the UKCAT. You'll need to provide evidence and you can apply via the UKCAT booking website. You can apply if you have received:

Free School Meals
16-to-19 Bursary
Education Maintenance Allowance
Further Education Discretionary Learner Support
The Full-Rate Maintenance Grant from Student Finance
The Full-Rate Young Students' or Independent Students' Bursary
Income Support
Job Seeker's Allowance
Employment and Support Allowance or Universal Credit
Child Tax Credit (or if you are from a family that has received Child Tax Credlt)
Income Support
Income-based Jobseeker's Allowance
Income-based Employment and Support Allowance
Universal Credit or Asylum Support

Universities That Rely Heavily on the UKCAT

Some medical schools will look heavily at the UKCAT score before they decide to invite you for an interview. The following schools have in the past relied heavily on UKCAT scores.

University of Aberdeen
Barts and the London School of Medicine
University of Dundee
University of Edinburgh
University of Exeter
University of Glasgow
King's College, London
University of Leicester
University of Manchester
University of Newcastle
University of Nottingham
University of Sheffield
University of Southampton
University of St Andrews

Universities That Don't Rely as Much on the UKCAT

A few schools use other data in combination with the UKCAT to make their decision, but some still have a minimum for the UKCAT scores. In the past these schools have included:

University of Birmingham
University of Buckingham
University of Bristol
Cardiff University
Hull York Medical School
Keele University
University of Liverpool

Plymouth University
Queens University Belfast
St George's, University of London
University of East Anglia

BMAT

There are eight U.K. universities which require the BMAT (BioMedical Aptitude Test) as well as A-Levels if you want to apply for medicine.

The BMAT is a two-hour, multi-section test that is taken on paper. You can sit it once a year, and you can either sit in September or October.

For the September test you need to register yourself, and you can do this online and then go to a test centre. The results are available from the end of September, so you can use the results to inform your UCAS choices. Please note that the September test is not accepted by the University of Oxford.

For the October test, it's all done through your school. Tell the exams officer at your school that they need to register you, and then you will be able to sit your exam at your school. Because the results of the October test aren't released until a month later, you won't know what your BMAT results are before you apply for UCAS. This is different from the UKCAT, where you get your results straight away. Because you have to wait until after you've submitted your UCAS application before you get your BMAT results, you won't be able to base your UCAS choices on how well you scored in the BMATs.

There are three sections to the test. Section One is an hour long and it's 35 multiple choice questions. You are not allowed to use a calculator for this. It is going to be verbal, spatial, and mathematical reasoning. There are going to be logic puzzles. There are going to be patterns. It's going to be problem-solving, and there are going to be logical assumptions that you will need to make. They want to see how you can tackle tricky situations.

Section Two is 30 minutes long, and this is a knowledge-based section. There are 27 multiple choice questions on biology, chemistry, physics and maths. It's going to be GCSE-level science and maths, but it's borderline AS-level in each of these subjects. You are not allowed a calculator for this section either. If you have not continued with each of these subjects, some revision may be required.

Section Three is 30 minutes long and it's a long-form answer. Here they're going to see how you respond to the situation posed, and will evaluate if you can communicate in good written English.

Just like any exam, you should study as many past examples as you can get your hands on. All the BMAT past papers are available on the Cambridge assessment website. You can download all of those for free.

Section One and Section Two are scaled from one to nine, with five being the score that the majority of people get—or roughly about half marks. If most people are getting half marks, this gives you an indication of how hard this test actually is. Very few people will get a six, and only the truly exceptional people are going to get a seven or above. Section Three is given a mark for the content between zero and five, and a mark for the English will be either an A, a C, or an E. This is marked by two different examiners, and then the overall mark is going to be a combination of the two marks from the different examiners.

The results are only valid for a year and you can only take the BMAT once a year, so make sure you're taking it at the right time of year, either September or October. If you're going to reapply later, then you're going to have to redo the BMAT for a second time.

Universities that Require the BMAT
Brighton and Sussex Medical School
University of Cambridge
University College London)
Imperial College London
Keele University (for international students only)
Lancaster University
University of Leeds
University of Oxford (will only accept October test results)

GAMSAT

This is a graduate medical school admissions test, and it's taken twice a year, in September and in March. It is going to be a long day if you decide to take this test, roughly nine hours, and you are not allowed to leave early.

There are three parts to the exam: It starts with ten minutes to read Section One, followed by 100 minutes to answer questions. You will be given five minutes to read Section Two, followed by 60 minutes to answer questions. Then you get a 60-minute break for lunch. Section Three is a long section. You get 10 minutes of reading, and then you have 117 minutes to answer questions on Section Three.

Section One is reasoning and humanities, with multiple-choice questions. Section Two is all about your written communication, and Section Three is multiple-choice questions on reasoning in biological and physical sciences. With the multiple-choice questions, there is no negative marking, so don't leave any questions blank in your answer booklet.

The scores will be weighted at the end, so you get a score for each section, and then you get an overall score. Section Three is weighted twice as much as Sections One and Two. You're going to need to check which universities require this for graduate medical school entry. Some of them do and some of them don't, and this is accepted in a large number of countries.

Interviews for Medicine

Medical school interviews can be really intense. Fantastic predicted grades, excellent test results, a brilliant personal statement and amazing references will mean absolutely nothing if the interviewer doesn't see you answer the questions with confidence.

The questions you will be asked are going to fall into four main groups. You will be asked about your motivation for becoming a doctor; your work experience and what you learned from it; your opinions or your ideas about popular topics; and then how you apply logic to strange and unfamiliar situations.

The exact style of the interview is going to vary slightly between institutions, but all of them will ask questions that fall into those four broad categories. It is a really good idea to spend some time mind-mapping each of those areas and writing down a few key points. Don't try and script answers, because you will inevitably get flustered in the interview if they ask the questions in a way you were not expecting. Just make a few key points on each area. Think of all of the things about your work experience, and all of your motivation behind becoming a doctor.

Although it varies, many students encounter a traditional interview where they face a panel that spends quite a long time asking questions. On the panel, there will inevitably be people writing down notes; there's going to be someone who looks really stern, someone who looks really happy, and then a few with blank faces who you can't tell anything from. This type of interview can be quite intimidating, but it's still very common.

A few places have moved towards a series of mini-interviews, where you go around having short conversations with lots of different people. It's one-on-one, which can be intense in its own right if you're used to the traditional style of interview. There could be some role-play involved, where you meet a patient and have to help in some way. Or there could be another situation that unfolds, and they want to see how you react to it.

During the interview, don't be afraid to ask for clarification. If you're not exactly sure what they're asking, ask them to expand upon it. Don't give them the answer that you think they are looking for. They want to admit *you*, not the person you think you should be. They are genuinely interested in what you have to say.

For some of the questions, there will be no right or wrong answer. They just want to see how you work through the problem, what your opinion is on the situation, and how you would deal with things. You can prepare for these interviews by making notes on each of the topics that follow.

Lastly, you need to be confident and believe in your abilities. You deserve to be in this interview, you deserve this place at medical school. Don't feel as though you have to hold back. Be confident and show them what an amazing person you are! You've gotten this far, after all. You got the interview based on your amazing predicted grades and your awesome personal statement, so now is the time to show them what a brilliant doctor you will be.

Common Interview Questions

You should aim to prepare answers for each of these questions before your interview. Don't learn them verbatim, as you may get flustered if you may a mistake. Think about a few key points for each question.

You as a doctor and your motivation

- Why do you want to be a doctor?
- How has the recent publicity about junior doctors' contacts made you feel?
- What is your motivation?
- What qualities are important for a doctor to have?
- Why did you choose to apply here?
- What do you find most interesting about medicine?
- Can you give me an example of a medical issue you're particularly interested in?
- Have you read any interesting articles recently?
- Can you give me an example of a recent medical breakthrough that really excited you?
- What is the most historically important medical innovation?
- Which was the most interesting dissection you've seen? (There are lots on YouTube!)
- Is dissection of cadavers an important tool for teaching?
- If you don't get a place at medical school, what will you do?
- What is the most appealing aspect of being a doctor?
- What are the least appealing aspects of being a doctor?
- What is the hardest part about being a doctor?
- What are your weaknesses?
- What are your strengths?

- Why do you deserve a place on this programme?
- What can you offer this medical school that other students can't?
- What extracurricular activities do you have that would mean you're going to be a good doctor? (Try to think of medical-related ones and non-medical-related ones.)
- Are there any new extracurricular activities that the university offers that you're planning on trying out?
- Is empathy important?
- Tell me about your extended project.
- What are your long-term career goals?
- Do you have a specialism in mind?
- What would be the five things you'd take to a deserted island?
- Which is more important, passion or effort?
- What three words would you use to describe yourself?
- Is evidence-based practice important?
- What do you think of PBL versus tutorials as a style of teaching?
- What do you think the work load is going to be like?
- How will you cope if you fall behind?
- What mechanisms do you have in place to deal with stress?
- Imagine you're a junior doctor, how would your patients describe you?
- How would you react if you made a mistake that led to a patient dying?
- What public health campaigns are you aware of?

Your work experience and what you got from it
- Has any one doctor inspired you?
- What have you learnt from the doctors you've been speaking to?

- Why is work experience important?
- What did you learn from your time doing work experience?
- During your work experience, did you see any difficult situations?
- What did you find challenging about your work experience?
- What was the best part about your work experience?
- Did you work experience change any of your previous views?

Application of logic to strange and unfamiliar situations
- How much does the moon weigh?
- What would a world without fire be like?
- How many notes are there in a song?
- Why do we wear clothes?

Your opinions or your ideas about popular topics
- Discuss the continuing problem of overuse of antibiotics.
- Should the NHS fund IVF?
- Should organ donation be 'opt-in' or 'opt-out'?
- Should the NHS fund public health campaigns?
- Should underage children be given contraception?
- Is the sugar tax a good idea?
- Australia doesn't pay childcare benefit to families that have not vaccinated their children, should the U.K. follow this model?
- There have been a number of recent cases in the news where doctors have wanted to discontinue treatment for terminally ill children, but the parents have wanted to continue. Who has the decision-making right and why?

- Should people who become ill due to their lifestyle contribute to the cost of their treatment?
- Should patients with HIV be made to inform their sexual partners?
- Should euthanasia be legal?
- Should abortion be legal?
- Should sex selection of a foetus be legal?
- Should the birth of 'saviour siblings' be legal?
- Should people be fined for attending A&E or calling an ambulance in inappropriate situations?
- Each year 854 women die from cervical cancer. The recent introduction of a vaccine against this aims to reduce those numbers. The same vaccine could prevent deaths from penile (134 yearly deaths) and anal (399 yearly deaths) cancer, should the NHS fund the vaccine for men as well?
- How much of a problem is 'health tourism'?
- Should the NHS spend more or less on mental health provisions?

Jenny's Story – My Interview for Medicine

Jenny has A-Levels in Physics (A*), Biology (A), Chemsitry (A) and Maths (A)

With my interview just around the corner, I can't deny how nervous I felt. It wasn't only that this university was one the of the few that I've always admired, I felt even more nervous because it was the only course I could picture myself studying.

I decided to arrive in the city the night before my interview, as I wanted to make sure I was well rested. Once I checked into my hotel, I got the opportunity to further explore the city that I would hopefully be spending a lot of time at in the near future.

I awoke the next morning feeling refreshed and ready to tackle my interview. Reminding myself of the advice my tutor gave me, "Relax, and be yourself," I headed on to my interview. I took a seat at the table opposite a lecturer and the head of the department. After a brief introduction to the panel, they proceeded to ask me several questions.

I was asked by the panel, "Why do you want to study this course?" I felt that early on in the interview, I wanted the panel to see how serious and passionate I was about studying this course. I shared with them how as a youngster I witnessed a close family receiving life-saving treatment from paramedics. This was the exact moment where I knew that when I grew up, I wanted to be in the position where I can apply myself to saving lives. For me, that led me to my decision to study and specialise in medicine.

They then discussed with me how tough a medicine degree can be for some people. I appreciated that they didn't sugar coat the course. It reiterated to me that if I chose to study medicine, I needed to be self-motivated. Self-motivation can only be achieved when you are absolutely certain that this is the path for you. We also discussed my work experience in hospitals. The subject then turned to medicine in the media. I informed them of a really cool medical trial I read about a few days prior in the newspaper. Both members of the panel seemed quite impressed with the fact that I keep an eye out for news related to medicine.

The panel also asked what I would do to combat the stress of the degree. To me, this was the perfect opportunity to discuss my extracurricular activities. I discussed my other interests in life and showed them that I'm not just a study fanatic. I am still very much a fun-loving teenager. I love water sports, and it is a form of relaxation and fun for me.

As the interview concluded, I was given the opportunity to ask my own questions. I asked the panel for their feedback on me and whether they feel I would be suited the course. I felt the interview was very positive and couldn't wait to hear back from the university.

Courses Related to Medicine, but Aren't Medicine

Many of the students I meet want to become doctors because they want to help people. But there are many ways that you can help people that don't involve being a doctor. Being a doctor doesn't pay very well, it's very stressful, and it has very long hours. There are loads of medically related degrees that you might not have considered.

Pharmacists are on the front line of medicine. If there's something wrong with you, and you can't get to a doctor or a hospital, you go and see a pharmacist. They analyse patients' symptoms, take their histories, interact with them, and make sure what they're taking is suitable and safe. A pharmacist is a brilliant career.

When someone collapses unexpectedly, the call goes out for "Is there a doctor in the house?", but what you really should be asking for is a paramedic. Paramedics are the people who save lives every single day. In a life-or-death situation, they can be much more useful than a doctor.

Biomedical sciences is a broad enough degree that if you decide you really want to be a doctor at the end, then you can follow a post-graduate course in that. But biomedical science, biochemistry, biology, or a degree in molecular biology will let you follow a path into research, into drug discovery, into cancer research, or into curing childhood illnesses. These paths all still help people, and if you get yourself a PhD, you can still call yourself a doctor.

Dentistry and ophthalmology have much better working hours, much better working conditions, and much less chance of someone dying on your watch. These are brilliant careers—and judging by how much my dentist goes on holiday, they pay really well, too!

Nursing or midwifery qualifications will give you a lot more daily interaction with people. When I have spent time in hospital with my son, I see the nurses about ten times as much as I see the doctors. The nurses and midwives are the people that you really get to know. They're the ones you pop in and say hello to if you happen to be passing by a ward. They're the ones who you give the presents to at the end. They're the ones who actually care for you on a daily basis.

Radiographers, audiologists, or physiotherapists and other specialists are highly trained and have such an important role in the medical field. They work within hospitals and medical centres, and they assist with numerous critical tasks, whether it's diagnosing patients and passing the information on to the doctors, or consulting with the doctors about what could be wrong. Very often a doctor won't be specialist enough to look at an X-ray or an ultrasound. They will pass it on to the radiologist, who will write a report and then send that back to the doctor. Physiotherapists help regain mobility, and their lives, on a daily basis. They have such an important role.

Maybe you've had the idea ever since childhood that you would be a doctor, but sometimes that idea can get in the way of you seeing all of these other awesome medically related careers that might be better suited to you. Because let's be honest, being a doctor is really hard. Their hours are bad, their pay is not great, and people die. It's incredibly, incredibly stressful. And there is absolutely nothing wrong with deciding that maybe you don't want to have a life that is that stressful.

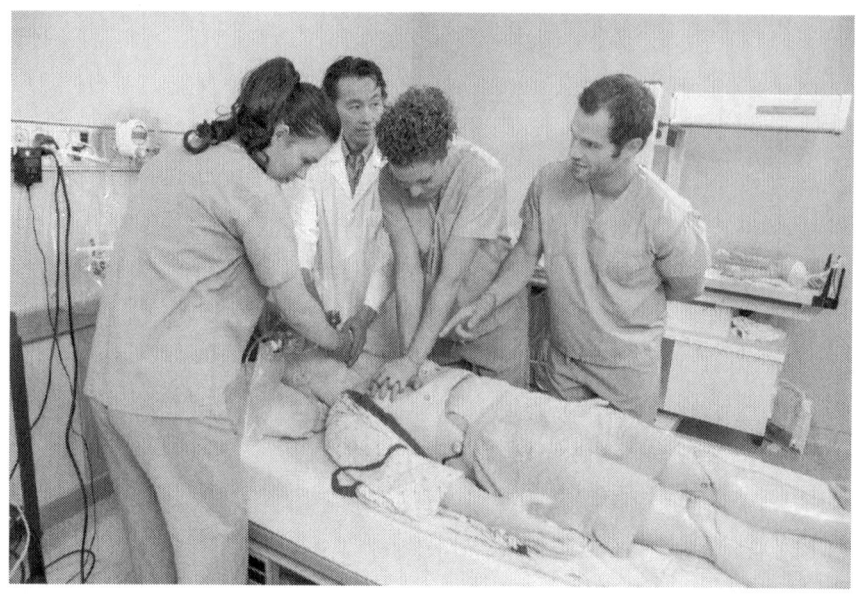

What to Do If You Don't Get a Place to Study Medicine

If you didn't get any offers in medicine, or if on results day you didn't get the grades that you need to take up your place in medicine, then do not despair.

There are five different things you can think about doing if you don't get your place to study medicine. It's a little bit different from other degrees because you can't go through Clearing, and you can't really go through Adjustment, either. There are not a lot of changes you can make after you apply, because there just aren't a lot of medical places out there.

Firstly, there is that fifth choice on your UCAS application. So, you can take that up if you want to. If you don't want to take up that fifth choice, then there are a few other things you can do.

Think about if medicine is really the right career for you. Why didn't you get a place? Was it something that happened in interview, and did you get any feedback from the interviewers? Or if you didn't get your grades, are you so far below that even if you apply next year, you are not going to get the place? If so, you can apply through Clearing to do a different course entirely. There are a large number of medically related degrees that might be better suited to you (see previous section), and these other degree courses might have places available through Clearing.

If you want to continue on the medical path, then there are a few different things you can think about. You can think about going to study abroad. Europe isn't that far away, and Ireland is very close. The majority of these medical schools teach in English, so not being able to speak a foreign language shouldn't be a problem. But please be aware that they all have different application deadlines, so you should definitely do your research.

You can consider doing an undergraduate, and then go for medicine as a graduate entry. You'll be a little bit older, but you'll also have much more life experience and confidence, which will put you in a better position when you apply as a graduate.

You could also take a gap year. I don't mean a gap year to go and work in the supermarket, I mean a proper gap year where you go off and get some amazing work experience, say volunteering in a hospital in a different country. Use this gap year to make your personal statements for your medical school application really shine. And then you can apply for the next year. The advantage of doing this is that you'll know what your grades are (and your BMAT and UKCAT scores, too), and you can apply to universities that are more likely to accept you based on your grades.

If your grades aren't quite high enough to go straight on to a medical degree, then you can have a look at doing medicine with a foundation year. This is just another year of study before your medical degree begins, and it provides with you the necessary information that you may have missed on your A-Levels. Then you can progress straight on to the normal medical degree. In some cases, but not all, the entry requirements for foundation courses are lower, so you can get in with all Bs instead of all As.

The other thing you can do is an Access course. A year-long Access course, either at college or at a university, can be linked to your medical degree. So if you are determined to become a doctor, but haven't got a place or haven't quite got the grades, then there are lots of other options out there for you.

Universities

How to Pick a University

How to pick university is potentially one of the most important decisions you have made in your life so far. It is a big decision, and you need to be getting it right.

When you're picking a university, there are a number of things to consider:

- City or campus location
- How far you are away from home
- University course combination
- Climate
- Social life
- Sports
- Most importantly, where you'll be happy

One of the first things that need to be taken into account is the type of location.

When we throw around the terms city and campus university, we're talking about two different types of location. You can have a campus university in or very close to a city, so campus universities are not always in the middle of nowhere. Campus universities just mean that they have everything in one place. Your first-year halls, your lecture theatres, the clubs, the bars, the cafes, the shops, the doctors, the students' union are all going to be in one centralized location. It's going to include things perhaps you didn't even think of, like mental health provisions, childcare provisions, or the library. That means you don't have to travel that far, especially in your first year when you're probably going to live on campus. You'll never have to leave campus if you don't want to.

For example, in the first year, you can roll out of bed at ten minutes to 8:00 and still make your 8:00 lecture. Because campuses are so centralized, there is also the perception that they're going to be a little bit safer, because typically only students and staff are on campus. You don't have to go very far to get back from the clubs or the pubs because it's a five-minute walk in an area that is very busy and full of other students. You don't have to jump in a taxi; you don't have to walk through a city late at night by yourself or get public transport. The other advantage is that wherever you go, you're going to bump into somebody that you know. If you walk into the library, there's going to be a table of people there working that you know, so you can sit down with them. If you have a spare five minutes and you want to go and grab a cup of coffee, that can quickly turn into an hour sitting down and chatting with people you know.

One of the main disadvantages of a campus university is that you don't get to see a lot of the city that you've moved to. You won't get to experience the culture, and you won't get to experience meeting other people. You can spend weeks of your life not leaving an area the size of a few square miles. While some people may like this, some people may not.

City universities are a different format. They are spread out within a city. Your halls may be a bus ride from your lecture theatre; your lecture theatre may be a bus ride or a long walk from the bars or the student union. You may walk past many university buildings—whether it's lecture theatres, the student health provision, or general offices—and you won't even know that they're part of the university. There are large chunks of major cities that are wholly owned by universities, and people wandering around will never even know. In between all of these university buildings, there are going to be non-university buildings. Shops, cafes, bars where anybody can go, because it's just a regular shop. And there are going to be people all over the place. If you're walking from one lecture theatre to another lecture theatre, you're just going to be walking down an ordinary street. You won't be able to turn to the person next to you and chat with them, because chances are they're not a student.

The big advantage to a city university is that you will experience what is going on in that city. You're going to come across things that you weren't expecting. If you isolate yourself in a campus university, you're not going to happen across stuff unexpectedly—but if you wander around a city, aimlessly perhaps, going from one place to another, you're going to come across new experiences and new people that you never expected. Some of these are going to be good, and some of these are going to be wrong. The disadvantage of a city university is that you have a lot further to travel, which can make it more expensive. The halls can be quite a long way from the lecture theatres.

The decision, in the end, is entirely up to you. You need to decide what type of university you think will fit you best. You should ask yourself what kind of university suits your personality, and where you're going to be happiest spending the next three, four, five, six years of your life.

Your social life may seem like a trivial thing, but you're going to be living at this university for a while. You need to consider your social life. It's not going to be the most significant consideration, but it is substantial. If you love going clubbing, going to bars, going out every night, maybe a quiet country university that doesn't have access to all those things may not be the best place for you. You need to pick a university that is going to fit in with your lifestyle.

The course choice is going to be the most important thing, so you need to look closely at the breakdown of the units in the course. What units do you cover in your first year? Is the first-year curriculum broad? Can you change course if you change your mind? If you are keen on one topic, pick a university that teaches it. Don't pick a university that has a good reputation if they don't teach the topics that you're interested in.

We also need to talk about the weather. My husband went to the University of Manchester, where it rains like every single time we go for a visit. It rains a lot, and I don't like rain. It messes up my hair and makes it all frizzy. I didn't want rain at university, so I went to Bath where it doesn't rain a lot. I know it's frivolous and I apologize for that, but I would not have been happy in Manchester. My husband wouldn't have been happy in Bath, because he loved Manchester. Your university decision is such a personal thing!

The other thing you need to consider is the distance from home. When I was picking universities, I applied to Imperial, Kings, Bristol Bath, and Southampton. I applied to three London universities, and when I was talking to my parents about where I would live, it went like: "Well, of course, you will live at home," and I was kind of like, "Oh, no, no I won't. Not going to go home when I am at university!"

So I immediately crossed off three London universities that I had applied for, and I was left with a choice of three. If you want to live at home, pick a university that is really close. If you don't want to live at home, *don't* pick a university that is really close!

There are going to be lots of different things you need to take into account when you decide whether or not you want to live at home for university. You may have responsibilities at home. You may have parents or children that you need to care for, which means you need to stay at home. You may have a great bedroom which you just don't want to leave. Would your parents let you come and go at whatever time? Is living at home going to be something that you need to do? Is it something that you want to do? Would it hamper your social life and thus hamper your university experience? I didn't want to move too far away from my parents, just in case everything went wrong. I didn't want to be more than three hours away from home, so I discounted the whole of the North of England and just stayed in the south. This turned out great, because I went to Bath, which is the best university in the whole world ever!

Accommodation and transport are also important considerations. If your accommodation is in one place, and all the pubs and clubs are in another place, but transport stops at 11 o'clock at night, that means you either have to walk home (which is a daft idea because you're going to be wearing high heels), or you'll have to find somewhere to stay or not go out at all. When you think about accommodation, you want to think about the price of accreditation. It is a lot cheaper to stay at home. Maybe if your parents are paying for university, perhaps they won't pay for accommodation. Obviously, the London accommodation is going to be expensive, and the other problem with London accommodation is that the universities are always looking at housing further out. I know lots of London universities that have their accommodation way out in the suburbs, so you're going to have a long commute into university every day, which is a little bit of a drag.

Sarah's Story – How I Picked My Uni

Sarah has A-levels in Drama (B), History (B) and French (C)

Choosing where I would be spending the next few years of my life was at the top of my to-do list. I was pretty certain of the type of course I wanted to study at university. This was my starting point. I made a list of all the universities that had the courses of my choice. To narrow this list down, I had certain specifications I needed for the university to possess.

One of these was distance. I knew even though it was the cheapest solution, I definitely did not want to be living at home. I would be turning 18 shortly before the start of university. This meant I would officially be an adult and I wanted to be free to make my own choices as an adult. Staying at home would mean having to continue doing the chores my parents had set for me and living by a curfew. It did not sound student-like and at all appealing to me.

Having said that, I also knew I wanted to be fairly close by my parents, just in case of home sickness or emergencies. I wanted to be able to reach them by one train journey at a maximum of two hours. This shortened my list of potential universities.

I then looked at the type of university I wanted to attend. There are two types—campus and city universities. With a campus, everything from student accommodation to study halls are located very close to each other. You could reach everything within 10 to15 minutes. A collegiate university tends to be a lot more widespread, e.g., your accommodation could be up to an hour away from the main university site. For me a campus site was far more appealing. It would mean I wouldn't have to spend further money on travel to attend my lectures. Being a big lover of libraries, I could work all night in the university library and reach home within minutes.

Another aspect I looked at was the surroundings of the university. I'm an introvert by nature and I love quiet surroundings. I narrowed my choices to cities that weren't as popular amongst the masses. This also meant the nightlife wasn't as exciting in my university choices as it was elsewhere. Bars and clubs are definitely not my scene of choice. I would much rather hang out with my friends at a tea room. Living costs and accommodation prices also played a big part in my shortlist. I didn't want to be paying out of my ears for everyday living.

Once I had a definite shortlist, I booked open days. Out of the whole process in choosing a university, this was the deciding factor. I'm a big believer in following your gut instincts. Once I visited a university, my instincts would immediately kick in and tell me whether or not this university would make me happy. I chose a university that definitely makes me happy and I couldn't be more proud of myself

Open Days

I am a firm believer that the most important factor in deciding where you're going to go to university is where you're going to be happiest. This is why open days are a fantastic opportunity for you to go to experience university life, and decide where you are going to be happy. When I was younger, I had a dream university. I'd planned on going there when I applied, and it was forefront in my mind that that was where I wanted to go to university. But when I actually went to the open date, I didn't like it. Even though I'd spent so much of my childhood going out to places close to it, and going to events that were associated with it, when I actually got there and met the students, I didn't like it. And then I ended up going to University of Bath because I felt happy there. I went to the open date, and I smiled. I walked out onto the amphitheatre, in the blazing sunshine, next to the lake, saw the looks of all of the happy students, and I knew this was where I was going to spend the next four years of my life. And they were four brilliant, amazing, happy years!

You are making a big decision. And this may be one of the first truly big decisions that you've had to make all by yourself. You've got to decide where you're going to be living for the next three, four, five, or even six years. This is a long time, and it's going to feel even longer if you end up somewhere that you're not happy. Reading prospectuses, looking at things online, and watching other people's videos is a great indication of where you might be happy. But pictures can be deceiving. They make somewhere small and overcrowded seem large and spacious. There is no substitute for actually going to the place and seeing how you respond to the environment. Open days are the perfect opportunity for seeing what you think of things.

Open days season kicks off early in June. This is great opportunity for a day off school just after your mock exams. I know that I definitely threw in a few cheeky extra ones where I wasn't actually intending on applying, just because I didn't fancy going into school on a particular day. Obviously, this is not something you should tell your teachers.

After June and July, it will quiet down a little bit, but most Saturdays up to the UCAS application deadline will have a few open days. You should try and visit as many as you can. You need to make a long list of places that you're interested in. Use the university profiles in this book to make a list of places you're interested in, and then go and visit them and see how they feel.

Register beforehand for the ones that you're interested in, and they might send you a goody bag. It is at this time of year that you start to accumulate a large number of free pens and post-it notes, as universities send these out as advertising. In the pack that they send you, there might also be a list of lectures. Have a look through them and sign up for the ones that you like. These lectures will likely cover a number of academic things, like the specifics of a given course or placement opportunities, but there will also be talks on the UCAS application process, financial aid, and how much It's going to cost you to live at that particular university. Try and go to as many of these lectures as possible. You want to be as informed as you can before you start making any firm decisions.

Remember, open days are the universities' opportunities to sell themselves to you. They are putting on everything they can to make them seem like the most amazing, most special, most brilliant place ever. Remember, you are worth a lot money to the university. You're going to be giving it to them directly in tuition fees, and indirectly in things like accommodation fees, the money that you spend on campus, and the money that you spend in the bars and the shops. They are trying to show off and entice you to come to their university. Now, if you are not impressed with the university when it's showing off, how impressed are you actually going to be on a day-to-day basis?

The students' union at the university will be out in force. Many of the people there are going to be volunteers, and if they're spending their time volunteering to show off how amazing their university is, chances are they love it there. Talk to them and ask them why they love it. Ask them why they're so enthusiastic. If there aren't people around who are looking enthusiastic about the university, ask yourself why that is. There are probably going to be some student guides as well. Now, these may be volunteers, or these may be paid guides. Sometimes the students that are paid to guide you around are a much better indication of what the university is like. As opposed to the super enthusiastic volunteers who think everything is absolutely amazing, paid guides might give you a bit more real insight into exactly what it is like at university. Ask them whether they're happy. Ask them whether they like it there. Ask them whether they're enjoying their course. Chances are, they will give you an honest answer.

Remember, these student guides and student union volunteers all know what it was like when they applied through UCAS. They were in the same position that you are in now. They know the hard decisions that you have to make, and they generally want to help you as much as they can. They want to answer the questions, they want to tell you how to make decisions, and they want to pass on their advice to you. They're generally really, really nice people who are there to help you. So ask them as many questions as you can. Find out what it is really like there before you commit yourself, your money, and your time.

Look at all the facilities you can. Most universities are large, interesting, and diverse places. But you need to find somewhere that suits you and where you're going to fit in. For example, is there somewhere on campus or close by where you can practice your faith? If you're interested in shopping and going out to bars, are there enough to keep you interested? If it's a 40 minute train journey away to the nearest decent set of shops, is that really going to work for you if that's your major pastime? If extreme sports are an absolute essential at the weekends, pick a university that offers a range of extreme sports.

The course and the type of university will be the main drivers in your decision, but don't forget, you're going to be living there for a very long period of time. So make sure you're going to fit in, and make sure you're going to be happy.

Ask a few questions about logistics. What time does the library shut? If the library shuts at 5 p.m. every day (which is unlikely for university libraries), that's not actually very useful. What's the Wi-Fi coverage like? If the Wi-Fi coverage doesn't actually extend to the accommodation, well, that's not very useful.

Try and ask as many questions as you can, so that when it's time to pick your university and your courses on your UCAS application, you have as much information as you possibly can.

University Vloggers

Ali Abdaal is studying Medicne at the University of Cambrdige https://www.youtube.com/user/Sepharoth64

Alicedoesphysics is studying Theoretical Physics at Lancaster University https://www.youtube.com/channel/UChw2nOY1TKsSqb-gktzHMUA. She has made an awesome video for this series on A-Level Physics https://youtu.be/Lu1nftOFfvo

AliciaTay is studying Law at the University of Bristol https://www.youtube.com/channel/UC7QYpzHCrrUG49mrXZL56RA

Angeliculture is studying at LSE https://www.youtube.com/user/BdotJelly

Astrid Franciszka is studying English Literature at the University of Cambridge https://www.youtube.com/channel/UC5PxioZ-lrEZIObY6IzViGQ

bluemangofrosting is studying Engineering at The University of Cambridge https://www.youtube.com/channel/UCklKbXYJwvqDYOXFUYlQcgQ

Charlotte Mulcahy is studying Biological Sciences at Lancaster University https://www.youtube.com/channel/UC1KeuwUVF98o0aJckgeHwbQ

Chidera Ota is studying Medicine at the University of Cambridge https://www.youtube.com/channel/UCeq4iBads31CT551gDJND5A. She has made an awesome video for this series on applying to study medicine https://youtu.be/wDp3CX-InuM

Courtney Daniella is studying Human, Social and Political Sciences at the University of Cambridge https://www.youtube.com/channel/UCy3BDnBwfMAMFpqt3j9jHvQ

Derin Adetosoye is studying at the London College of Fashion https://www.youtube.com/user/beautybyderin

Dylan - Student Vlogs is studying Economics and Finance at the University of York https://www.youtube.com/channel/UCpMNCbnIjxci0LUs4MVqFdQ

Eve Benent is studying Modern Languages at the University of Oxford https://www.youtube.com/channel/UCD2h_l6FMIta19ronaayedg

Eve Cornwell is studying Law at the University of Bristol https://www.youtube.com/channel/UCM8qRGoiaLwmMv31L7xeeEQ

EverythingJodie is studying at the University of Nottingham https://www.youtube.com/channel/UClM44VPQEqRLc2adihmjZ5g

Grace Fit U.K. is studying Music at the University of Oxford
https://www.youtube.com/channel/UC1QbgAuzMDsWn7eCtImRB7Q

Helen Lily is studying Economics and Management at the University of Oxford
https://www.youtube.com/channel/UCFzhOljgMOEMnWQt66UZkiA

HeyOlivia is studying Biomedicine at the University of Bristol
https://www.youtube.com/channel/UC9fr_J4crNnfuIFt-GrZh0g

Holly Gabrielle is studying Natural Science at the University of Cambridge
https://www.youtube.com/channel/UCUJy393uwl2PTQIMwha8gQg

Ibz Mo is studying Psychology at the University of Cambridge
https://www.youtube.com/user/ibstarsns

Imani Shola is studying at the University of Cambridge
https://www.youtube.com/channel/UCblFTK49k4YvzZ7MeXXXjdg

Jack Edwards is studying English Literature at Durham University https://www.youtube.com/user/thejackexperience

Jake Wright was studying Computer Science at the University of Cambridge
https://www.youtube.com/user/jaketvee

Joe Binder was studying at the University of Cambridge
https://www.youtube.com/channel/UCjKEegxSq5T309TCCSwmhHw

KikeA is studying Law at the University of Nottingham
https://www.youtube.com/channel/UCNAwFGljsnlIgP9yJUBsXBA

Luke Birch is studying at the University of Lincoln
https://www.youtube.com/user/TheLukeBirch

Miss Hanake is studying Japanese at the University of Oxford
https://www.youtube.com/user/MissHanake

Miss Varz is studying at the University of Oxford
https://www.youtube.com/channel/UC0a0jgB33-HHcAm84UFfPgw

MollyatOxford is studying Classics and English at the University of Oxford
https://www.youtube.com/user/readingismycupoftea

Noo Stenning is studying Biochemsitry at the University of Bath https://www.youtube.com/user/PrincessEmeraldNoo

PaigeY is studying Natural Science at the University of Cambridge
https://www.youtube.com/channel/UCqVgG1Tu_23FnA2vPqC_igw

Parth G is studying Physics at the University of Cambridge
https://www.youtube.com/user/InfamousPillarKid

Poppy Barr is studying Psychology at the University of Exeter https://www.youtube.com/user/PoppyBbeauty. She has made an awesome video for this series on starting university https://youtu.be/RIHvy7a8Ct0

Rosie Crawford is studying Law at the University of Oxford https://www.youtube.com/user/NeonMartian817

Ryhan Hussain is studying Medicine in Bulgaria https://www.youtube.com/channel/UCg2u5o5dvS5iIu74rRO5x1w

Senthooran Khan is studying Medicine at the University of Cambridge https://www.youtube.com/channel/UC_5rL_WhCNhOuXst0g9Jrvg

Shirley Bekker was studying at the University of Cambridge https://www.youtube.com/channel/UCs1twMBmc-RxV4HNulKJCGQ

Simon Clark was studying Physics at the University of Oxford https://www.youtube.com/user/SimonOxfPhys. He has now just finished a PhD at The University of Exeter.

TheKingBeth is studying Maths at University of Southampton https://www.youtube.com/user/TheKingBeth

This is mani is studying Computer Science at the University of Oxford https://www.youtube.com/channel/UC3TD7PqzopTRpmwdqNXPASQ

Tim Stewart is studying at University of Birmingham
https://www.youtube.com/channel/UCOLHjlVufLbOSh2a50Q
Pesw

Unjaded jade is studying Biology
https://www.youtube.com/channel/UC4-uObu-
mfafJyxxZFEwbvQ

Viola Helen is studying at the University of Oxford
https://www.youtube.com/channel/UCzf3VsJqDDWp-
v938ewpT8g

Matt's Story - Open days

Matt did the EPQ and A-Levels in Biology (C), Maths (D) and Geography (D)

In order to attend a university open day, you have to book your place online through the university's website. You can't just show up, as you have to go to an actual course talk which takes place at specific times on specific days. When you arrive, you have to register with a university representative before you can go into your allotted course talk. These talks typically last anywhere from 30-90 minutes and are not only a great way to learn more about the course you're interested in, but also as a way to meet potential lecturers and course mates. Once the talk is finished, you can also attend the accommodation and campus tours which are going on throughout the day (or if you arrive particularly early, you can even do this before your course talk begins).

Not only are the open days important for learning about your course choices and what the university can offer you, but they can also help give you a feel for what it will be like to live there. The best thing about the open days is that everyone is in the same boat. Nobody has any expectations of you, and its stress free. At this point, it's the universities that are trying to sell themselves to you.

Of course, not everyone is able to attend open days, and you may find yourself at a university you haven't seen in person yet (in my case it was the only one of my choices I didn't get to see beforehand, but I had been looking into it). That being said, you should definitely try to go to at least one open day for each uni you are interested in just to get a feel for the atmosphere if nothing else. And the great thing about university open days is that if you can't make it to one of them, they hold several throughout the year.

Ata's Story - Open Days

Ata has A-levels in Maths (C), Media (C) and PE (C).

Although I was pretty adamant about the universities I wanted to apply to, I still felt it was a good idea to visit the universities of my choice in the flesh. Booking an open day is fairly easy with the advances of modern technology. You register your name and contact information online. This is followed swiftly by a confirmation email. In particular one open day clearly stood for me, and coincidentally this happened to also be my first choice.

I took a two hour train journey on the day. I was told that some student representatives would be at the train station to welcome me. I felt this was such a nice touch as I've never visited this city before and it would ensure I wasn't walking around like a lost lamb. As I got off at my stop my eye instantly noticed a sea of red shirts. I made my way to them, they offered me a water bottle and one student representative escorted me to the coach stand.

We arrived at the university within ten minutes and I was definitely blown away. The buildings have been standing since the past century and they definitely had a unique sense of character to them. Inside the university I was given a welcome pack (which included some yummy snacks). I was told I had the opportunity to book a tour of the university if I chose to do so. As I was alone and this was my first ever visit, I booked myself into tour of the university.

There were five other people with me on the tour. The student representative was very friendly. He asked everyone individually where we had travelled from and the courses we had hoped to study. He told us he would make sure to take us to each department we were interested in. We were all able to ask him questions about his experience at the university, the social life, and even job opportunities available locally whilst studying.

We stopped at each department of our choice for half an hour each. We were given a brief ten minute introduction into the subject. We were then able to meet and speak with the tutors from the specific departments. I asked one of the tutors on a course I was interested in what he expects from his students, amongst other questions. He told me of a practical session that was to be held later on that I could attend.

We were taken to an outside area where free burgers were being cooked for visitors. This really put the university in high esteem for me, as they had thought of everything to make us feel welcome. I headed off to the practical session by myself, and it was very informative. Before leaving for my train I took a quick visit to the university library. It was definitely the library of my dreams. The open day really gave me a sense of the university and made me excited for my future.

The Teaching and Excellence Framework (TEF)

In the middle of 2017, a new university ranking system went into effect: the Teaching and Excellence Framework, or TEF. This ranking gives gold, silver, or bronze ratings to the universities that decided to take part, nearly 300 different universities in all. The stated aim of this new ranking system was to allow students to make a more informed choice, but universities that gained bronze or above are the ones that are allowed to raise their tuition fees. It is a voluntary scheme, so not every university is going to be ranked. The rankings take into account the facilities, student satisfaction, dropout rates, and employment or study after university.

However, the rankings don't take into account any of the classes or any of the labs; nor did any of the assessors visit the universities or talk to any students. And some of the big universities are not happy because they got bronze, which was not the result that they expected.

So how much attention should we be paying to these gold, silver, or bronze rankings? Well, these were given to a university as a whole, not for an individual course, so they completely miss out on the fact that the university that you want to go to may be a specialist in doing this one particular course, or they may have this one specific lecture, or they may do this one specific combination. It was given to the whole university. Thus the TEF completely misses out on the nuances, the niches, the unique things about universities.

Gold TEF

The Arts University Bournemouth; Aston University; Bangor University; The University of Bath; The University of Birmingham; Bishop Grosseteste University; The University of Buckingham; University of Cambridge; The Conservatoire for Dance and Drama; Coventry University; De Montfort University; University of Derby; University of Dundee; The University of East Anglia; The University of Essex University of Exeter; Falmouth University; The University of Huddersfield; Imperial College London; University of Keele; The University of Kent; The University of Lancaster; The University of Leeds; University of Lincoln; Liverpool Hope University; Loughborough University; University of Newcastle upon Tyne; The University of Northampton; The Northern School of Art; Norwich University of the Arts; The University of Nottingham; Nottingham Trent University; University of Oxford; University of Portsmouth; The Royal Academy of Music; The Royal Central School of Speech and Drama; Royal College of Music; Royal Northern College of Music; The Royal Veterinary College; University of St Andrews; The University of Surrey.

Silver TEF

University of Gloucestershire; University of Greenwich; Heriot-Watt University; University of Hertfordshire; The University of Hull   ; King's College London; Leeds Arts University; Leeds Beckett University; Leeds Trinity University; The University of Leicester; Cardiff Metropolitan University; Cardiff University; University of Central Lancashire; University of Chester; The University of Chichester; City, University of London; University of Durham; Liverpool John Moores University; University College London; London South Bank University; The University of Manchester; Manchester Metropolitan University; Middlesex University; Newman University;

University of Northumbria at Newcastle; Oxford Brookes University; Queen Mary University of London; Ravensbourne; The University of Reading; The Royal Agricultural University; Royal Holloway, University of London; The University of Sheffield; Sheffield Hallam University; South & City College Birmingham; University of St Mark & St John; St Mary's University, Twickenham; Staffordshire University; University of Sunderland; University of Sussex; Swansea University; Teesside University; The University of Warwick; The University of West London; University of the West of England, Bristol; University of Winchester; University of Worcester; Wrexham Glyndŵr University; University of York

Bronze TEF

Solent University; University of Southampton; St. George's, University of London; University of Suffolk; Trinity Laban Conservatoire of Music and Dance; University of Wales Trinity Saint David; The University of Westminster; University of Wolverhampton; York St John University; Kingston University; The University of Liverpool; London Metropolitan University; The London School of Economics and Political Science; The School of Oriental and African Studies; University of Plymouth; Roehampton University; The University of Salford.

Are Leagues Tables Important?

There are lots of university league tables out there, and some of them are making impressive claims. But picking the right university is a massive decision, so how much should be based on league tables?

I am a firm believer that the best university for you is the one that you are going to be happiest at, not one that comes in higher or lower on a league table. Apart from that, there are so many different league tables that most universities can claim to be the top of this one, or the top five in that one, just depending on how they manipulate the data. You need to be wary of any claim that you come across. For instance, whether Oxford or Cambridge is at the top will switch depending on how the university league tables have decided to do their rankings, but those two are always going to be at the top.

Depending on which one you read, the league tables generally will only give you a rough sense of the university. The tables give you a general indication of where to start looking, because you can see which universities are consistently in the top 10, which ones are consistently middling, and which ones are consistently below 150. But the league tables do not tell the whole story. I would recommend that while you're reading the tables, move over to the right a little bit and look at the raw data. There you will see the different bits that make up the rankings.

There are general categories that most of league tables use, they may be called slightly name different in each table, but most of them use these broad categories.

Student satisfaction - this is based on students' opinions, students' experiences, how well the university met their expectations. How did the university live up to all they thought it was going to be? This can be slightly tricky because if a student has high expectations, or a whole group of students high expectations, of a university and the university just gave them a good education, then the students can give the university a poor rating. Whereas if students have really low expectations in university and they gave a good education, then the students could give them a really high rating. This one is based on opinion, students' opinion. How did they feel, what did they feel like at university?

Research - this has very little impact on you as an undergraduate, since you'll be in lectures and you'll be in labs, and you generally won't be involved in actual research.

UCAS points – the level UCAS points you need to get in there. This can be useful, especially if you can sort the list by UCAS points. If you know roughly how many UCAS points you're going to get based on your predicted grades, you can look at the universities in that range. Go a touch higher, go a bit lower, but it might give you some universities that you haven't thought of to go and have a look at.

Financial prospects - this can be useful one because it tells you how many graduates got graduate-level jobs. It's not overall employment because it doesn't take into account how many graduates got non-graduate-level jobs like working in Tesco's. It can help you determine which ones have good career services, which ones have good links for the industry. It doesn't, however, take into account the local economy or the location of the university.

Student-staff ratio – this is another one you need to be wary of because it can look excellent on paper but doesn't give you any indication of what it's going to be like in reality. Having a low student-staff ratio where there are lots of staff to students doesn't mean these staff are going to be available to students. Doesn't mean the staff are going to answer their emails or have office hours or be available to talk to you. You're never going to know this until you get to university.

How much money a university's spending - This is data you need to be wary of because they might just put a load of money into infrastructure, which as an undergraduate you will never ever see. Just because they have a lot of money to flush around doesn't mean it's going to impact you as an undergraduate in any way at all.

Results - what percentage of students got a good result, a first or a two one? You do need to be a touch wary about this because results are handed out by the university. There's not a centralized exam board across the country. It is the university's decision. There is some extent of moderation, but it is generally down to university. A university may tend to hand out more if they want to rise up league tables.

League tables can give you some good information, they can give you some general information, places to go and look at, but they are a very crude tool for differentiating between one university and another university. The best thing to try and work out is the university going to be a good fit for you, are you going to be happy there, are you going to enjoy the course that you're on, are you going to want to be there for three, four, five years.

Aarav's Story - How I Picked My University

Aarav has A-Levels from a internatinonal school in Shanghai, these are in Maths (A), Further maths (B), Biology (B) ad Phsyics (B)

Admit it or not, there are a numerous universities across the country, and every one of them offers diverse experiences and distinctive courses. The university you study in and pass out from would make a noteworthy part in portraying your future, and the way that there are various decisions, and it can confuse and make you choose the wrong choices. Choosing a university goes much past picking one that is strategically situated or offers school fees that you have the means to pay. There are numerous things to keep an eye out for to guarantee that the university is an ideal choice for you.

While trying to pick out the perfect university for myself, the first thing I was on the lookout for was the quality of education that the university offers. The quality of education provided by a university was the principal item for me and since all universities are not established to be equal, I definitely had to choose one based on some of these vital factors. There are different factors that affect the quality of education, for instance, the school curriculum, technique of lecturing and the department's lecturers and professors. The leading universities have certified lecturers who have great years of experience and this is one of the principal reasons why these universities give the most outstanding quality of training.

Not just that, I also checked for the school facilities and accommodation because as an international student, I would need a place to stay and which would most likely be the university hostel. The facilities provided by the institution are some of the time insufficient for the number of students they admit and this can be a major concern a person's academics are being disturbed due to the lack of facilities. So I made sure to look at the amenities and facilities of the school ahead of time. Always note that accommodation is an important factor. The cost, access to the institution, and roommates all assume a role in deciding whether or not if the accommodation would be suitable for you.

Additionally, as an international student from a not so rich background, the cost of the education was also a priority for me. The best for me would be a scholarship program and based on my research, and I am amazed to say almost all universities in U.K. offer scholarship programs and some of them let go of the educational cost charges altogether. It is also a great idea to find out about the scholarships you are qualified for so that you can reduce the cost of your education. The tuition fees is a main part of the total cost and getting a scholarship makes sure that the cost falls inside your financial budget. Finally, I was able to ask a few of the students at the university about the employment outlook after passing out. I asked how simple or difficult it is when attempting to apply for a job after graduating from school. With this, I was able to get good feedback on future employment and I'm happy I chose the university where I am today.

Russell Group Universities

There are a few different ways to determining which universities you should aim for. One way is to look at the Russell Group Universities, which is a collection of 24 universities in the U.K.

At the moment, the group consists of:
- University of Birmingham
- University of Bristol
- University of Cambridge
- Cardiff University
- Durham University
- University of Edinburgh
- University of Exeter
- University of Glasgow
- Imperial College London
- King's College London
- University of Leeds
- University of Liverpool
- London School of Economics & Political Science (LSE)
- University of Manchester
- Newcastle University
- University of Nottingham
- University of Oxford
- Queen Mary, University of London
- Queen's University Belfast
- University of Sheffield
- University of Southampton
- University College London (UCL)
- University of Warwick
  University of York

If you look at the Russell Group website, their statistics are all really good. Students coming out of Russell Group universities have high employment rates and their research is excellent, and all of their stats are great across the board.

Admission to the Russell Group is not based on league tables. the Russell Group is comprised of 24 great universities but they are not the top 24. Just because a university isn't in the Russell Group doesn't mean it's a bad university. There are loads of great universities that aren't in the group, so it shouldn't be your only determining factor. Certainly, the Russell Group has a certain prestige, but it's important not to get fixated on labels. The most important thing is picking a university where you will be happy, regardless of what kind of label it has.

Red-Brick Universities

The term Red-Brick University tends to be associated with snobbery and elitism, but not in the way you think. We've all heard the phrase, but first we need a little bit of a history lesson to determine whether or not these schools are worth aiming for.

Oxford was the first university established in England, all the way back in 1096. (Which is, like, a crazy long time ago!) Cambridge was founded in 1209 after a few Oxford dons got into an argument. A few more universities were established in Scotland and Northern Ireland over the next couple hundred years, but there were not very many until the Industrial Revolution and the introduction of compulsory education. Between 1900 and 1909, the U.K. got six new universities all at once. These were Birmingham, Liverpool, Leeds, Manchester, Sheffield, and Bristol, and they were built using ubiquitous red bricks of the time. Hence the name.

These universities were set up to teach the skills that were in-demand at the time: engineering, science, or anything that was needed for industry. At the time, their admission requirements were much broader and much more open than the admissions of Oxford and Cambridge. They still only admitted men, but it wasn't a collegiate system, and they were much more open to people of different backgrounds and different religions. And the old school universities didn't like this one little bit. They looked down at these new sticks universities that opened up, and they coined the term Red Brick as kind of a derogatory, sneery term to describe them.

A lot has changed since then. These six universities still get called 'Red Brick' schools, but the name has shifted from derogatory to conveying a sense of quality and legacy. While the Red Brick universities aren't formed into any specific group, they are still referred to that way to distinguish them from the later 'Plate Glass' universities that were built in the '50s and '60s. There were dozens of Plate Glass universities built in the popular style of the era, and all of a sudden Red Brick became a good thing!

Later, in 1992, there was another massive increase in the number of universities in the U.K. Many of these were polytechnical colleges, or polytechnics being converted into universities. Once again, the term Red Brick came to distinguish the old guard of universities built between 1900 and the Second World War. But does it really matter? It basically just means that you're going to an old university—but not a really, *really* old university.

Former Polytechnics

In 1992, the Further and Higher Education Act allowed loads of colleges and technical colleges to take on the name of university. This led to confusion as many new universities popped up, institutions changed their names, and former polytechnics got a bit of a reputation.

For instance, the city of Oxford has the University of Oxford, but then Oxford Brookes Universities popped up. Because the University of Oxford is very famous, there was never going to be much confusion there, but take Birmingham as an example. Birmingham has the University of Birmingham and Birmingham City University, and from the names, it's not very obvious which one is the old Red Brick university and which one is the former polytechnic. And the league tables are just going to say Birmingham, while the University of Portsmouth and the University of Brighton give absolutely no indication of their origins at all. But Portsmouth, Brighton, Birmingham City, and Oxford Brookes all used to be colleges, technical colleges, or polytechnics.

Many students are confused about whether or not they should go to a university because it used to be polytechnic. They wonder if they are any good, and if they should go to them or not. This question is tough for me to answer, because it's so individual to you. It depends on the course that you're looking for, and it depends whether the university is a good fit for you. The age of a university, the reputation of a university, or the former name of a university has no bearing on whether you're going to be happy there. It has no bearing on whether it's going to provide a good education for you or whether you're going to be successful there. Not wanting to go to a university just because it's a former polytechnic is just snobbery, and it's not going to get you very far. There is so much more to consider when picking a location, and the main thing is whether you think you'll be happy there.

Bethan's Story - Choosing my University

Bethan did year 13 twice, she came out with A-levels at ABB

Choosing a university is a process that I think changes from person to person. You have to consider whereabouts you would like to be living; whether or not you'll live in halls or commute from home, and of course what subject it is you want to be studying. There are several different tools to help with this decision, the main one being the league tables which are updated annually and also include the grade/UCAS point requirements for each university (and you can filter this search accordingly to your own interests to see which universities have the best results for your chosen subject).

The five universities that I chose to put on my application were Southampton, Brighton, Northampton, Lincoln and Exeter. I actually found it all lot easier to choose universities that I was interested than I was expecting. They all offered the course I was looking for, but it was actually the atmosphere/environment that won me over in each case. As I was moving away from home, I wanted to experience a completely different style of life and all five of my choices offered that. I think the most vital thing to remember is that whilst it's nice to have ambitious goals, its important and in your best interests to be realistic, otherwise you might end up disappointed with the outcome. Only you are aware of your own capabilities, so don't force yourself into applying for something you know you just won't be able to meet the requirements for.

Conservatoires

If you want to study music, dance, or drama, then university might not be the right place for you. You might be better off at a specialist conservatoire.

Now conservatoires sound very fancy or maybe a little bit strange, but they're just specialist music, dance, and drama colleges. And each one is going to be very different and offer distinct specialisms. This could be based on the teachers that they have on staff, or it could be based on the area that they're in. So if you're thinking about applying to a conservatoire, you need to do your research and find which one is going to be the best fit for you, your skills, and where you want to take your career in the future. The experience at a conservatoire is going to be quite different to a standard university experience. It is going to be very practiced-based and very performance-based. There are not going to be a lot of lectures going on, which means it will likely be much more intense. You're only going to be working from nine to five with performances in the evening, and you may have a block of an academic week and then a block of a performance week. You are going to get a lot of exposure to the professional world.

Because conservatoires are geared toward producing professionals, your teachers will likely also be professionals active in their respective fields. You're going to be doing performances at prominent places in the evening, and you're going to be exposed to the culture, the atmosphere, and the experiences of a professional musician, dancer or actor.

The application process is the same through the UCAS system, but you'll also need to submit a portfolio or do an audition, maybe one or two audition pieces as part of the application process. It is much more like a full-time job, a full immersion experience, as opposed to going to a university and having large chunks of time to do independent study. You're going to be expected to be working and rehearsing, either by yourself or in groups, for large chunks of time. But is it going to be one of the best experiences for you if you know that this is the direction you want your career to take.

The following conservatoires can be applied for via UCAS:

Royal Birmingham Conservatoire
Bristol Old Vic Theatre School
Leeds College of Music
Royal Academy of Music
Royal College of Music
Royal Conservatoire of Scotland
Royal Northern College of Music
Royal Welsh College of Music and Drama
Trinity Laban Conservatoire of Music and Dance

The Open University

The Open University has been around since the 1970s, but what it offers is still fresh, innovative, and radically different to what the other universities offer. It can offer you a real chance to get a degree if you cannot follow a more traditional route.

When we're talking about the Open University, everything you think you know about traditional university doesn't apply anymore. The Open University is a distance-learning university, which means you don't go to lectures. There are no fixed times, and you don't have to move away from home. You have set assignments to work on, activities to do, videos to watch, podcasts to listen to, but you can do all of these in your own time. You can do them when the kids are napping, when you're on the bus, or when you're on your lunch break—whenever you can find a spare bit of time. You'll get sent a pack of books, CDs, and DVDs in the post when you start the course, so you don't have to rely on a reliable internet connection. (But if you want, you can download all the videos onto an app on your phone or tablet, so you can take them around with you in your pocket.) This means if you have other responsibilities, you can study when it suits you. This is ideal for people with care responsibilities, or for people who have already started working but want a boost in their career.

The Open University is one of the most prominent universities in the world, but you may only infrequently have interactions with other students. If you do want interaction, thankfully they have a massive online community that is there to support you. You have a personal tutor who is going to be available to you via phone, via email, and quite often in the chat room as well. Courses start at different points throughout the year—currently February, April, and October—and the application deadline for these courses is generally about a month to six weeks beforehand. Applications aren't made by UCAS, so you get to skip the process that other students have to go through. Instead, the applications are done directly to the university.

When you sign up, you can pick which modules you want to do straight away, so you've got a little bit of certainty about what your course is going to be made up from. It costs a lot less than a traditional university because you pay per module. A 30-credit module is £1,432, and a 60-credit module is £2,864. Full-time study is 120 credits a year, which comes to £5,728. That's a lot less than the traditional universities are charging, which often comes to £9,000 a year. You also pay as you go, so you don't have to pay the whole lot up front. You can pay for your next module when you're ready to study it, so you can take the time to save up for the modules, and pay for them when you're prepared to study them.

The majority of courses don't have any entry requirement. You can do an Access course beforehand if you don't feel quite ready to jump straight into a degree-level course. This will help you if you haven't done any A-Levels or it's been a really long time since you were in education. You do need to have a set level of Engllsh, so generally a C, as well as a four or a five at GCSE. You also need to be able to use a computer to access the course content, so you need a basic level of computer competency.

If your mobility or your physical or mental health means that you can't attend a traditional university, the Open University makes a huge point of being accessible as possible. They have grants and bursaries that are available to help you, and they adjust assessments and exams to suit your needs. All the course materials are available in a wide range of formats. There is a time limit for each module, but these are really achievable. You have 16 years to get enough credits to complete a full degree. They have an excellent tool on their website to help you determine whether you can do it full-time, part-time, or whether you just need to do a few modules a year.

They also offer open degrees, which are fantastic things. These are completely unstructured, and you just build up enough credits to be honoured with a degree. You need 360 credits for a degree, and an open degree lets you pick any topics that you'd like to study.

The Open University is an excellent option for many people. If you've got caring responsibilities, if you've got financial responsibilities, or if your physical or mental health limits you from attending a traditional university, then the Open University can help you get a degree in a way that potentially you didn't think was possible.

MOOCs

MOOCs are 'massive open online courses'. But what are they, should you be doing them, are they any good, and what qualifications can you get from them?

Now online courses are not an EU thing, but Open University has been running like this for years. When I was at university, I did one of my modules online, but recently there has been a massive explosion in them. They now have a fancy new name, MOOCs. The thing that is different about these is that they are open. You can study the course for free. You only pay if you finish, and only if you want to get an actual qualification or a real certificate to prove that you've done the course. All the studying, all the videos are free and open to everybody.

These courses can then be used as part of credit towards a degree, so if you're applying to university, these can be a useful way to show that you're interested and that you've put a bit of effort in. You don't necessarily have to pay for the qualification, but the fact that you can talk about doing it is going to be really valuable in interviews. If you want to have a look at all the courses that are available, the significant provider in the U.K. is called Future Learn. You can just go to their website and look at all the courses they're providing from excellent universities all over the world.

At the moment, you can't get full degrees in the U.K. by doing open online courses (you can get complete degrees online via the Open University, however; see previous section). But if you're thinking about trying something out, then MOOCs are a fantastic way to start.

Oxbridge

What's So Different about Oxbridge?

Oxford and Cambridge are two of the U.K.'s oldest universities, and they consistently rank at the top of the world's university league tables. But they are a little different from other universities in the U.K.

The biggest difference is the college system, where you apply to a specific college within the university. Your college is where you're going to spend the majority of your time, whether it's socializing, eating, studying, or sleeping. While lectures and labs are university-wide, tutorials, supervisions, and seminars are often college-wide.

This means that not every college can offer every single course, and there may be only one or two other people at your college doing the same course as you. You can expect these tutorials and supervisions to be very small and very intense. I've gone through all of the colleges at Oxford and Cambridge, and later in this chapter I have listed which colleges offer which courses.

The timings and workload at Oxford and Cambridge is going to be very different to other universities. You can expect to be working weekends, and you can expect the workload to be very high. However, you're only going to be at university for three terms, and these three terms are only eight or nine weeks long. That's less than 30 weeks at university across the whole year, so you have a lot of time to relax over those holidays.

While other universities have large lectures, Oxford and Cambridge do a lot of their teaching in tutorials or supervisions. Due to the small size of the colleges, these can often be one-on-one with some of the world's leading academics. These happen on a daily or weekly basis, and these can be quite intense, because if you don't know what you're talking about, you're really quite stuck and exposed.

Due to the age of Oxford and Cambridge, some of the colleges are very traditional and very formal. Some of the newer ones are much more relaxed, but some of the older ones still insist that you wear gowns to formal dinners, which can happen weekly. These are sit-down, served three-course meals where you're expected to observe excellent etiquette the entire time. If this isn't your thing, then maybe you should look at a different university, or look at some of the more modern colleges.

The last difference you need to know about Oxford and Cambridge is that you can only apply to one. You can only apply to either Oxford or Cambridge, but not to both. The deadline for applications is the 15th of October, which is earlier than the normal U.K. deadline. Picking clothes is almost as hard as picking a university, because you need to find somewhere that you're going to fit in, and somewhere you're going to be happy for the next three or four years of your life.

Oxford or Cambridge – What is the Difference between the Two?

You may have been dreaming about studying at Oxford or Cambridge for years—ever since you were small and knew what going to university actually was—but now time has come to make the decision, so how do you decide between the two? The tricky thing is you can only apply to one. You can only put either Oxford or Cambridge down as one of your choices on your UCAS application form. You cannot fill up your UCAS application form with lots of different choices at Oxford or Cambridge, or a combination of the two.

These universities are often lumped together under the name Oxbridge, but they are actually quite different even though they have a lot in common. They're both very, very old. They're very traditional, both still have a formal setting. They always rank at the top of the world's university league tables, or very close to the top. They're going have similar styles, with tutorials, supervisions, and small, intimate teaching styles alongside the large theatres and the large labs, but there are some important differences between the two of them.

The most important difference is going to be the course. While Oxford and Cambridge are similar, they don't actually offer the same courses. For example, Oxford will offer separate degrees in Biological Sciences, Chemistry, and Physics, whereas Cambridge offers a Natural Science degree where you select your modules along the way as your interests develop, but you're not guaranteed that you're going to come out with a Physics degree. Oxford does Politics, Philosophy, and Economics (PPE) all bundled together in one degree, whereas Cambridge will offer you a degree in Economics, or in Philosophy, or a degree in Politics and History. Cambridge offers degrees in Veterinary Science, in Land Management, in Architecture, and Asian and Middle Eastern Studies, whereas Oxford offers degrees in Oriental Studies and Fine Arts. Even the degrees that have the same title at the two universities may be completely different. You need to delve deep into the modules and check that the degree you're applying for actually suits you. If there's a particular section of Classics that you're really, really interested in, one university might offer it and the university may not offer it. Check you're actually applying for a course that you want to study. Don't just apply to the university based on the name or their reputation because you think it'll suit you better later in life. Apply to a course that you want to study.

Both Oxford and Cambridge are going to require fantastic A-Level grades, with a typical offer being all As, with one or two of those As being A stars. They use different ways to differentiate between excellent grades, and they will use this to decide upon who to interview and who is going to get to play. Only about half of the courses at Cambridge have a pre-interview assessment. Many of these will require you to submit written work beforehand, or there will be an assessment on the day.

The only real way you can determine whether you prefer Oxford or Cambridge or Cambridge or Oxford is going to visit them and seeing what they're actually like, seeing where you think you'll be happiest, seeing which one suits your personality better. Cambridge is slightly smaller and some of the amenities are bit further out, which may require you to catch a bus every morning. Oxford has slightly larger population, and it's also slightly more compact, which means that it is known to be ever so slightly livelier—but when you compare either Oxford or Cambridge to a place like London or Manchester, then it's size and liveliness don't really compare to the big cities.

There are so many different holidays at Oxford and Cambridge that even if you want one that's a bit quieter in a livelier city, you're going to find that. There are a few other small idiosyncrasies between the universities, which probably won't have a massive impact on whether you decide to go there or not. For example, Oxford requires you to wear academic dress when you're sitting exams, and Cambridge doesn't. These are really small, small things. The best thing is to do as much research into the course that you want to do, and then go and visit the cities and see what you actually think of them. Things like open-top bus tours will give you a really good overview of the whole city. I also recommend that you talk to people while you're there. See if they're happy there, and see if you would fit in!

How do Oxbridge Colleges work?

Not only do you need to pick a university and a course, but if you're applying to Oxford and Cambridge you need to pick a college as well, and sometimes this can be the hardest part because every college has a really distinctive personality.

On your application form, you need to fill in the college code for Oxford and Cambridge to indicate which college you want to apply for. You can also fill in an open application, but this is a slightly different process that we will cover in a separate section. The most important thing when picking a college is trying to find somewhere that you are going to be happy and fit in for the next three, four, potentially five years. Once you've picked a college, you'll be interviewed by that college, not by the university as a whole. This means that two people who are applying for the same course but at different colleges might have quite different interview experiences.

When you eventually get to Oxford or Cambridge, most of your actual learning will take place within the college environment, including all of your tutorials and your supervisions. The college is going to have a few lecturers and academics associated with it, and they are going to offer the course that they teach through the college. The more popular courses are taught at the majority of colleges, but the rarer courses aren't going to be taught at every single college. There are a large number of colleges at each university, which means each college is actually quite small, generally having less than 500 students. The size of the college and the range of courses offered at Oxford and Cambridge means that you might be the only person—or one of a small group—in your year studying your course. This structure means that your tutorials and supervisions are going to be very intimate, and they will likely be with some of the world's leading academics.

Even though the college system is small and more intimate, it doesn't mean that there will be only 10 people in the whole university doing your course—it just means there are only a few people at your college doing your course. You will meet all the other people doing the same course as you when you convene for big lectures. You'll certainly get to know the other students in your college who are studying the same course as you, but your lectures and labs are going to be university wide, and these could have hundreds of people in them. These are going to be quite impersonal, so you won't get the same level of interaction as you would inside your college.

Some of the brilliant unique things about Oxford and Cambridge are the tutorials and supervisions. This is where you get to have that on-going academic conversation, where you get to draw out ideas, where you get to sit down and actually talk about things that you're interested in.

Unless you choose to eat out, the majority of meals are going to be served within the college, so you can get a nice cooked breakfast every morning and then dinner in the evening. Some of the colleges are very formal, so dinner in the evening is going to be formal. This means you'll have to wear academic dress gowns or other formal wear, and you'll be expected to use proper etiquette and respect throughout a three course meal. On the other hand, some colleges just have standard canteens.

The majority of your social life, at least for the first year, is going to be within the college. They will all have their own common rooms where everyone sits around and chats, and some also have bars where you can go and socialize and have a drink if you want to. They're going to have their own clubs, and they're going to have a large number of groups, societies, and events to welcome the freshers (or the first years) to the college. The colleges are really like a big extended family, and they welcome you with open arms when you start in first year.

Every college has lots of facilities that you'd expect a normal university to have—places for you to study, places for you to eat, libraries where you can do your work. Of course, the wider university has much larger facilities, but if you don't want to travel too far from your room to study, then each college will have a place for you to do that.

How Do You Pick a College?

There are quite a few things you need to consider when picking your college. You may have heard lots about one college, or you may have had relatives or older friends who have gone to a different college, but it may not be easy to get into the college of your choice.

The first thing you need to check is whether or not a specific college offers the course that you want to do. Later in this book I've listed which courses you can do at which specific college, which should help you narrow down your choices. Some of the colleges at Cambridge are single sex, some of the colleges only admit graduates, and some of them only admit mature students. The first thing you need to do is work out which ones you can actually apply to.

Then we need to think about whether the personality of the college fits your personality and your style. Some of them are very old and very traditional, and if you don't think you're going to get on well with that, then maybe pick a slightly more modern college that does things slightly differently.

The best way you're going to be able to do this is by actually visiting the college. There is very little substitute for actually going someplace and getting the feeling for it. I know for some of you that's not going to be easy to do, so check out the profiles of the college in this book or watch YouTube videos about students sharing their lives at the college.

Location could be a big factor for some of you. Some of the colleges are tucked right up in the centre next to all the lecture theatres, bars, and cafes, but they're also right in the middle of the tourist centre, so a tourist might think it'd be brilliant to take a photo of you studying in your room. If you don't want to be right in the middle of things, there are colleges that are a little bit further out. Oxford is quite compact, so nothing's more than about half an hour away, but Cambridge is a bit more spread out. These are student towns, thankfully, which means that there are loads of buses and a large number of students cycle everywhere. It is very common to see more bikes than cars on the road.

You're going to need to look at facilities that a college actually offers, including the clubs. If you are absolutely passionate about one particular sport, don't go to a college where you can't do it. If you know that you want to sing in a certain position in a choir, have a look at which colleges have an opening for that position for that year. All of these are listed and are constantly changing on the Oxford and Cambridge website, so those are the best place to go look at for that information.

For some of you accessibility is going to be a concern. You're going to need accessible accommodation and accessible facilities, and some colleges are better set up for that than others.

The most important thing when you are picking a college is finding somewhere that you are going to be happy. You're going to be living there, you're going to be studying there, you're going to be socializing there. The main focus of your life while you're at Oxford and Cambridge is going to be college-based, so please pick somewhere that you are going to be happy, not somewhere other people think you're going to be happy, and not somewhere you're going just because it has a great reputation.

Mature-student colleges
Mature students are over 21 when they start university.

Oxford – Harris Manchester and Wycliffe Hall.
Cambridge – Hughes Hall; Lucy Cavendish College (women only); St Edmund's College; and Wolfson College

Graduate-only colleges
Oxford – Campion Hall; Green Templeton College; Kellogg College; Linacre College; Nuffield College; St Antony's College; St Cross College; and Wolfson College.
Cambridge – Clare Hall and Darwin.

Single-sex colleges
Cambridge (Women only) – Murray Edwards; Newnham; and Lucy Cavendish

Oxford College Information

College Summaries

Balliol College is a prosperous educational community in the heart of Oxford. It was established to develop education at both undergraduate and graduate levels. The college takes both undergraduate and undergraduate students. Presently the school has 373 undergraduate students and 279 postgraduate students. Both male and female students are also admitted by the school with the percentage of sixty per cent and forty per cent, respectively. Apart from academic activities, a lot goes on at Balliol: hall dinners, chapel services, speaker lunches, debates, concerts, plays, sport, society meetings and much more. Balliol has an exceptional kitchen, which provides lunch and dinner seven days a week throughout term time.

Brasenose College admits both undergraduate and postgraduate students into the college with adequate facilities for both types of student. The college has 367 students and 203 postgraduate students presently in the college. Brasenose College also admits both male and female students into the college. Currently, the percentage of male students and female students are fifty-six and forty-four per cent, respectively. For undergraduates, the centre of all social doings is the Junior Common Room, and for graduates, it is the Hulme Common Room. Brasenose faces the west flank of Radcliffe Square at the other end of the Radcliffe Camera in the centre of Oxford. The JCR plays a dominant part in the life of the undergraduate community. Offering social, entertainment, and wellbeing provisions to the students, the elected group addresses many features of student life and communicates with the governing body and graduate student councils.

Christ Church offers admission for both undergraduates and postgraduates students. As it stands, the college has 428 undergraduate students and 164 postgraduate students. In addition, the college also takes male students and female students. The percentages of both sexes are fifty-nine per cent and forty-one per cent, respectively. For accommodation, the structures of Christ Church are the cathedral (one of the tiniest in the country, which also serves as the college sanctuary), a great hall, dual libraries, two bars, and common rooms for academics, graduates and undergraduates. There are also gardens and a neighbouring sportsground and boat-house. Accommodation is usually provided for all undergraduates and for some graduates, although some accommodation is off-site. Members of the school are normally expected to dine in hall, where there are two sessions every evening, one informal and one formal.

Corpus Christi College accepts both postgraduate and undergraduate students. Currently, the college has small population of undergraduate students greater in number than the postgraduate students. This college also accept both male and female applicants into the college, but accepts more male students than female students. As at now, the percentage of male students in the college is fifty-five per cent while the percentage of females in the college is forty-five per cent. Corpus Christi College was established in 1517 as a centre for novel learning in the University of Oxford. The college enjoys an unsurpassed location, overseeing gardens and fields yet within five minutes' stroll of the city centre and the Bodleian Library. Modern accommodation, with internet connection in every apartment, is made available for all undergraduates and for most postgraduates. The College also owns exceptional facilities for sport, music and drama.

Exeter College presently accepts both female and male students, although the population of male students within the college is greater than the population of the female students. The percentage of female to male students is forty-five and fifty-five per cent, respectively. Accepting both postgraduates and undergraduate students, the population of undergraduate students in the college right now is medium-sized. The College is the fourth oldest in Oxford and has occupied its present place on Turl Street since 1315, a year after it was established. At the moment, Exeter is home to various communities of fellows and students from every continent. The college has a mixed-voiced choir and it's also involved in sports like rugby, hockey, netball and cricket, etc.

Harris Manchester College accepts both postgraduate and undergraduate students, but the college admits more postgraduate students than undergraduate students. Female students and male students are present in the college, but the percentage of female students in the college is slightly greater than the population of male students in the college. The percentage of female students is fifty-two while the population of male students in the school is forty-eight per cent. The college is located in Mansfield Road in central Oxford. The social life of the students within the college includes sport, and fellows are usually expected to dine in the Arlosh Hall, where there is a twice-weekly formal dinner to which students wear jackets, ties, and gowns.

Hertford College accepts both male and female students, and the population of male students in the college is lesser than the population of female students, with fifty-two per cent of the population being female students while the male students are forty-eight per cent of the population. Both postgraduate and undergraduate students are accepted by the college, and there is a medium sized population of undergraduate students in the college while the number of postgraduate students in the college is small. It is situated at Catte Street in the centre of Oxford, right opposite the main gate to the Bodleian Library. Students are accommodated for the full three or four years of their study and the social activities of students in the college include music and sport activities such as college boat clubs and rugby.

Jesus College accepts both undergraduates and postgraduate students, but the college has more undergraduate students with medium population of undergraduate students while the population of postgraduate students in the college is small. Both male and female students are present in the college, but the students in the college are mostly male students. Fifty-six per cent of the students in the college are male while the remaining forty-four per cent are female. Jesus College is located at the centre of the city, between Turl Street, Ship Street, Cornmarket Street and Market Street. Students from the college partake in a range of social activities such as sport, and some participate with student journalism for *Cherwell* or *The Oxford Student*. The Turl Street Arts Festival is held yearly in partnership with Exeter and Lincoln Colleges.

Keble College is a college that accepts both male and female students, although more male students are present in the college than female. Within the college, the male students represent sixty-one per cent of the population, while female students represent thirty-nine per cent. The college has more undergraduate students than postgraduate students. There is medium-sized population of undergraduate students in the college. Keble College is bounded to the north by Keble Road, to the south by Museum Road, and to the west by Blackhall Road. The college has a sports teams, and it also prints a termly magazine called *The Brick* which is a gossip magazine for the students.

Lady Margaret Hall accepts undergraduate students and postgraduate students. As it stands, the population of undergraduate students in the college is medium-sized, while the postgraduate students are smaller in number. Lady Margaret Hall also accepts both male and female students into the college in equal percentages; at present there are fifty per cent male students and fifty per cent female students in the college. The college is positioned beside the River Cherwell at Norham Gardens in north Oxford, next to the University Parks. Accommodation is continuously made available for undergraduates for three years of their study, and provided for a portion of postgraduate study. The students are involved in activities like football, rowing, and other sports.

Lincoln College accepts both undergraduate students and postgraduate students into the college, although the population of undergraduate students in the college is small, while the population of the postgraduate students is smaller than that of the undergraduate students. Both female and male students are accepted by the college, with the percentage of fifty-one per cent and forty-nine per cent for male students and female students, respectively. Lincoln College is located on Turl Street in central Oxford. This college provides accommodation for all undergraduate students, and almost all postgraduate students are also given accommodation. The social life of the students involves the use of the Junior Common Room and the Middle Common Room.

Magdalen College admits both postgraduate students and under-graduate students, with a medium population of undergraduates. The population of postgraduate students is almost half of the population of the undergraduates. The college accepts both male and female students into the college. Presently, the female student population is forty-one per cent of the total population, while the male students in the college represent fifty-nine per cent. The college is close to the River Cherwell. There are many social clubs in the college and the social life of the students involves activities like college boat, hockey, football, rugby, squash and others forms of college sport.

Mansfield College is a college that accepts undergraduate and postgraduate students, even though the population of the undergraduate students is small, and the population of postgraduate students is smaller than the population of the undergrads. Both female and male students are present in the college; the percentage of female students in the college is forty-four per cent while that of male students is fifty-six percent. The college is situated on Mansfield Road, close to the centre of Oxford, south of the Science Area. The social life of the students within the college involves various sports like the Mansfield College Boat Club and other student organisations.

Merton College accepts male and female students into the college. Right now, the female students in the college represents forty-four per cent of the total student population, while the population of male students represents fifty-six per cent. Merton College accepts both postgraduate and undergraduate students, although the population of the undergraduate students is small. The social activities in the school includes some school traditions like students dressing in formal academic costumes and moving backwards around the Fellows' Quad drinking port at the Time Ceremony. Other social activities include sport and different student societies.

New College is another Oxford college that accepts both undergraduate and postgraduate students. It has a medium population of undergraduate students, and there are fewer postgraduate students in the college. The college also accepts both male and female applicants. The current statistics in the college indicates that the male students are fifty-five per cent of the total population of students while the female student population is forty-five per cent. The social student life within the college includes the use of the junior common room for various social activities by the undergraduate students, and the middle common room by the postgraduate students. The students of the college are also involved in sport, such as rowing.

Oriel College has both postgraduate and undergraduate students. As it stands, the population of undergraduate students in the college is medium-sized with a smaller population of postgraduate students. The college accepts male and female students; the population of male students is greater than that of the females. The population of male students in the college is up to fifty-five per cent while the female students are forty-five per cent. Accommodation is available for all undergraduates, and for a number of the postgraduates. Students usually dine in the hall, where there are double sittings every evening, one informal and one formal, except on Saturdays, where there is only an informal sitting. Arts, journalism and rowing are other social activities in the college.

Pembroke College accepts both undergraduate and graduates into the college. The population of the undergraduates is medium, and it is higher than the population of the postgraduate students in the college. The college also accepts both female and male students with the percentage of forty-four and fifty-six, respectively. The college has a junior common room for the undergraduate students in the college, and it's notable for its artistic wealth and sporting prowess. The sport activities of the college include rugby, hockey, crickets, women boxing, polo and darts. Pembroke College has a very strong sporting status across the Oxford university.

The Queen's College is a college that admits both undergraduate students and postgraduate students. The size of the undergraduate students is medium and the population of postgraduate students in the college is lower than the population of undergraduate students in the college. The college admits female and male students, with the population of the male students slightly higher than the population of the female students in the college. The male students are fifty-three per cent of the student's population, while the female students are forty-seven per cent. The college boasts an active society that participates strongly in intercollege sport competitions. There are also different student societies in the college and, as one of the bigger colleges, it hosts triennial Commemoration balls.

Regent's Park College admits both postgraduate and undergraduate students into the college. The population of the undergraduate students is small while the population of the postgraduate students is far lower than that of the undergraduate students in the college. The college also admits both male and female students into the college, but the population of female students in the college is greater than that of the male students in the college. The female students in the college represent fifty-seven per cent of the population, while the male students represent forty-three per cent. The college is located in central Oxford, just off St Giles'. Students are given access to accommodation in the first and final years of study only. There are sports teams in football, rowing, netball and basketball in the college. The junior common room in the college is used for other social activities.

St Anne's College admits both male and female students into the college. Presently, the percentage of the female and male students in the college is fifty per cent, respectively, which means there are equal numbers of male and female students in the college. The college also accepts both postgraduate and undergraduate students. The population of postgraduate students is lesser than the medium-sized population of undergraduates. The social activities among the students of the college include sport and societal activities. St Anne's college has sport teams for majority of the sports in Oxford University, and competes in inter-collegiate tournaments.

St Benet's Hall is a permanent private hall that accepts undergraduate students and postgraduate students. The size of the undergraduate student's population is small and there are few postgraduate students in the college. Both female and male students can be admitted into the college, although the population of male students in the college is higher than the population of the female students. The percentage of the male student population is eighty-one per cent, compared to nineteen per cent for females. The college has a Joint Common Room (JCR) which is available for the use of both the undergraduate and postgraduate students of the college. The social activities of the college include sport, which is primarily focused on rowing.

St Catherine's College admits both female and male students into the college. Currently the population of the male students in the college is higher than that of the female students. The male student population is greater than the population of the female students. The male students admitted into the college are fifty-five per cent of the total student's population while that of the female students is forty-five per cent. Both undergraduate students and postgraduate students are admitted into the college. The population of the undergraduate students is large and the college has a significant number of postgraduate students. The college make merry of its patron saint every year with a special Catz Night dinner, and the major sport activity in the college is rowing.

St Edmund Hall accepts both undergraduate and postgraduate students. There is a medium-sized population of undergraduate students in the college, which is larger than the number of postgraduate students. The college also accepts both male and female students with the percentages of fifty-six and forty-four per cent, respectively. St Edmund Hall is situated just off Queen's Lane, near the High Street, in central Oxford. There are three common rooms for student social activities. The main social activities in the college are creative writing (there is a weekly creative writing workshop), drama, and sport.

St Hilda's College offers admission for postgraduate students and undergraduate students. The population of the undergraduate students in the college is medium-sized. The college admits both male and female students, and the current population is almost equal, with fifty-one and forty-nine per cent for male and female students, respectively. St Hilda's College is situated at the eastern end of the High Street, across the Magdalen Bridge. The major social activity in the college is sports. St Hilda's College is well known for women's rowing, because the college used to only admit female students.

St Hugh's College is a college that admits both undergraduate students and postgraduate students. The size of the undergraduate student population is medium and the population of postgraduate students in the college is smaller. The college also accepts female and male students into the college; the current male population of the school is fifty-five per cent while the female population is forty-five per cent. The college occupies a rectangular site in North Oxford. St Hugh's College is large enough to accommodate every undergraduate and most of its postgraduates for the duration of their studies. There are common rooms for undergraduate and postgraduate students, and the social activities of the students include sport and music, among others.

St John's College accepts both undergraduate students and postgraduate students into the college, although the population of undergraduate students in the college is medium-sized, while the population of the postgraduate students is smaller. Both female and male students are accepted by the college, with the percentage of fifty-five per cent and forty-five per cent for males and females, respectively. The college occupies a central position on St

Giles'. The college offers accommodation to all undergraduates within the college throughout the period of their studies. Social activities in the college include dining, sport, and drama.

St Peter's College admits both male and female students into the college. Presently, the percentage of females and males in the college is forty-six and fifty-four per cent, respectively. The college also accepts both postgraduate and undergraduate students, with the population of postgraduate students being much smaller than the medium-sized undergrad population. St Peter's College has sports teams competing in rowing, cricket, football, table football and rugby competitions. Rowing is a common sport in the college. The student-run junior common room offers a range of social occasions during the academic year, alternating from formal events to casual parties.

Somerville College accepts both undergraduate and postgraduate students into the college. There is a medium-sized population of undergraduate students in the college, and the population of undergraduate students is larger than the population of the postgraduate students. The college also accepts both male and female students. The population of the male and female students in the school is almost equal, with percentages of forty-nine and fifty-one per cent, respectively. The college is situated in the Science Area and Jericho, at the southern end of Woodstock Road. The college has facilities for rowing and music, and has a strong reputation in both social activities.

Trinity College admits both postgraduate and undergraduate students. Right now, the population of undergraduate students in the college is medium-sized, with a smaller population of postgraduate students. The college accepts male and female students; the population of male students is greater than that of the females. The male population in the college is up to fifty-five per cent, while the female students are forty-five per cent. The college was established on land previously occupied by Durham College. The major social activities in the college are sports and music.

University College is a college that accepts both undergraduate and postgraduate students. There is medium-sized population of undergraduate students in the college while there are fewer postgraduate students. The college also accepts both male and female applicants into the college. The current statistics indicates that the male students are fifty-five per cent while female students are forty-five per cent. The college is located on the High Street and its grounds are bounded by Merton Street and Magpie Lane. The social activities in the college include the *Alternative Prospectus*, which is written and produced by existing students for forthcoming aspirants of the college. The grace of the college is the longest in the University.

Wadham College admits both undergraduate and postgraduate students into the college. The size of the population of the undergraduate students is large, with fewer postgraduate students in comparison to the population of the undergraduate students. Female students and male students can be admitted into the college. The population of the male students represents fifty-four of the total student's population while the population of female students is forty-six per cent. Wadham Gardens is adjacent to the college. Undergraduate students admitted by the college are given accommodation for the first and final years of their studies. The college has a strong student union that controls the social activities of the college.

Worcester College admits both undergraduate students and postgraduate students. The size of the undergraduate student population is medium, and the population of postgraduate students in the college is lower than the population of undergraduate students. The college also accepts female and male students; the current male student's population of the school is forty-nine per cent, while the female population is fifty-one per cent. The major social activity within the college is sports, Worcester has a reputation in hockey, football and cricket. This is one of the few colleges that has its own sporting grounds.

Wycliffe Hall accepts both male and female students into the college. Presently, the percentage of the female and male students is forty-seven and fifty-three per cent, respectively. The college also accepts both postgraduate and undergraduate students into the college. St Anne's College population of postgraduate students is lesser than its small-sized population of the undergraduates, and the population of the postgraduate students is also small. There is a common room for all the students of the college and the students are involved in social activities like sport and fellowship groups associated within the college.

Distance of Oxford Colleges from City Centre

Less than 5 minute walk:

Lincoln College; Brasenose College; Jesus College; Exeter College; Oriel College; Corpus Christi College; Christ Church; Balliol College; Hertford College; Trinity College; Merton College; University College; Pembroke College; St Peter's College; The Queen's College

5 to 10 minute walk:

Wadham College; New College; St Edmund Hall; Harris Manchester College; St John's College; Magdalen College; Worcester College; Regent's Park College; Mansfield College; Keble College; St Benet's Hall

10 to 15 minute walk:

St Hilda's College; Somerville College; St Catherine's College; St Anne's College; Wycliffe Hall

15 to 20 minute walk:

Lady Margaret Hall and St Hugh's College

These times are assuming a 20 minute/mile walking pace. Just because some colleges are close to town doesn't mean that they are also close to the lectures theatres and labs, however. The majority of students cycle, so picking St Hugh's doesn't mean you'll be isolated from the rest of university social life.

What Course Can You do at Which Oxford College?

Archaeology and Anthropology is offered at: Harris Manchester College, Hertford College, Keble College, Magdalene College, St Hugh's College, St John's College, and St Peter's College.

Biochemistry (Molecular and Cellular) is offered at: Brasenose College, Christ Church College, Corpus Christi College, Exeter College, Hertford College, Lady Margaret Hall College, Lincoln College, Magdalene College, Merton College, New College, Oriel College, Pembroke College, The Queen's College, St Anne's College, St Catherine's College, St Edmund Hall College, St Hilda's College, St Hugh's College, St John's College, St Peter's College, Somerville College, Trinity College, University College, Wadham College and Worcester College.

Biological Sciences is offered at: Balliol College, Brasenose College, Christ Church College, Hertford College, Jesus College, Keble College, Lady Margret Hall College, Magdalene College, Merton College, New College, Pembroke College, The Queen's College, St Anne's College, St Catherine's College, St Hilda's College, St Hugh's College, St John's College, St Peter's College, Somerville College, Wadham College, and Worcester College.

Biomedical Sciences is offered at: Balliol College, Corpus Christi College, Exeter College, Keble College, Lincoln College, Magdalene College, New College, The Queen's College, St Anne's College, St Catherine's College, St Edmund Hall College, St Hilda's College, St Hugh's College, St John's College, Somerville College and University College.

Chemistry is offered at: Balliol College, Brasenose College, Christ Church College, Corpus Christi College, Exeter College, Herford College, Jesus College, Keble College, Lady Margret Hall College, Lincoln College, Magdalene College, Merton College, New College, Oriel College, Pembroke College, The Queens College, St Catherine's College, St Edmund Hall College, St Hilda's College, St Hugh's College, St John's College, St Peter's College, Somerville College, Trinity College, University College, Wadham College and Worcester College.

Classical Archaeology and Ancient History is offered at: Balliol College, Brasenose College, Christ Church College, Corpus Christi College, Exeter College, Keble College, Lady Margaret Hall College, Lincoln College, Magdalene College, Merton College, Oriel College, Regent's Park College, St Anne's College, St Hilda's College, St John's College, Somerville College, University College, Wadham College and Worcester College.

Classical Archeology and Ancient History is offered at: Balliol College, Brasenose College, Christ Church College, Corpus Christi College, Exeter College, Keble College, Lady Margaret Hall College, Lincoln College, Magdalen College, Merton College, Oriel College, Regent's Park College, St Anne's College, St Hilda's College, St John's College, Somerville College, University College, Wadham College and Worcester College.

Classics is offered at: Balliol College, Brasenose College, Christ Church, Corpus Christi College, Exeter College, Jesus College, Lady Margaret College, Magdalen College, Merton College, New College, Oriel College, The Queen's College, Regent's Park College, St Anne's College, St Benet's Hall College, St Hilda's College, St Hugh's College, St John's College,

Somerville College, Trinity College, University College, Wadham College, and Worcester College.

Classics and English is offered at: Brasenose College, Corpus Christi College, Exeter College, Harris Manchester College, Jesus College, Lady Margaret College, Magdalen College, Oriel College, The Queen's College, Regent's Park College St Anne's College, St Hugh's College, Trinity College, University College, Wadham College and Worcester College.

Classics and Czech (with Slovak) is offered at: Brasenose College, Christ Church College, Jesus College, Magdalen College, The Queen's College, St Anne's College, St John's College, Somerville College, University College, Wadham College, and Worcester College.

Classics and Celtic is offered at: Christ Church College, Exeter College, Jesus College, Merton College, The Queen's College, St Anne's College, St John's College, Wadham College, and Worcester College.

Classics and Oriental Studies is offered at: Balliol College, Brasenose College, Christ Church, Exeter College, Harris Manchester College, Lincoln College, New College, Oriel College, The Queen's College, St Anne's College, St Benet's College, St Hilda's College, St Hugh's College, St John's College, Somerville College, Trinity College, University College, Wadham College and Worcester College.

Computer Science is offered at: Balliol College, Christ Church College, Hertford College, Jesus College, Keble College, Lady Margaret College, Magdalen College, Merton College, New College, Oriel College, St Anne's College, St Catherine's

College, St Hugh's College, St John's College, Somerville College, University College and Worcester College.

Computer Science and Philosophy is offered at: Balliol College, Christ Church College, Herford College, Lady Margaret Hall College, Merton College, New College, Oriel College, St Anne's College, St Catherine's College, St John's College and University College.

Earth Sciences (Geology) is offered at: Exeter College, St Anne's College, St Edmund Hall, St Hugh's College, St Peter's College, University College and Worcester College.

Economics and Management is offered at: Balliol College, Brasenose College, Christ College, Exeter College, Harris Manchester College, Hertford College, Jesus College, Keble College, Lady Margaret College, Merton College, New College, Pembroke College, St Catherine's College, St Edmund College, St Hilda's College, St Hugh's College, St Peter's College, Trinity College, Wadham College and Worcester College.

Engineering Science is offered at: Balliol College, Brasenose College, Christ College, Exeter College, Harris Manchester College, Hertford College, Jesus College, Keble College, Lady Margaret College, Lincoln College, Magdalen College, Mansfield College, New College, Oriel College, Pembroke College, St Anne's College, St Catherine's College, St Edmund's College, St Hilda's College, St Hugh's College, St John's College, St Peter's College, Somerville College, trinity College, University College, Wadham College and Worcester College.

English Language and Literature is offered at: Balliol College, Brasenose College, Christ College, Corpus Christi College,

Exeter College, Harris Manchester College, Hertford College, Jesus College, Keble College, Lady Margaret College, Lincoln College, Magdalen College, Mansfield College, Merton College, New College, Oriel College, Pembroke College, The Queen's College, Regent's Park College, St Anne's College, St Catherine's College, St Edmund Hall College, St Hilda's College, St Hugh's College, St John's College, ST Peter's College, Somerville College, Trinity College, University College, Wadham College and Worcester College.

English Language and Czech (with Slovak) is offered at: Brasenose College, Christ Church College, Jesus College, Magdalen College, The Queen's College, St Catherine's College, St John's College, St Peter's College, Somerville College, University College, Wadham College and Worcester College.

English and Celtic is offered at: Christ Church College, Exeter College, Jesus College, Merton College, The Queen's College, St Anne's College, St Catherine's College, St John's College, St Peter's College, Wadham College and Worcester College.

European and Middle Eastern Languages are offered at: Brasenose College, Christ Church College, Jesus College, Magdalen College, New College, Pembroke College, The Queen's College, St Anne's College, St Hilda's College, St Hugh's College, St John's College, Somerville College, University College, Wadham College and Worcester College.

Fine Art is offered at: Brasenose College, Christ Church College, Exeter College, Lady Margaret College, Magdalen College, New College, The Queen's College, St Anne's College, St Catherine's College, St Edmund College, St Hugh's College, St John's College and Worcester College.

Geography is offered at Brasenose College, Christ Church College, Hertford College, Keble College, Mansfield College, Regent's Park College, St Anne's College, St Catherine's College, St Edmund College, St Hilda's College, St John's College and St Peter's College.

History is offered at: Balliol College, Brasenose College, Christ Church College, Corpus Christi College, Exeter College, Harris Manchester College, Hertford College, Jesus College, Keble College, Lady Margaret College, Lincoln College, Magdalen College, Mansfield College, Merton College, New College, Oriel College, Pembroke College, The Queen's College, Regent's Park College, St Anne's College, St Benet's Hall College, St Catherine's College, St Edmund Hall College, St Hilda's College, St Hugh 's College, St John's College, St Peter's College, Somerville, Trinity College, University College, Wadham College and Worcester College.

History (Ancient and Modern) is offered at: Balliol College, Brasenose College, Christ Church College, Corpus Christi College, Exeter College, Keble College, Lady Margaret College, Lincoln College, Magdalen College, Merton College, New College, Oriel College, The Queen's College, Regent's Park College, St Anne's College, St Hilda's College, St Hugh's College, St John's College, Somerville College, Trinity College, University College Wadham College and Worcester College.

History and Economics is offered at: Balliol College, Brasenose College, Harris Manchester College, Jesus College, New College, Oriel College, Pembroke College, Regent's Park College, St Anne's College, St Catherine's College, St John's College, St Peter's College, Somerville College, Wadham College and Worcester College.

History and English is offered at Balliol College, Corpus Christi College, Exeter College, Harris Manchester College, Jesus College, Merton College, Pembroke College, The Queen's College, Regent's Park College, St Catherine's College, St Hilda's College, St Hugh's College, St Peter's College, Somerville College and Wadham College.

History and Portuguese is offered at: Brasenose College, Christ Church College, Exeter College, Herford College, Jesus College, Magdalen College, Merton College, Pembroke College, The Queen's College, St Anne's College, St Catherine's College, St John's College, St Peter's College, Wadham College and Worcester College.

History and Politics is offered at: Balliol College, Brasenose College, Christ Church College, Corpus Christi College, Harris Manchester College, Herford College, Jesus College, Keble College, Lady Margaret College, Lincoln College, Magdalen College, Merton College, New College, Oriel College, Pembroke College, The Queen's College, Regent's Park College, St Anne's College St Catherine's College, St Edmund Hall College, St Hilda's College, St Hugh's College, St John's College, St Peter's College, Trinity College, University College, Wadham College and Worcester College.

History of Art is offered at: Christ Church College, Exeter College, Harris Manchester College, Lincoln College, St Catherine's College, St John's College, St Peter's College, Wadham College and Worcester College.

Human Sciences is offered at: Harris Manchester College, Hertford College, Keble College, Magdalen College, Mansfield College, St Benet's Hall College, St Catherine's College, St Hugh's College, St John's College and Wadham College.

Law (Jurisprudence) is offered at: Balliol College, Brasenose College, Christ Church College, Corpus Christi College, Exeter College, Harris Manchester College, Herford College, Jesus College, Keble College, Lady Margaret Hall College, Lincoln College, Magdalen College, Mansfield College, Merton College, New College, Oriel College, Pembroke College, The Queen's College, Regent's Park College, St Anne's College, St Catherine' College, St Edmund Hall College, St Hilda's College, St Hugh's College, St John's College, St Peter's College, Somerville College, Trinity College, University College, Wadham College and Worcester College.

Material Science is offered at: Corpus Christi College, Mansfield College, The Queen's College, St Anne's College, St Catherine's College, St Edmund Hall College and Trinity College.

Mathematics is offered at: Balliol College, Brasenose College, Christ Church College, Corpus Christi College, Exeter College, Hertford College, Jesus College, Keble College, Lady Margaret College, Lincoln College, Magdalen College, Mansfield College, Merton College, New College, Oriel College, Pembroke College, The Queen's College, St Anne's College, St Catherine's College, St Edmund Hall College, St Hilda's College, St Hugh's College, St John's College, St Peter's College, Somerville College, Trinity College, University College, Wadham College and Worcester College.

Mathematics and Computer Science is offered at: Balliol College, Christ Church College, Corpus Christi College, Exeter College, Jesus College, Keble College, Lady Margaret College, Magdalen College Merton College, New College, Oriel College, St Anne's College, St Catherine's College, St Hugh's College,

St John' College, Somerville College, University College, Wadham College and Worcester College.

Mathematics and Philosophy is offered at: Balliol College, Brasenose College, Christ Church College, Corpus Christi College, Exeter College, Jesus College, Lady Margaret Hall College, Magdalen College, Merton College, New College, Oriel College, Pembroke College, The Queen's College, St Anne's College, St Catherine's College, St Hilda's College, St Hugh's College, St John's College, St Peter's College, Somerville College, University College, Wadham College and Worcester College.

Mathematics and Statistics is offered at: Balliol College, Brasenose College, Christ Church College, Corpus Christi College, Exeter College, Jesus College, Keble College, Lady Margaret Hall College, Lincoln College, Magdalen College, Mansfield College, Merton College, New College, Oriel College, The Queen's College, St Anne's College, St Catherine's College, St Edmund Hall College, St Hilda's College, St Hugh's College, St John's College, St Peter's College, Somerville College, Trinity College, University College, Wadham College and Worcester College.

Medicine is offered at: Balliol College, Brasenose College, Christ Church College, Corpus Christi College, Exeter College, Herford College, Jesus College, Keble College, Lady Margaret Hall College, Lincoln College, Magdalen College, Merton College, New College, Oriel College, Pembroke College, The Queen's College, St Anne's College, St Catherine's College, St Edmund Hall College, St Hilda's College, ST Hugh's College, St John's College, St Peter's College, Somerville College, Trinity College, University College, Wadham College and Worcester College.

Modern Greek and Arabic is offered at Christ Church College, Jesus College, Pembroke College, The Queen's College, St John's College and Wadham College.

Modern Greek and Beginners' Russian is offered at: Brasenose College, Christ Church, Jesus College, Lady Margaret Hall College, New College, The Queen's College, St Catherine's College, St Peter's College and Wadham College.

Modern Greek and Linguistics is offered at: Brasenose College, Christ College, Exeter College, Jesus College, Pembroke College, St Catherine's College and St Peter's College.

Music is offered at: Christ Church College, Corpus Christi College, Exeter College, Herford College, Jesus College, Keble College, Lady Margaret Hall College, Lincoln College, Magdalen College, Merton College, New College, Oriel College, Pembroke College, The Queen's College, St Anne's College, St Catherine's College, St Hilda's College, St Hugh' College, St John's College, St Peter's College, Somerville College, Trinity College, University College and Worcester College.

Oriental Studies is offered at: Balliol College, Christ Church College, Harris Manchester College, Herford College, Mansfield College, Pembroke College, The Queen's College, St Anne's College, St Benet's Hall College, St John's College, University College and Wadham College.

Philosophy and Czech (with Slovak) is offered at: Brasenose College, Christ Church College, Jesus College, Magdalen College, The Queen's College, St Catherine's College, St John's College, St Peter's College, Somerville College, University College, Wadham College and Worcester College.

Philosophy and Celtic is offered at: Christ Church College, Exeter College, Jesus College, Merton College, The Queen's College, St Catherine's College, St John's College, St Peter's College, Wadham College and Worcester College.

Philosophy, Politics and Economics (PPE) is offered at: Balliol College, Brasenose College, Christ Church College, Corpus Christi College, Exeter College, Harris Manchester College, Hertford College, Jesus College, Keble College, Lady Margaret Hall College, Lincoln College, Magdalen College, Mansfield College, Merton College, New College, Oriel College, Pembroke College, The Queen's College, Regent's Park College, St Anne's College, St Benet's Hall College, St Catherine' College, Edmund Hall College, St Hilda's College, St Hugh's College, St John's College, St Peter's College, Somerville College, Trinity College, University College, Wadham College and Worcester College.

Philosophy and Theology is offered at: Christ Church College, Harris Manchester College, Jesus College, Keble College, Lady Margaret College, Mansfield College, Oriel College, Pembroke College, Regent's Park College, St Benet's Hall College, St John's College, St Peter's College, Trinity College, Worcester College and Wycliffe Hall College.

Physics is offered at: Balliol College, Brasenose College, Christ Church College, Corpus Christi College, Exeter College, Hertford College, Jesus College, Keble College, Lady Margaret Hall College, Lincoln College, Magdalen College, Mansfield College, Merton College, New College, Oriel College, Pembroke College, The Queen's College, St Anne's College, St Catherine's College, St Edmund Hall College, St Hilda's College, St Hugh's College, St John's College, St Peter's

College, Somerville College, Trinity College, University College, Wadham College and Worcester College.

Physics and Philosophy is offered at: Balliol College, Brasenose College, Christ Church College, Corpus Christi College, Herford College, Lady Margaret Hall College, Magdalen College, Merton College, Oriel College, Pembroke College, The Queen's College, St Catherine's College, St Hilda's College, St Peter's College, University College, Wadham College and Worcester College.

Psychology (Experimental) is offered at: Brasenose College, Christ Church College, Corpus Christi College, Harris Manchester College, Jesus College, Lady Margaret Hall College, Magdalen College, New College, Pembroke College, The Queen's College, St Anne's College, St Catherine's College, St Edmund College, St Hilda's College, St Hugh's College, St John's College, Somerville College, University College, Wadham College and Worcester College.

Psychology, Philosophy and Linguistics is offered at: Brasenose College, Christ Church College, Corpus Christi College, Harris Manchester College, Jesus College, Lady Margaret Hall College, Magdalen College, New College, Pembroke College, The Queen's College, St Anne's College, St Catherine's College, St Edmund College, St Hilda's College, St Hugh's College, St John's College, Somerville College, University College and Worcester College.

Religion and Oriental Studies is offered at: Christ Church College, Harris Manchester College, Lady Margaret Hall College, Pembroke College, Regent's Park College, St Benet's Hall College, St John's College and St Peter's College.

Theology and Religion is offered at: Christ Church College, Harris Manchester College, Keble College, Lady Margaret Hall College, Mansfield College, Oriel College, Pembroke College, Regent's Park College, St Benet's College, St John's College, St Peter's College, Trinity College, Worcester College and Wycliffe Hall College.

Cambridge College Information

Cambridge College Summaries

Christ's College admits both undergraduate and postgraduate students into the college. The population of the undergraduate students in the college is large, with a small population of postgraduate students. The college also admits mixed sex into the college. The population of male students in the college is slightly higher than the population of female students, at fifty-eight and to forty-two per cent, respectively. The college is centrally located, with direct access to shops and cafes in the city centre. Christ's College has various facilities in place to sustain a range of clubs, teams and societies that carry various social activities within the college.

Churchill College admits both male and female students, but the population of male students in the college is greater that the population of female students. The male population of the college is seventy per cent of the total population, while the females represent twenty-one per cent. Both undergraduate and postgraduate students are admitted to Churchill College. The population of undergraduate students in the college is large and greater than the population of postgraduate students. The college is located on the borders of the University, away from the traditional centre of the city. There are various social events and sport activities within the college.

Clare College offers admission for postgraduate students and undergraduate students. The population of the undergraduate students in the college is large. The college admits both male and female students, with an almost equal distribution of fifty-two and forty-eight per cent for male and female students, respectively. Clare has an excellent reputation as one of the most musical colleges in Cambridge, and many students there can play different musical instruments. Rowing with Clare Boat Club is the major sporting activity in the college.

Corpus Christi College accepts both undergraduate and graduates into the college. Although the population of the undergraduates can be described as small, it is still higher than the postgraduate population. The college accepts both female and male students, with the percentage of forty and sixty per cent, respectively. Corpus Christi College provides accommodation for both postgraduate and undergraduate students in the college, although some of the students don't stay in the college. The Corpus Challenge with Oxford University and rowing are the major social activities in the college. There is a play room in the college for drama.

Downing College accepts both undergraduate students and postgraduate students, although the population of undergraduate students in the college is medium-sized, while the population of the postgraduate students is lower than that of the undergraduate students. Both female and male students are accepted by the college, with a percentage of sixty-six per cent to thirty-four per cent for male and female students, respectively. The students of the college are actively involved in student politics at the University. The college has various sport teams, like men's football, men's and women's rugby, tennis and ultimate frisbee. Downing College Boat Club is also successful.

Emmanuel College accepts male and female students into the college. Right now, the population of male and female students is almost the same. The female students in the college represent forty-nine per cent of the total student population, while male students represent fifty-one per cent. Emmanuel College accepts both postgraduate and undergraduate students into the college, although the population of the undergraduate students is large. The Emmanuel College Students' Union (ECSU) represents every undergraduate student at the college, and it runs a shop, a bar, and a common room, as well as provides money for sports and other societies.

Fitzwilliam College accepts both postgraduate and undergraduate students. Currently, the college has large population of undergraduate students greater in number than the postgraduate students. This college also accept both male and female applicants, but it accepts more male students than female students. As of now, the percentage of male students in the college is sixty-three per cent while the percentage of females in the college is thirty-seven per cent. The main social activities among students at the college are music and sports. Fitzwilliam College is customarily strong in football, rugby union, and table tennis, and has an excellent reputation for music among other colleges.

Girton College accepts both undergraduate students and postgraduate students into the college, although the population of undergraduate students in the college is large, while the population of the postgraduate students is smaller. Both female and male students are accepted by the college, with a percentage of fifty-three per cent and forty-seven per cent for male to female, respectively. Girton College is located on the peripheries of the village of Girton. The common social activities in the college are sport, music and student societies. The college provides sports fields for cricket, football, hockey, lacrosse, netball and volleyball.

Gonville & Caius College accepts both undergraduate students and postgraduate students into the college, although the population of undergraduate students in the college is small, and the population of the postgraduate students is even smaller. Both female and male students are accepted by the college, with a percentage of fifty-one per cent and forty-nine per cent for males and females, respectively. The main social activities in the school are music and sports. Gonville & Caius College is known for its choir and the Caius Boat Club. Caius Jazz is a music event that takes place almost every term in the college bar.

Homerton College is a college that accepts both undergraduate and postgraduate students. There is large population of undergraduate students in the college, and the population of the postgraduate students is also large. The college accepts both male and female applicants, and the current statistics indicate that male students are thirty-seven per cent of the total population of students, while females are sixty-seven per cent. Students are involved in social traditions, and the major sport in the college is rowing with the Homerton College Boat Club.

Hughes Hall accepts undergraduate students and postgraduate students. As it stands, the population of undergraduate students is small, while the postgraduate students are larger in number. Hughes Hall is one of the colleges that accepts more postgraduates than undergraduate students. The college accepts both male and female students, but there are more male students than female, with sixty-one per cent to thirty-nine per cent, respectively. The main college location is near the centre of Cambridge. College societies, sports, and music are the main social activities.

Jesus College accepts both undergraduate and postgraduate students. There is large population of undergraduate students in the college, while there are fewer postgraduate students. The college accepts both male and female applicants, and the current statistics indicate that male students are fifty-seven per cent of the total population while the female student population is forty-three per cent. The college is located close to Cambridge. The college is known for a relaxed and entertaining environment with numerous social and sport activities. Also, dinners are served for five days every week in the college's Formal Hall.

King's College admits both postgraduate and undergraduate students into the college. The population of the undergraduate students is medium-sized, while the population of the postgraduate students is far lower than that of the undergraduate students. The college also admits both male and female students into the college, but the population of males is greater than females. The female students in the college represent forty-three per cent of the population, while the male students represent fifty-seven per cent. King's College is located beside the River Cam and is opposite King's Parade in the middle of the city. The college has its own student unions, and several informal events and sport activities occur in the college.

Lucy Cavendish has both postgraduate and undergraduate students. Right now, the population of undergraduate students in the college is small with an equal population of postgraduate students. The college accepts only female students; the college is one of the few colleges in Cambridge that do not accept any male students. There is a student union in the college, and the social activities within the college include college parties, societal activities, sports such as rowing, and Formal Hall with no high table.

Magdalene College accepts both undergraduates and postgraduate students, but the college has more undergraduate students than postgrads. Both male and female students are present in the college; fifty-four per cent of the students in the college are male students while the remaining forty-six per cent are female students. Magdalene College is bounded by Magdalene Street, Chesterton Lane and the River Cam. College Grace and May Ball are the main social activities in the college.

Murray Edwards College has both postgraduate and undergraduate students. Right now, the population of undergraduate students in the college is medium sized with a lower population of postgraduate students. The college is another college under Cambridge University that accepts only female students; the college is exclusively for female students. The college provides accommodation for undergraduates throughout the course of study, but accommodation is only available for some postgraduates. The students are involved in various social activities such as sport and other social events.

Newnham College is a college that accepts undergraduate and postgraduate students even though the population of the undergraduate students is large and the postgraduate population is much lower. This college is another college in the university that does not accept male students. Dinner is served to students in Formal Hall seven days of the week, and students at the college now also have a contemporary buttery where they can relax. The college has several student societies, including clubs for rowing, football, netball, tennis, and many other sports.

Pembroke College offers admission for postgraduate students and undergraduate students. The population of the undergraduate students in the college is medium-sized. The college admits both male and female students; the current population of both female and male students is almost equal, but there are slightly more male students than female students in the college; fifty-three and forty-seven per cent, respectively. There are several clubs and societies established by the students, including Pembroke College Boat Club and the college's dramatic society, the Pembroke Players.

Peterhouse admits both postgraduate and undergraduate students into the college and the population of the undergraduate student is small while the population of the postgraduate students is even smaller. The college admits both male and female students into the college, but the population of male students in the college is greater than that of the female students. The male students in the college represent fifty-seven per cent of the population, while female students represent forty-three per cent. There are different clubs and societies in the college and the students are also involved in sports and music.

Queens' College accepts undergraduate students and postgraduate students. The size of the undergraduate student population is large and there are many postgraduate students in the college. Both female and male students can be admitted into the college, although the population of male students in the college is higher than the population of the female students. The percentage is fifty-seven and forty-three per cent, respectively. The college is a part of the easily identifiable structures in Cambridge, and Queens' College borders the river Cam. Accommodation is made available for every undergraduate student and many postgraduate students. The major social activities in the college are sports and May Ball.

Robinson College accepts male and female students into the college. Right now, the population of male students is greater than the population of female students, with females representing forty per cent of the total student population, with males making up the other sixty per cent. Robinson College accepts both postgraduate and undergraduate students into the college, although the population of the undergraduate students is medium-sized. Like other colleges, this college has leisure amenities such as a junior common room, middle common room, TV room, art room, café and bar for their students. Sports and formal halls are also carried out in the college.

Selwyn College accepts undergraduate and postgraduate students, even though the population of the undergraduate students is medium-sized and the postgraduate population is much smaller. Both female and male students are present in the college, but the population of male students is higher than the population of female students, at fifty-five to forty-five per cent, respectively. The social activities in the college include sport (which is predominately rowing), informal societies, various dining halls, use of common rooms for entertainment, and formal halls.

Sidney Sussex College has both postgraduate and undergraduate students. As it stands, the population of undergraduate students in the college is medium-sized with smaller population of postgraduate students. The college accepts male and female students; the population of male students is greater than that of females. The population of male students in the college is up to sixty-three per cent of the student's population, while the female students are thirty-seven per cent of the student's population. The social activitiess in the school include music; in particular, the college choir has a good reputation among other Cambridge colleges. Other social activities are sports and student societies.

St Catharine's College admits both undergraduate and postgraduate students into the college. The size of the population of the undergraduate students in the college is large, with fewer postgraduate students in comparison to the population of the undergraduate students. Female students and male students are admitted to the college, and the population of male students represents fifty-two per cent while the female students are forty-eight per cent. The college is positioned right in the middle of Cambridge. Hockey, rowing and racquet are the important sports in the college. There are several societies in the college for various social activities.

St Edmund's College accepts both undergraduate and graduate students. St Edmund's College is a college that admits majorly postgraduate students, and the population of the undergraduates can be described as small. The college accepts both female and male students with the percentage of thirty-one and sixty-nine per cent, respectively. The college is situated on Mount Pleasant, about ten minutes' stroll northwest of the middle of Cambridge. There is a formal hall where students are expected to wear their gowns, and sport activities are not common in the college.

St John's College admits both postgraduate and undergraduate students into the college. The population of the undergraduate student is large, while the population of postgraduate students is far smaller. The college admits both male and female students into the college, but the population of male students in the college is greater than that of the female students. Female students represent forty-one per cent of the population, while the male students represent fifty-nine per cent. This college is popular for its choir, its fellows' accomplishments in a range of different sporting contests, and its yearly May Ball. Accommodation is available for all undergraduates and some postgraduates.

Trinity College is a college that admits both undergraduate students and postgraduate students. The size of the undergraduate student's population is large and the population of postgraduate students in the college is smaller than the undergraduates. The college accepts female and male students; the current male student's population of the school is sixty-three per cent while the female population is thirty-seven per cent. There are several societies in the college and the main sport is rowing, which is part of the annual May Ball.

Trinity Hall accepts undergraduate students and postgraduate students. The size of the undergraduate student population is medium, and there are fewer postgraduate students in the college. Both female and male students can be admitted into the college, although the population of male students in the college is higher. The percentage of the male and female students is fifty-four and forty-six per cent, respectively. There is a common room for undergraduates where informal activities take place. There is an annual event in the college called June Event where students are entertained.

Wolfson College accepts male and female students into the college. Right now, the female students in the college represents thirty-six per cent of the total student population while the population of male students is sixty-four per cent. Both postgraduate and undergraduate students are accepted into the college, although the population of the undergraduate students is small. The population of the postgraduate students is higher than that of the undergraduates. Wolfson College is popular for its entertaining events, which entice guests from numerous other colleges of Cambridge. These events comprise formal dinners, concerts, dancing nights, and music displays.

Distance of Cambridge Colleges from City Centre

Less than 5 minute walk:
Christ's College; Clare College; Corpus Christi College; Downing College; Emmanuel College; Gonville & Caius College; King's College; St Catharine's College

5 to 10 minutes walk:
Jesus College; Pembroke College; Peterhouse; Queens' College; Sidney Sussex College; St John's College; Trinity College; Trinity Hall

10 to 15 minute walk:
Magdalene College and Newnham College

15 to 20 minute walk:
Hughes Hall; Lucy Cavendish; Murray Edwards College; Robinson College; Selwyn College; St Edmund's College

Over 20 minute walk:
Churchill College; Fitzwilliam College; Wolfson College

Over 30 minute walk:
Girton College and Homerton College

These times are assuming a 20 minute/walk walking pace. Cambridge is more spread out than Oxford, but has a very extensive bus network and the majority of students ride bicycles.

What Courses Can You Do at which Cambridge College?

Anglo-Saxon, Norse and Celtic is offered at: Christ's College, Churchill College, Clare College, Corpus Christi College, Downing College, Emmanuel College, Fitzwilliam College, Girton College, Gonville & Caius College, Homerton College, Hughes Hall, Jesus College, King's College, Lucy Cavendish, Magdalene College, Murray Edwards College, Newnham College, Pembroke College, Peterhouse, Queens' College, Robinson College, Selwyn College, Sidney Sussex College, St Catharine's College, St Edmund's College, St John's College, Trinity College, Trinity Hall and Wolfson College.

Archaeology (Celtic) is offered at: Christ's College, Churchill College, Clare College, Corpus Christi College, Downing College, Emmanuel College, Fitzwilliam College, Girton College, Gonville & Caius College, Homerton College, Hughes Hall, Jesus College, King's College, Lucy Cavendish, Magdalene College, Murray Edwards College, Newnham College, Pembroke College, Peterhouse, Queens' College, Robinson College, Selwyn College, Sidney Sussex College, St Catharine's College, St Edmund's College, St John's College, Trinity College, Trinity Hall and Wolfson College.

Architecture is offered at: Christ's Church College, Churchill College, Clare College, Corpus Christi College, Downing College, Emmanuel College, Fitzwilliam College, Girton College, Ginville & Cauis College, Jesus College, King's College, Lucy Cavendish Magdalen College, Murray Edwards College, Newnham College, Pembroke College, Peterhouse, Queen's College, Robinson College, Selwyn College, Sidney Sussex College, St Edmund College, St John's College, trinity College, Trinity Hall College, Wolfson College,

Asian and Middle Eastern Studies is offered at: Christ's College, Churchill College, Clare College, Corpus Christi College, Downing College, Emmanuel College, Fitzwilliam College, Girton College, Gonville & Caius College, Homerton College, Hughes Hall, Jesus College, King's College, Lucy Cavendish, Magdalene College, Murray Edwards College, Newnham College, Pembroke College, Peterhouse, Queens' College, Robinson College, Selwyn College, Sidney Sussex College, St Catharine's College, St Edmund's College, St John's College, Trinity College, Trinity Hall and Wolfson College.

Chemical Engineering is offered at: Christ's College, Churchill College, Clare College, Corpus Christi College, Downing College, Emmanuel College, Fitzwilliam College, Girton College, Gonville & Caius College, Homerton College, Hughes Hall, Jesus College, King's College, Lucy Cavendish, Magdalene College, Murray Edwards College, Newnham College, Pembroke College, Peterhouse, Queens' College, Robinson College, Selwyn College, Sidney Sussex College, St Catharine's College, St Edmund's College, St John's College, Trinity College, Trinity Hall and Wolfson College.

Classics is offered at: Christ's College, Churchill College, Clare College, Corpus Christi College, Downing College, Emmanuel College, Fitzwilliam College, Girton College, Gonville & Caius College, Homerton College, Hughes Hall, Jesus College, King's College, Lucy Cavendish, Magdalene College, Murray Edwards College, Newnham College, Pembroke College, Peterhouse, Queens' College, Robinson College, Selwyn College, Sidney Sussex College, St Catharine's College, St Edmund's College, St John's College, Trinity College, Trinity Hall and Wolfson College.

Computer Science is offered at: Christ's College, Churchill College, Clare College, Corpus Christi College, Downing College, Emmanuel College, Fitzwilliam College, Girton College, Gonville & Caius College, Homerton College, Hughes Hall, Jesus College, King's College, Lucy Cavendish, Magdalene College, Murray Edwards College, Newnham College, Pembroke College, Peterhouse, Queens' College, Robinson College, Selwyn College, Sidney Sussex College, St Catharine's College, St Edmund's College, St John's College, Trinity College, Trinity Hall and Wolfson College.

Economics is offered at: Christ's College, Churchill College, Clare College, Corpus Christi College, Downing College, Emmanuel College, Fitzwilliam College, Girton College, Gonville & Caius College, Homerton College, Hughes Hall, Jesus College, King's College, Lucy Cavendish, Magdalene College, Murray Edwards College, Newnham College, Pembroke College, Peterhouse, Queens' College, Robinson College, Selwyn College, Sidney Sussex College, St Catharine's College, St Edmund's College, St John's College, Trinity College and Trinity Hall.

Trinity Hall is offered at: Christ's College, Churchill College, Clare College, Downing College, Fitzwilliam College, Gonville & Caius College, Homerton College, Hughes Hall, Jesus College, Lucy Cavendish, Magdalene College, Pembroke College, Queens' College, Robinson College, Selwyn College, St Edmund's College, St John's College and Wolfson College.

Engineering is offered at: Christ's College, Churchill College, Clare College, Corpus Christi College, Downing College, Emmanuel College, Fitzwilliam College, Girton College, Gonville & Caius College, Homerton College, Hughes Hall, Jesus College, King's College, Lucy Cavendish, Magdalene

College, Murray Edwards College, Newnham College, Pembroke College, Peterhouse, Queens' College, Robinson College, Selwyn College, Sidney Sussex College, St Catharine's College, St Edmund's College, St John's College, Trinity College, Trinity Hall and Wolfson College.

English is offered at: Christ's College, Churchill College, Clare College, Corpus Christi College, Downing College, Emmanuel College, Fitzwilliam College, Girton College, Gonville & Caius College, Homerton College, Hughes Hall, Jesus College, King's College, Lucy Cavendish, Magdalene College, Murray Edwards College, Newnham College, Pembroke College, Peterhouse, Queens' College, Robinson College, Selwyn College, Sidney Sussex College, St Catharine's College, St Edmund's College, St John's College, Trinity College, Trinity Hall and Wolfson College.

Geography is offered at: Christ's College, Churchill College, Clare College, Corpus Christi College, Downing College, Emmanuel College, Fitzwilliam College, Girton College, Gonville & Caius College, Homerton College, Hughes Hall, Jesus College, King's College, Lucy Cavendish, Magdalene College, Murray Edwards College, Newnham College, Pembroke College, Queens' College, Robinson College, Selwyn College, Sidney Sussex College, St Catharine's College, St Edmund's College, St John's College, Trinity College, Trinity Hall and Wolfson College.

History is offered at: Christ's College, Churchill College, Clare College, Corpus Christi College, Downing College, Emmanuel College, Fitzwilliam College, Girton College, Gonville & Caius College, Homerton College, Hughes Hall, Jesus College, King's College, Lucy Cavendish, Magdalene College, Murray Edwards College, Newnham College, Pembroke College, Peterhouse,

Queens' College, Robinson College, Selwyn College, Sidney Sussex College, St Catharine's College, St Edmund's College, St John's College, Trinity College, Trinity Hall and Wolfson College.

History and Modern Languages is offered at: Christ's College, Churchill College, Clare College, Corpus Christi College, Downing College, Emmanuel College, Fitzwilliam College, Girton College, Gonville & Caius College, Homerton College, Hughes Hall, Jesus College, King's College, Lucy Cavendish, Magdalene College, Murray Edwards College, Newnham College, Pembroke College, Peterhouse, Queens' College, Robinson College, Selwyn College, Sidney Sussex College, St Catharine's College, St Edmund's College, St John's College, Trinity College, Trinity Hall and Wolfson College.

History and Politics is offered at: Christ's College, Churchill College, Clare College, Corpus Christi College, Downing College, Emmanuel College, Fitzwilliam College, Girton College, Gonville & Caius College, Homerton College, Hughes Hall, Jesus College, King's College, Lucy Cavendish, Magdalene College, Murray Edwards College, Newnham College, Pembroke College, Peterhouse, Queens' College, Robinson College, Selwyn College, Sidney Sussex College, St Catharine's College, St Edmund's College, St John's College, Trinity College, Trinity Hall and Wolfson College.

History of Art is offered at: Christ's College, Churchill College, Clare College, Corpus Christi College, Downing College, Emmanuel College, Fitzwilliam College, Gonville & Caius College, Homerton College, Hughes Hall, Jesus College, King's College, Lucy Cavendish, Magdalene College, Murray Edwards College, Newnham College, Pembroke College, Peterhouse, Queens' College, Robinson College, Selwyn College, Sidney

Sussex College, St Catharine's College, St Edmund's College, St John's College, Trinity College, Trinity Hall and Wolfson College.

Human, Social, and Political Sciences is offered at: Christ's College, Churchill College, Clare College, Corpus Christi College, Downing College, Emmanuel College, Fitzwilliam College, Girton College, Gonville & Caius College, Homerton College, Hughes Hall, Jesus College, King's College, Lucy Cavendish, Magdalene College, Murray Edwards College, Newnham College, Pembroke College, Peterhouse, Queens' College, Robinson College, Selwyn College, Sidney Sussex College, St Catharine's College, St Edmund's College, St John's College, Trinity College, Trinity Hall and Wolfson College.

Land Economy is offered at: Christ's College, Clare College, Emmanuel College, Fitzwilliam College, Girton College, Gonville & Caius College, Homerton College, Hughes Hall, Jesus College, Lucy Cavendish, Magdalene College, Murray Edwards College, Newnham College, Pembroke College, Queens' College, Robinson College, Selwyn College, Sidney Sussex College, St Catharine's College, St Edmund's College, St John's College, Trinity College, Trinity Hall and Wolfson College.

Law is offered at: Christ's College, Churchill College, Clare College, Corpus Christi College, Downing College, Emmanuel College, Fitzwilliam College, Girton College, Gonville & Caius College, Homerton College, Hughes Hall, Jesus College, King's College, Lucy Cavendish, Magdalene College, Murray Edwards College, Newnham College, Pembroke College, Peterhouse, Queens' College, Robinson College, Selwyn College, Sidney Sussex College, St Catharine's College, St Edmund's College,

St John's College, Trinity College, Trinity Hall and Wolfson College.

Linguistics is offered at: Christ's College, Churchill College, Clare College, Corpus Christi College, Downing College, Emmanuel College, Fitzwilliam College, Girton College, Gonville & Caius College, Homerton College, Hughes Hall, Jesus College, King's College, Lucy Cavendish, Magdalene College, Murray Edwards College, Newnham College, Pembroke College, Peterhouse, Queens' College, Robinson College, Selwyn College, Sidney Sussex College, St Edmund's College, St John's College, Trinity College, Trinity Hall and Wolfson College.

Mathematics is offered at: Christ's College, Churchill College, Clare College, Corpus Christi College, Downing College, Emmanuel College, Fitzwilliam College, Girton College, Gonville & Caius College, Homerton College, Hughes Hall, Jesus College, King's College, Lucy Cavendish, Magdalene College, Murray Edwards College, Newnham College, Pembroke College, Peterhouse, Queens' College, Robinson College, Selwyn College, Sidney Sussex College, St Catharine's College, St Edmund's College, St John's College, Trinity College and Trinity Hall.

Medicine is offered at: Christ's College, Churchill College, Clare College, Corpus Christi College, Downing College, Emmanuel College, Fitzwilliam College, Girton College, Gonville & Caius College, Homerton College, Jesus College, King's College, Lucy Cavendish, Magdalene College, Murray Edwards College, Newnham College, Pembroke College, Peterhouse, Queens' College, Robinson College, Selwyn College, Sidney Sussex College, St Catharine's College, St Edmund's College, St John's College, Trinity College, Trinity Hall and Wolfson College.

Medicine (Graduate Course) is offered at: Hughes Hall, Lucy Cavendish, St Edmund's College, and Wolfson College.

Modern and Medieval Languages is offered at: Christ's College, Churchill College, Clare College, Corpus Christi College, Downing College, Emmanuel College, Fitzwilliam College, Girton College, Gonville & Caius College, Homerton College, Hughes Hall, Jesus College, King's College, Lucy Cavendish, Magdalene College, Murray Edwards College, Newnham College, Pembroke College, Peterhouse, Queens' College, Robinson College, Selwyn College, Sidney Sussex College, St Catharine's College, St Edmund's College, St John's College, Trinity College, Trinity Hall and Wolfson College.

Music is offered at: Christ's College, Churchill College, Clare College, Corpus Christi College, Downing College, Emmanuel College, Fitzwilliam College, Girton College, Gonville & Caius College, Homerton College, Hughes Hall, Jesus College, King's College, Lucy Cavendish, Magdalene College, Murray Edwards College, Newnham College, Pembroke College, Peterhouse, Queens' College, Robinson College, Selwyn College, Sidney Sussex College, St Catharine's College, St Edmund's College, St John's College, Trinity College, Trinity Hall and Wolfson College.

Natural Sciences is offered at: Christ's College, Churchill College, Clare College, Corpus Christi College, Downing College, Emmanuel College, Fitzwilliam College, Girton College, Gonville & Caius College, Homerton College, Hughes Hall, Jesus College, King's College, Lucy Cavendish, Magdalene College, Murray Edwards College, Newnham College, Pembroke College, Peterhouse, Queens' College, Robinson College, Selwyn College, Sidney Sussex College, St

Catharine's College, St Edmund's College, St John's College, Trinity College, Trinity Hall and Wolfson College.

Philosophy is offered at: Christ's College, Churchill College, Clare College, Corpus Christi College, Downing College, Emmanuel College, Fitzwilliam College, Girton College, Gonville & Caius College, Homerton College, Hughes Hall, Jesus College, King's College, Lucy Cavendish, Magdalene College, Newnham College, Pembroke College, Peterhouse, Queens' College, Robinson College, Selwyn College, Sidney Sussex College, St Catharine's College, St Edmund's College, St John's College, Trinity College, Trinity Hall and Wolfson College.

Psychological and Behavioral Sciences is offered at: Christ's College, Churchill College, Clare College, Corpus Christi College, Downing College, Emmanuel College, Fitzwilliam College, Girton College, Gonville & Caius College, Homerton College, Hughes Hall, Jesus College, King's College, Lucy Cavendish, Magdalene College, Murray Edwards College, Newnham College, Pembroke College, Queens' College, Robinson College, Selwyn College, Sidney Sussex College, St Catharine's College, St Edmund's College, St John's College, Trinity College, Trinity Hall and Wolfson College.

Theology, Religion, and Philosophy of Religion is offered at: Christ's College, Clare College, Corpus Christi College, Downing College, Emmanuel College, Fitzwilliam College, Girton College, Gonville & Caius College, Homerton College, Hughes Hall, Jesus College, King's College, Lucy Cavendish, Magdalene College, Murray Edwards College, Newnham College, Pembroke College, Peterhouse, Queens' College, Robinson College, Selwyn College, Sidney Sussex College, St

Catharine's College, St Edmund's College, St John's College, Trinity College, Trinity Hall and Wolfson College.

Veterinary Medicine is offered at: Churchill College, Clare College, Downing College, Emmanuel College, Fitzwilliam College, Girton College, Gonville & Caius College, Homerton College, Jesus College, Lucy Cavendish, Magdalene College, Murray Edwards College, Newnham College, Pembroke College, Queens' College, Robinson College, Selwyn College, Sidney Sussex College, St Catharine's College, St Edmund's College, St John's College, Trinity Hall and Wolfson College.

Open Applications

You may have dreamt about going to Oxford and Cambridge for years, but now that application time has actually come around and you have to pick a college, making that decision can be really tricky. If you can't decide on which college to go to, you can make an open application.

When you're filling in your UCAS application form, you need to put down your college code. If you want to make an open application, you just put a nine (9) in that box to indicate an open application. Bear in mind that you can still only make one application to either Oxford or Cambridge, so you can't make a direct application to a specific college and one application which is open. You can still only apply once.

When they get all of the applications in, the open applications are allocated to whichever college received fewer applications for that subject in this particular year (for whatever reason). You will be assigned to whichever college has space for students in your subject.

However, this doesn't mean it's going to be easier for you to get in. Oxford and Cambridge have very high standards and a very large number of applicants. An open application just means you're going to get assigned to a college, not that's it's going to be any easier for you to get in. They're not going to accept somebody who doesn't meet their standards just to fill up space. If they don't think they have students of the right calibre, they're going to look to the pooled applicants, or the reallocated applicants, instead of taking somebody who's applied direct.

After your application has been allocated to a college, it will be treated exactly the same as if you had applied directly. The college will interview you, the college will decide to take you on, and the college will let you know whether you got in or not. The only thing different about an open application is the fact that you don't have to decide where you go. This can be tricky because you are going to be spending a large amount of your time within the college, and you may not like the college or the style of college where you eventually end up.

Pooled or Reallocated Applications

For Oxford and Cambridge, you apply directly to the college, but the colleges are very small. They may only have one or two spaces for each course, each year. Now, if you're an excellent candidate, but there are more excellent candidates at that particular college, then you may get sent to a different college. If a college thinks you are an excellent student, and you've only just missed out on a place there because of the large number of excellent students applying this year, then at Cambridge they'll put you into a "pool". At Oxford, it's called "reallocation".

Colleges that have spaces—or feel that the people who applied directly to them weren't quite up to standard—can look at pooled or reallocated students. The colleges all want the best students for their particular culture, so they would rather have a better student who applied to a different college, as opposed to somebody who applied directly to them but didn't quite meet up to their standards.

Oxford and Cambridge do their initial interviews in the first few weeks of December. If a college has a large number of really good applicants that year, or if it thinks you would fit in really well somewhere else, then they can choose to send you to a different college. Oxford and Cambridge do this slightly differently.

Oxford does everything in one day. If you go for an interview at Oxford, you might have an interview at the college you applied to, and then you might have a follow-up interview at a different college. All of the Oxford interviews—both the initial interviews and the reallocation interviews—are all done in one day.

Cambridge does things across two days. They have the initial interviews in December then applicants go into a pool, and then in the beginning of January, students might get called back for a second interview by a second college. Cambridge sends about a quarter of its applicants to the pool, and then about a quarter of those end up getting a place at a different college.

If you get sent to a pool—or if at Oxford you get sent to a different college to be interviewed for reallocation—you may get an offer from your initial college, you may get an offer from a new college, or you may get rejected. And there is absolutely nothing you can do about this. You don't get a second choice of college. You have no influence over which college gives you an offer. You can state your preference when you apply, but it is just a preference.

Zeus's Story - Account of an Oxford University Graduate

I asked Zeus to write about why he picked Oxford and how he found life studying there. He talks about specifics for chemistry (the degree he studied) but the ideas can be applied to any course.

I'll start with a little bit of background about myself to give some context to the rest of the account. I'm Zeus, 22, a British citizen and I'm studying for my second Master's degree here in Pharmacology at Hertford College, Oxford. My first Master's is in Chemistry from Corpus Christi College, Oxford. I hope to give you a flavour for the admissions and interview process, the day-to-day life as an Oxford student, and along the way I'll tell you things I wish I knew five-and-a-half years ago when initially applying here.

During my A-Levels, which are studied between the ages of 16-18 in the U.K., I achieved A*AAA in Chemistry, Physics, Biology and Mathematics, respectively, which gave me a solid foundation to all of the sciences and opened many doors in terms of choosing what degree to apply for. I was always technically and analytically minded, and therefore my A-Level choices were a natural decision to make.

During my A-Levels, I thoroughly enjoyed Chemistry as it suited my individual mindset and way of working. My teachers were incredibly supportive of my Chemistry education, and my due to my high marks and interest in the subject, I was encouraged to apply to Oxford. That's where the ball really got rolling. Chemistry isn't the most oversubscribed university course, and through UCAS (U.K. university admissions), we are given five options which can include one of either Oxford or Cambridge. Cambridge doesn't offer straight Chemistry, only Natural Sciences, and being quite direct-minded and focused, Oxford's Chemistry program seemed more suitable for me.

It's very important for everyone to thoroughly research the universities you are interested in before applying. I think it's worth visiting as many websites as possible, getting a real feel for the course, what it entails, the city, the wider picture, and then shortlist a handful of universities that you're interested in. It is **hugely** beneficial to attend open days and get a real feel for the place and meet some of the people affiliated with the university. Oxford has open days a few times per year, which are really well organised.

The university is divided into individual colleges and so the open days entail visiting both the department you are interested in and any specific colleges. When applying, you can either decide to submit an open application (where the university assigns you to a college) or a direct application to a college. Either way, you become a member of a college upon your successful admission to the university. I'll discuss this more later.

At the open days here in Oxford, the colleges will be open in which you are allowed to look around, be given tours by current students of the college and see accommodation, dining hall, chapel and where you'll be spending the next few years (at least!). Whilst it's not feasible to visit all 38 colleges of Oxford in a day, again it comes down to checking out the websites and trying to get an initial feel for which colleges you'd like to visit on the open days. There are some websites out there that'll help you decide which colleges, such as *The Student Room*, and *http://www.chooseoxfordcollege.co.uk/*

College choice is so individual and depends on such a wide range of things like: state / private school balance, accommodation quality, location around the city, college size, etc. You really need to think about what you're looking for in a college. The open days are incredibly useful and full of friendly students and staff, and maybe you'll even the chance to meet other prospective applicants along the way.

Corpus Christi is a small college and I was attracted to that, as my sixth form college was also small. It's a reputable college and is known for being incredibly friendly whilst highly academic, but also a good location in the city (and an excellent library). It's really about finding what works for you. You just need to do the most research that you can in preparation for applying and open days, etc.

In terms of applying, it really does boil down to two factors: showing your academic excellence and an ability to express your passion for the subject and potential to excel in it. As Oxford is hugely competitive, it's a challenge to really portray these things, but again, it comes down to excellent preparation and thinking outside the box – what can I do that's a little bit different to others?

Even though work experience / shadowing is not necessary for Chemistry, unlike Medicine, I still knew that it'd give me a competitive advantage amongst most other candidates who didn't do those things. It certainly wouldn't do any harm, right? I spent a couple of days at a paint company seeing the chemistry behind paint processing. In their personal statement, most people discuss books which they've read around the subject (which is highly recommended), but it's always about proving to the admissions tutors why you are different, why you are capable of being an Oxford student, and why you want to study the course that you are doing. Taking part in Olympiads but also attending conferences and seminars is another cool and somewhat unique way to demonstrate your passion, beyond a standard extended project that more and more people are doing now. It's a good talking point for interviews, too.

In terms of college choice, a lot of people play the "statistics game" thinking that commonly undersubscribed colleges (I won't name any names) are easier to get into than the more popular and prestigious colleges. This is really **not** the case. The only advice I would give in terms of college choice from an admissions point of view is: know the type of academic interest that the college tutor has. Read up on what they do, what they like and their way of talking (or typing). It's surprising how much information you can gather, and this is really important in terms of the interview.

The interview itself is incredibly academic and probably won't involve questions such as "why Oxford?" or "why this subject?" That's not to say they won't be asked, though! The whole purpose of the interview is to see if you are suited to the tutorial system of Oxford. As an Oxford undergraduate, your tutor will give you a week's worth of work to do, which you'll discuss in a one-to-one, or two-students-to-one-tutor format every week. The whole purpose of the interview is to demonstrate that you can be engaging, interactive and suggest answers and thought processes to the problems that they throw at you. It's less about getting the right answer, but more about verbally expressing your thought processes and your willingness to try. Don't come out with "don't know" *answers, instead ask, "could you please give me a little hint?" Try to work with them; it's to replicate what you'll be doing every week for three years.*

The interview is as much about making sure Oxford is right for you as it is you being right for Oxford. Don't be afraid to get the wrong answer, but verbally express your thinking and show willingness to try. Your interview may be based around interesting bits of Chemistry that you've stated on your personal statement, so make sure you know everything you've listed on there exceptionally well, as well as all of your current A-Level syllabus work. It's not about seeing how much Chemistry you've crammed into your brain, but your ability to think, reason and interact, showing a potential for growth and improvement. They are likely to ask things related to their area of interest; for example, a Physical Chemistry tutor isn't likely to ask you on Organic Chemistry, so you can direct your preparation according to the interviewer and their specialisms.

The interviews are all conducted in December (probably just before you finish for the Christmas break) and you'll typically have 2-3 interviews over the span of a couple of days. The interviewing college will provide free accommodation for that period where you can get a little snippet to life at Oxford, and when you're not being interviewed, you can meet other students, college staff and have a look around the city. The same is offered for international students and is, as far as I know, the same for a local student.

All of the offers are made on the same day in January to commence studies in October. In the meantime, the college that offered you a place will send you a college contract and other slightly boring documents to complete so that everything's in place for when you arrive at Oxford. A lot of people go onto the forums, such as The Student Room, to try to connect with their course mates before they arrive at Oxford. I found that really useful and nice to know some people for when I arrived.

Upon arrival to Oxford, the first week is known as "fresher's week" and is essentially an induction week: you get to meet your peers, other people in the college, lots of socialising, lots of induction talks, getting familiar with your department and meeting your tutors. It's an action-packed week, and there's lots of opportunities for partying for the outgoing types, but the small and friendly collegiate system means there are also excellent opportunities for the more introverted types at Oxford. There's absolutely something and somebody for everyone here at Oxford. In fresher's week, you'll also attend "fresher's fair" where you can meet and sign up to a lot of societies, clubs and even get free pizza! It's a great opportunity to take up a sport, join a society or a club and really branch out and make new connections.

Life at Oxford is, unsurprisingly, very difficult. It's a steep learning curve and requires you to really get to grips with managing your time, stress levels and finding the appropriate work-life balance. I've learned much more about how to deal with life and what it throws at you than any academic knowledge I've attained here at Oxford. The short (8 week) but intense terms really set you up to deal with anything. The skills and attributes of an Oxford graduate are sought at much more than just the knowledge you've acquired.

You really do need a passion for your subject because it's really hard going here. It's a means to an end, though. It's only a few years and it's going to pay off for the rest of your life. Should you get through it, you'll really reap the awards. Oxford is a great place to make connections, to network and to develop your confidence and open your mind to new cultures and ways of life, as it is so diverse here. That experience and immersion is invaluable, you can't put a price on it. Sometimes I think about if I'd have gone to a more "normal" university, maybe I would have had a more fun and well-rounded experience. But it really is what you make it; if you manage your time really well, stay on the ball and keep your head straight, you'll be able to lead a balanced life and enjoy yourself in the process. Fall behind on work and get lazy, you'll suffer. There are many lessons I'm still learning about Oxford to this very day, after five years here, and you never stop learning. You'll hit the ground and be dragged around a fair few times by the rigour here, but you'll get up stronger.

I take so much pride to think where I've come over the past five years since my school days, what I've learned, overcome and achieved here in Oxford. There's no better place; you are truly at a world-leading university with the brightest minds, talking about a subject that you should (!) have a passion for and love talking about. If your subject keeps you up at night, if you love solving problems and remain curious—if you live, breathe and sleep your subject—Oxford is the place for you. Do your research, ask the right questions, prepare yourself for what will probably be the most challenging few years of your life; that's all you can do.

How to Write a Personal Statement for Oxford or Cambridge

There are two things Oxford and Cambridge are looking for. They are looking for excellent grades, and passion for a subject. You need to get these across in your personal statement, but writing it can be hard. For instance, you cannot say: "I've always wanted to go to Oxbridge for my entire life," because as soon as other universities see that, they're going to reject you straight away. Remember, all of the universities see one personal statement, so you can't tailor it too much towards one course or one university, because as soon the other universities realized what you've done, you're just going to go straight in the 'no' pile. It's really, really tricky to get across your passion and your interest while keeping it as broad as possible. The worst thing would be to write a personal statement that is tailored for Oxford, then all the other universities reject you, and then Oxford refuses you as well. We don't want that to happen. We want you to get a place.

Most Oxford colleges have some form of additional admissions requirement, typically either a test or written work, so you are going to have the opportunity to show off how awesome you are. Cambridge sends you an email afterward, asking for more information. This is the Supplementary Application Questionnaire, and this is where you describe if there's anything you love about Cambridge, the course, or people you want to work with. This is great opportunity to include things that you can't put on your UCAS application.

In your personal statement, you need to convey the fact that you live and breathe the subject you are applying to study. It's going to be hard, it's going to be intense, it's going to be full on. You need to prove to Oxford or Cambridge that you can cope with that much intensity all focused around a tiny little subject. You need to tell them what has motivated you to apply for the course, and why you're going to be perfect for it. Most everyone applying to Oxbridge has perfect A-Levels, so you need to distinguish yourself. You have to be independent and motivated, and it helps if you have gone out and done something on your own initiative, like volunteering. Oxbridge does not want wishy-washy people who are kind of like, "Aw, yeah, maybe I'll do this course. Maybe I'll do that course." They want people that are going to live and breathe that course.

So make sure that you are coming across as enthusiastic, committed, and sincere, but don't use all those clichéd phrases like, "I have wanted to study medicine ever since I was born." Because you haven't. OK? I have a two-year-old. He does not want to study medicine. He wants to hit things with a hammer and play trains. Oxbridge wants to know about any interest you have within the field. A common question is "Tell me something you're interested in." If you can't answer that question confidently, then you are going to have a problem. You need to be interested in the course you are studying. If you want to go out and study medicine, become interested in medicine. If you want to go and study natural sciences, start reading "New Scientist," and find something you are interested in. You are going to need to way to develop or to express your enthusiasm for the subject and the things that you have found out on your own, outside of your course. Oxbridge does not want people that can just regurgitate the A-Level course back to them, because that's boring, and honestly, it's not that hard. Just remembering stuff that your teacher has told you is not going to get you into Oxbridge.

Get your passion across, but make it genuine. Don't make it fake, because they'll be able to see through that straight away. If you have a certain career in mind, and the course is a natural progression for that, then let them know. If you want to go work for Médecins Sans Frontières, and a medical degree is a stepping stone for that, then great. You have a career plan. You have a passion. Let them know, because these are the sort of passionate, committed people that Oxbridge wants to see.

Extracurriculars are only meaningful if they are relevant. Admissions tutors are not necessarily going to care about the fact that you were in the Scouts if you are applying for a journalism degree, but writing for the school newspaper is going to be relevant for English. It's not the number of extracurriculars that you have, it's the quality of them.

Oxbridge is also not interested in who your parents are or who you know. They want to find the truly academic students, the ones that are truly going to excel. You could have had the most amazing work experience on paper, but if you haven't gotten anything out of it, or if you can't talk about it passionately in your interview, then it doesn't mean a thing. But if you volunteered in a lab or a hospital or a vet's office, and you learned new ideas and asked important questions, then this is the kind of thing that Oxbridge is looking for. Your work experience doesn't have to be glamorous or exclusive; just make sure it reflects you and your personality. If it's relevant, write it down; if it's not, leave it out!

Perhaps most importantly, please avoid all of the websites that say they will write your personal statement for you, or the websites that show you examples to follow. Admissions tutors can see that a mile off, and it will not help you in anyway at all. There are loads and loads of example personal statements out there, and while it's good for you to see what other people have written, it's not worth plagiarizing anything—even on accident. This is the worst thing you can do with a personal statement. Do not end up copying someone else's, because UCAS will check to see if you've plagiarized it. And if you have plagiarized it, then that's it. It's straight out the window. You've got no chance at all. So do not plagiarize your personal statement. You can read previous statements to get inspiration, but under no circumstances should copy even a single sentence.

Supplementary Application Questionnaire (SAQ)

If you are applying to Cambridge, 48 hours after submitting your UCAS application, you'll be asked to fill in the Supplementary Application Questionnaire (SAQ) to give Cambridge some more specific information about you. This is a great way to include specific information (like your love of Cambridge) that you can't put down on your UCAS application.

The SAQ will be sent via email and you'll need to complete it by the 22nd of October.

There are a number of different sections to the questionnaire. They are going to ask for a photograph and some personal details, including BMAT score (if applying for medicine), education (any specific modules or units you've covered in you A-Levels), and qualifications. You can also include any additional Information that you want them to know about you and why you are applying to Cambridge.

Additional Entry Requirements for Courses

With fewer year 12 students taking AS-Levels when applying to university, you apply with only your predicted grades and your GCSE results. This has increased the emphasis on additional exams before the interview to help selection of the best candidates.

If you are sitting a combined subject, then expect to take the admission test for both.

Oxford

Biomedical Sciences - Biomedical Admissions Test (BMAT)
Chemistry - Thinking Skills Assessment (TSA) Section 1
Classics or Classics and Oriental Studies - Classics Admissions Test (CAT).
Classics and English - Classics Admissions Test (CAT) and English Literature Admissions Test (ELAT)
Classics and Czech (with Slovak) or Classics and Celtic - Classics Admissions Test (CAT) and Modern Languages Admissions Tests (MLAT)
Computer Science or Computer Science and Philosophy - Mathematics Admissions Test (MAT)
Economics and Management - Thinking Skills Assessment (TSA)
Engineering - Physics Aptitude Test (PAT)
English Language and Literature - English Literature Admissions Test (ELAT)
English and Czech (with Slovak) or English and Celtic - English Literature Admissions Test (ELAT) and Modern Languages Admissions Tests (MLAT)

European and Middle Eastern Languages - Modern Languages Admissions Tests (MLAT) and Oriental Languages Admissions Test (OLAT)

History or History and Economics - History Aptitude Test (HAT) and Thinking Skills Assessment (TSA)

History (Ancient and Modern) or History and English or History and Politics - History Aptitude Test (HAT)

History and Portuguese - History Aptitude Test (HAT) and Modern Languages Admissions Tests (MLAT)

Human Sciences - Thinking Skills Assessment (TSA)

Law - National Admissions Test for Law (LNAT)

Materials Science - Physics Aptitude Test (PAT)

Mathematics or Mathematics and Computer Science or Mathematics and Philosophy or Mathematics and Statistics - Mathematics Admissions Test (MAT)

Medicine - Biomedical Admissions Test (BMAT)

Modern Languages (Modern Greek and Arabic; Modern Greek and Beginners' Russian; Modern Greek and Linguistics) - Modern Languages Admissions Tests (MLAT)

Music - Practical test

Oriental Studies or Religion and Oriental Studies - Oriental Languages Admissions Test (OLAT)

Philosophy and Czech (with Slovak) or Philosophy and Celtic - Modern Languages Admissions Tests (MLAT)

Philosophy, Politics and Economics (PPE) - Thinking Skills Assessment (TSA)

Physics or Physics and Philosophy - Physics Aptitude Test (PAT)

Psychology (Experimental) or Psychology, Philosophy and Linguistics - Thinking Skills Assessment (TSA)

Cambridge

A large number of course require submission of one or pieces of work before interviews. These include: Anglo-Saxon, Norse, and Celtic; Archaeology; Architecture; Asian and Middle Eastern Studies; Classics; Economics; Education; Geography; History; History and Modern Languages; History and Politics; History of Art; Human, Social, and Political Sciences; Music

Several more can require assessment at interview: Engineering; Linguistics; Modern and Medieval Languages; Philosophy; Theology, Religion, and Philosophy of Religion.

English Literature - English Literature Admissions Test (ELAT)
Land Economy - Thinking Skills Assessment (TSA)
Law - Cambridge Law Test
Natural Sciences - Natural Sciences Admission Assessment (NSAA)
Maths - Sixth Term Examination Paper in Mathematics (STEP)
Medicine - Biomedical Admissions Test (BMAT)
Modern and Medieval Languages - Modern and Medieval Languages Test
Psychological and Behavioural Sciences - Thinking Skills Assessment (TSA) and essay

Cambridge Natural Science Admissions Assessment

If you're applying for Natural Science at Cambridge after you've submitted your UCAS application in October, there are a few more hoops you need to jump through. Before interviewing, you'll need to pass the Cambridge Natural Science Admissions Assessment, or the NSAA. The content of this is going to be based on A-Levels and the most common A-Level combinations. These are A-Level Biology, Chemistry, Physics, Maths and Further Maths. Psychology does not count as a science for Cambridge, and most people are going to be taking three or four A-Levels and an AS out of the sciences and the maths. Some colleges like Magdalene, Trinity, and St. John's are going to require you to do a further written assessment at your interview, but the NSAA comes before this. This is done in early November, a couple of weeks after your UCAS applications needs to be in. You have to be registered for this in advance, and you can't do this yourself. Your school exams officer has to register you for the NSAA. This is a proper exam and has to be done under exam conditions.

What they are looking at Cambridge are people who know the A-Level specification inside out but can apply it and go above and beyond. This is to differentiate exceptional students from everyone else who's getting A*s in Maths, everyone else who's getting those A*s in Chemistry or Physics and Biology. Let's assume that everyone sitting the assessment on that day has A*s and knows the A-Level specification perfectly. What this test does is challenge you to take the knowledge that you have and apply it in different ways to different things. There are two sections for this assessment: Part One, which is multiple choice, and Part Two, which is a long answer. Part One is 80 minutes of multiple choice, and includes five sections: A is Maths, B is Physics, C is Chemistry, D is Biology, and then E is like tough Maths combined with Physics. You have to do section A (Maths) and then two others from Physics, Chemistry, Biology or Further Maths. Three sections in total. Each section has 18 questions, so you're going to need to do 5 questions in total. You are not allowed a calculator, and they are multiple choice questions. These questions are meant to be hard. Even the best and brightest A* students are expected to struggle. It's not just whether you can get the answer right or not, it's how you try to answer the question.

In Part Two, you have to answer two questions from a list of six questions: two Biology, two Chemistry, two Physics. You get 40 minutes to do these questions, and these are long questions. There are going to be diagrams; there are going to be graphs. You are allowed a calculator for this, and you should write down all of your workings, because they're interested in the process of you getting the answer as well as you just coming up with the solution.

The content for the NCAA is going to be mainly based on Year 12 A-Levels. There is a long list over on the website if you haven't done A-Levels, way too long for me to include here. There isn't going to be any negative marking, so it's worth you trying every single section. For example, if you can't do part A, then you can go on and maybe try part E, D, or C. You don't have to do it in order, either. Some of the bits link, but some of the bits don't link. If you can't do the first part of the Chemistry questions, then try and do some of the other ones.

Remember, this assessment is meant to be hard, so you're going to have to know all of the content well. Be prepared to do some out-of-the-box thinking, be ready to be challenged, and try not to stress it so much.

The Cambridge Natural Science Admissions Assessment specimen papers and past papers are available on their website. These are worth doing, as are Olympiad papers for each subject and the Cambridge Lower Sixth Chemistry Challenge (C3L6) papers.

Oxbridge Interviews

Interviews at Oxford and Cambridge are slightly different from interviews at other universities. They're really testing you to see if you're the right person for that college.

When they decide who to interview, they're going to be looking at your predicted grades. They're going to look at your personal statement, your references, and for Cambridge, the supplementary additional questionnaire (SAQ) as well. If you are invited, these interviews happen in the first three weeks of December. These are interviews within the college that you have applied to, or the college you've been allocated to if you've made an open application. The subject tutor, the director of studies, or the person in the college who is actually responsible for the teaching of that course is going to be the person leading the main interview. You may get a second interview or a third interview with the admissions tutor for that college as well. The exact details are going to vary depending on which college and which subject you apply to. You can expect between one and three interviews, and they could last between 20 and 45 minutes. You could have a more academic and subject-based one, and then you might have a more general one as well. If you get invited for interview, you will be given details of exactly what to expect so it won't be a surprise when you arrive there on the day. Some subjects are also going to ask you to do a written test on the interview day.

The main interview is going to be like a conversation about the subject. It will follow the style of tutorials or supervisions at Oxford and Cambridge, so that the admissions tutor can really see whether you're going to be suited to academic life there. The questions are going to be based around your subject, but they're not always going to be straightforward. The admissions tutor isn't going to expect you to have covered this in school, and they're not going to expect you to know what the answer is straight away. They're interested in talking through the problems with you. They're interested in how you get from point A to point B. Because this will follow the teaching style of tutorials or supervisions, this is a good opportunity to see if this approach works for you.

If you don't understand something, then just ask the tutor to explain it to you. This isn't a test on how well you know everything. It's more about logic and how you think things through. They know people are going to come from very different backgrounds and very different educational experiences, so it's not about how much you know, because your grades will show that. The interview is designed to find something that may not come through in your grades or in your personal statements.

The questions aren't going to be trick questions. They're not designed to trip you up, but they are going to be tricky questions. You're going to need to show that you can apply logic and bring different things together. It will show that you can adapt to changing situations and assimilate new information without getting flustered. They can ask you questions about the subject you've applied for, the wider subject area, or things you've written in your personal statement. It's a really good idea to go over your personal statement again and look at any notes you've made from your work experience. It's really important that you don't lie in your personal statement, otherwise it will come out in your interview.

At Oxford, you may get sent to a second college for an interview if you are reallocated. They may send you to a certain college if they're oversubscribed for that subject, or if they think you're a good candidate but not quite the right fit for the college. See the previous section on pools and reallocations for more information.

Depending on how long you're expected to stay, most colleges will offer you accommodation and meals for your interview, and in some circumstances they will reimburse you for travel as well. If you're an overseas student, there are lots of overseas locations and tutors who do the Oxford and Cambridge interviews in other countries.

Oxbridge Interview Timeline and Dates

BMAT registration deadline: 1st October
UCAS applications deadline: 15th October
Pre-interview assessment registration ends: 15th October.
COPA deadline: 19th October
SQA deadline: 22nd October
Date of pre-interview assessments: 31st October
Interviews: early December
Pool interviews: early January
Decision: end January

UCAS Applications – Applying

How to Start Writing Your Personal Statement

Starting to write your personal statement can sometimes feel like the hardest thing in the world. This is because so much of what you write in your personal statement will determine what university you get into, your course, and potentially your future career.

But don't worry—we'll walk you through it! One of the best tricks when sitting down at a blank page is to not worry about starting at the beginning. If you know what you want to say in the middle, then start there. Sometimes just putting something, anything, down on the page is the best way to start, and then you can work back from there. If you're not sure what to write in a paragraph, make a list of key points that you want to get in there. Focus on the stuff you want to tell other people about you: what makes you really awesome and what you can do.

Set a timer on your phone, then just sit down and type. Put down whatever comes into your head. It doesn't have to be good. Don't read it back; it doesn't have to be sensible. Sit there and type, and make it a brain dump onto the computer or onto a bit of paper. When the timer goes off, after five minutes just have a look at what you've written. It may be absolute rubbish, and that's fine; or it may be absolute gold, and that's even better!

Your main focus should be explaining why you picked this subject at university. You need to be able to answer this question really confidently, because you need to it make a main part of your personal statement and they're probably going to ask you about it during any interviews. Spend some time thinking about why you love the subject and then write about it. Hopefully, this should come quite easy to you! What are you good at? What have you achieved in your life? What are your talents? Make a list of your achievements and then try and fit them in.

If you are not sure what you love about that subject or what you're good at, ask other people who live in the same house as you and who have spent a lot of time with you. They may have some insight on why you love a subject if you're always pestering them to visit a museum or asking them such-and-such a question. They may remember some award that you got two years ago that you didn't think was important but would impress the universities; or they may remember a writing competition that you entered, or something else that you achieved. Sometimes thinking about yourself so intently can be a bit freaky, so ask other people for help. Be sure to take notes when they give you their responses.

Once you've got all of your lists and your random notes, you can try and sort out a paragraph outline.

Structure of your Personal Statement

Your personal statement needs to stand out. It needs to be a tool that means you end up in the 'yes' pile instead of the 'reject' pile. And the way you structure it can have a massive impact on the opinion of the person reading it.

Your personal statement is a short insight into you as a person. I say short because it's 4,000 characters, and it's hard to get across how amazing you are in only 4,000 characters. The box that you have to fit it into is a limited size, so it can be tempting just to write one large block of text to try and squash as much in there as possible.

But that is hard to read, and you have to think about the admissions tutor for a little bit here. They probably have thousands of personal statements, references, predicted grades, and applications to look through, so the more comfortable a personal statement is to read, the better it is on the eyes. The more structured it is, the more it's going to flow—which means it will be interesting and engaging for the tutor.

It is a good idea to structure the paragraphs around key concepts. These should be: why you want to study the course, how suited you are to study the course, and then everything else.

You should start off with the most important thing: why you want to explore the subject. Admissions tutors look for students who are interested in the course they are studying. Students who can stick it out for three full years of intense study on one subject. They want students who love the subject, so explain why you love architecture, why you'd make a brilliant vet, why you want to know more about the Russian Revolution or environmental politics.

Your next paragraph is the most significant part. This is where you prove to the admissions tutor that you are passionate about this subject, that you have done the background to show how much you want to study this subject. Here you should share anything that you've done to show how engaged you are. Talk about your EPQ, any MOOCs that you've done, books that you've read, courses you've been on, lectures, shows—anything to show how passionate you are about this subject. Show the admissions tutor that you've gone above and beyond what your A-Levels have taught you. Show them you haven't just sat there and absorbed the A-Levels passively, but you've gone and found out information independently. If you've done any relevant (and relevancy is vital) volunteer or work experience, put that in there. Talk about what you've gained from it, what research you've done, any possible future careers, any essential competitions you've entered or won, or how you've engaged with the online community, possibly setting up a blog or doing some YouTube videos. This should be the most significant section, and it should show off how especially suited you are to study this course.

Lastly, you should include all of the other fantastic things that you've done. These are things which aren't necessarily very relevant to the course, but have given you loads of exciting experience. Working a part time job demonstrates that you're reliable, that you can turn up, that you're hard-working, that you're not scared of 8 o'clock on a Saturday morning. Any volunteering shows that you can work with other people and that you can be relied upon. Any projects where you've worked with other people will highlight your excellent communication skills. An admissions tutor is going to read hundreds of personal statements from students, all of whom are doing the same A-Levels and have the same predicted grades, so your personal statement is the way to make you stand out and show off how fantastic you are.

Harrison's Story - Applying for University

Harrison suffered the loss of his father during his A-Levels, subsequently he resat year 13. It was noted in his reference that his grade were not a true reflection of his potential due to circumstancecs. He has A-Levels in chemistry (B), Maths (D) and Biology (D)

The application process was actually fairly simple. Luckily in my case, it was all done through the 6th form using UCAS. All I had to do was supply the relevant information: which universities I was applying for (5 in total; 1 firm choice and 1 insurance choice), the courses, personal information, etc. The most difficult part for me was probably the personal statement. You have to write a short 4,000 character essay which includes hobbies, interests, any relevant experiences you may have been through (in relation to what you're applying for). Like with any application, you have to sell yourself with the personal statement, so creativity is the way to stand out, which can be difficult given how small the character limit is. Another stressful part of the application process is applying for the student loans. This is done on the student finance website where you put in your personal information, which uni you will be attending, your chosen course, where you'll be living during your study (in my case 3 terms), whether you'll have financial dependants and whether or not you're expecting to work during your study. As I was living at home still, the next part of the finance application falls to student finances contacting my parents to provide personal financial information in order to gage which level of maintenance loan I was eligible for.

How to Make Your Personal Statement Stand Out

It can be tricky differentiating yourself as an amazing person from all the other people who have the same grades as you. Admissions tutors read hundreds if not thousands of UCAS forms and personal statements every single year, and they have to put them into piles. They have to put them into a 'yes' pile, a 'no' pile, and a 'maybe' pile. We want to make sure that yours goes into the 'yes' pile and not into the 'no' pile. So how do you make sure that your personal statement stands out as amazing?

When you're writing your personal statement, remember that it goes to lots of different places, not just one place, so don't start talking about how amazing this university is or how you've always wanted to study this part of the course, because you'll get immediately rejected by all of the other universities where that doesn't apply. If you don't get into the university that you started talking about, then we're in a little bit of a tricky situation. To avoid this, make sure your UCAS application is general enough to cover everywhere you apply, but still talks about the course that you are applying for.

This is really complicated if you're applying for two different courses. If you are torn between two courses, you should consider composite degrees like liberal arts or natural science. The majority of the time students are only going to be applying for one course at different universities. Take Biochemistry as an example: there may be a slight deviation in course to Biomedical Sciences or Biochemistry with a year abroad, but most of you are only going to be applying for one course. Start talking about why you want to do that course.

Admissions tutors want people who are interested in studying that course. They don't want people turning up just because they think it's what they should be doing next. They want people who are interested in what they're going to be studying. They do not just want blank slates that they can fill up with information. Don't go overbroad and list every single book you've ever read to show you're interested in literature. Give them really strong bits of information. Give them the bits that emphasize what your strengths are and what your achievements are. You need to keep it within the character limit, of course, but also keep it modest while showing how awesome you are. I know this is going to be hard, but remember, the admission tutors *want* to admit you.

Now you need to let your personality shine through in your personal statement. It needs to be bubbling with everything that makes you awesome and amazing so that personal tutors really feel like they get to know you in your personal statement. When you're giving your evidence of things that make you fantastic—your strengths, your achievements, what makes you interested in the subject—make sure it is your voice coming across. Don't make it dull, don't make it bland, don't make it something that somebody else could have written. Make sure it's personal to you.

When you are talking about what reading you have done, don't just pick the bestsellers. I was talking to someone who does economics admissions, and he said every single person raves on about how they've read Freakonomics, and that's boring. Even I've read it, and I'm not doing economics at university! Talk about books that you've read that are not the bestsellers, or maybe from slightly less well-known authors. Maybe they were the ones that inspired you. If you haven't read any books yet, spend the next few weekends reading some books or doing something extra outside the course. What talks or podcasts have you listened to? What exhibitions have you been to? This applies to basically every single course. You can find at least one book on any course, so read it; hopefully you'll like it. If you don't like it, read another book. Find one that you do like.

You should also talk about what you've done over and above your A-Levels that makes you right for the course. This is important, because university is hard. I talk about this big jump from GCSE to A-Level, and then there's another big jump from A-Level to university. You are expected to be a lot more independent. You have to prove to the admissions tutor that you are capable of being independent, and that you are starting to do it already by finding extra stuff outside the course that is going to enhance your subject knowledge. If you have a long-term plan, share that with the tutors. If you know that you want to go work in research, or you know you want to go and be a journalist in this newspaper or something, then tell the admissions tutors. Say this in your personal statement. This is part of letting your personality shine through.

For your personal statement, you have 4,000 characters. Way back when, when I did mine, you had to type it out on a bit of paper, and then you'd have to take it (and your paper UCAS form) down to the nice lady in the photocopying room, and then you'd spend five minutes trying to photocopy your personal statement so it fit exactly in the box on the UCAS form. It was a bit of a nightmare, and I still remember all these years later how totally traumatic it was! These days, obviously, it's all done on computer, which is a lot easier. You do not want to cram as much stuff in there as possible because admissions tutors are going to be reading a lot. You want to make it nice and easy for them to read, so you need to consider paragraphs. You need to consider lines in between paragraphs as well, because proper spacing will make it look nicer and easier to read. Go back and read your UCAS form on the UCAS website because some special characters and formatting doesn't copy and paste across from Word. It's important that you make sure it looks okay on the UCAS website as well as on Word.

How to Show Passion for a Subject

The first trick is to find something to be passionate about, and this is hard. You're going to need to do a lot of reading, and you're going to need to do a lot of research. If this is a struggle, just remember that you don't have to develop a life-long, overwhelming passion for something. You can have a passion for something just for a couple of months, until university interviews are out of the way and you've got a place sorted, and then you can forget about it. It is unlikely that the admission tutor is going to come back six months later and want to talk about it again. You just need to get the passion across in your application form and in your interview.

Start by thinking which parts of your A-Levels interest you and which parts of your future degree course interest you. Start reading, either buying books or going to library and reading general magazines in your subject. There are loads of specific magazines in every single area that you can think of. There's going to be engineering, architecture, fashion design. There is going to be a niche magazine for your subject. New Scientist is an obvious one for science-types, so go buy a few issues and flip through it to see if anything catches your eye. If something does, do a little bit more research on it. Go and look at what the authors were writing, go back and see if you can get your hands on the papers, go and see if you can find some books about it. Ask your teachers, because your teachers generally are going to like reading books on their subject. I know that in the corner of my classroom I have piles and piles of science books and general books that people can just borrow to read whenever they want to. I lend these out, and then people come back and swap them like a little science library in the corner of my classroom.

Getting your passion across in your interview is relatively easy if you've got a good subject that you can talk about for, say, 15 minutes. But getting that across in your UCAS application form can seem a little bit harder. There are a number of different ways you can show this.

The extended project (EPQ) or extended essay comes in really useful. Most schools offer this, and you can do it on pretty much anything you like. But if you do it on something that you've talked about in your UCAS application, you're killing two birds with one stone, and you're getting your passion for the subject across in your UCAS application. For example, if you wanted to go and do medicine at university, there is very little point in doing your extended project on bridges, because that is not going to impress the university admissions tutor in any way at all. But if you wanted to do engineering at university, and you did your extended project on bridges and how they revolutionized transportation, then that's the sort of thing that is going to get passion across to your university tutors.

The other thing that you can do is look for writing competitions or start writing for magazines. We're not talking about the big magazines, but for example, the Young Scientists Journal is run by students aged 12-20. Keble College at Oxford has a yearly essay competition in theology and religion. These are just a few examples from a wide range. Even if you're not planning on applying to Oxford, getting an award or a mention from a writing competition is going to look amazing on your UCAS application form. If you can't find anywhere that will publish it, think about publishing it yourself. I do a lot of self-publishing on YouTube and on my website. If you started up a series of videos or blog posts about boats and the engineering behind sails, and you wanted to apply to do nautical engineering, that would show a long-term dedicated interest.

The last way that you can get your passion across is by competitions. Each year there is an Olympiad for each science and maths. You have to do it via your schools, and your teacher has to organize it. I'm sure if you go and ask your teacher very nicely, they would help you out!

What NOT to Write in Your Personal Statement

You have to remember that the person reading your personal statement has read hundreds, if not thousands, of them, and they're a little bit bored. If they see something in your personal statement that they don't like, you're going straight in the 'no' pile. You need to avoid putting things in the personal statement that are going to put people off.

First of all, do not be negative. Do not say, "I know my school says I got a 'B,' but I should have gotten an 'A' because my school's rubbish." Nobody wants to hear that. Don't be negative about your school, and don't be negative about yourself. Don't say, "I could've gotten an 'A' if I had worked a little bit harder."

Don't exaggerate how amazing you are, because admissions tutors are experienced in working out the truth from an exaggeration. If you did a day's work experience somewhere, do not exaggerate and turn this into a week's work experience or a month's work experience. If you once upon a time helped out on the school newspaper, this does not all of a sudden turn you into the editor of the school newspaper.

Every single university admission tutor that I talk to hates clichés, especially, "Ever since I was a child, I wanted to be a…" No, you didn't. I have a child; he doesn't want to be a doctor/architect/dancer. He wants to make a mess and play with Mommy's iPad. You might have wanted to be a mechanical engineer for a long time, but not ever since you were born.

Avoid words or sayings like, "I'm passionate about..." If you are passionate about your subject, then you should have a load of evidence to prove that you are passionate about your subject. You shouldn't have to tell someone that you're passionate about it, because like every other personal statement, people are passionate about things. Don't tell them, show them. Give them examples.

Stop throwing in overused words, that are off-putting to people reading your personal statement. Just be genuine and be honest.

It's great if you can get people to help you with your personal statement, but be wary of them rewriting it too much. Your parents, your grandparents, your teachers talk in a very different language than you. If you start coming out with language that sounds false, or language that sounds too old, or if it sounds like you've just used a thesaurus for every single word in there, that is going to look a bit odd. If your personal statement sounds like it's written by someone in their 50s or 60s, the admissions tutors are will be able to tell. By all means, take advice from parents, grandparents, and your school tutors, but do not change it so much that it doesn't sound like your voice. Universities want to admit you, not your parents. Do not let someone else write the entire thing for you, because again, that's going to sound fake. And in the interview, the tutor may say, "In your personal statement, I found this bit interesting." If you've got no idea what they're talking about, they're going to smell a rat.

We've covered it before, but I'll say it again: do NOT plagiarize any part of your statement. There are loads and loads of examples out there on the internet, but UCAS runs a plagiarization check on everything that comes through, and if you've plagiarized even a section of your personal statement, then UCAS will reject it.

The temptation for people that are writing personal statements is to include quotes from works they have found inspirational. You don't get a lot of space in your personal statement, so don't waste it telling the admission tutor what somebody else said. Admissions tutors are not interested in what someone else is saying; they're interested in what you are saying.

Do not just list every single thing you have ever done, because that's really dull. If it is something that is interesting enough to be in your personal statement, then turn it into a sentence or into a mini-paragraph. It is pointless listing every single thing you've ever done. Just pick out the most important, the most relevant parts and then expand upon that.

When you're writing something down, don't just make this general sweeping statement about your future or your work experience. Give evidence. Don't just say, "I've worked really hard looking into this." Back it up with some evidence. What have you done? What have you read? What have you done outside of school to go above and beyond what your teachers have been doing? What are you doing to prove to the people reading your personal statement that you're not just the same as everyone else, that you're better than everyone else? Give them examples, and avoid general sweeping statements.

The admissions tutors are not interested in ancient history. They're not interested in things that you did when you were five. They're not interested in things that you did when you were 12. They may be relevant, but that's a very long time ago. You need to give them examples that are recent. You need to give them examples that are relevant.

Do not waffle. Now you do not have a lot of space to fill, so make sure the information you're getting across is relevant, important, and interesting.

Don't tell jokes. Your friends may find you hilarious, but maybe the admissions tutor may not share your sense of humour, so don't.

Jacob's Story - What the Application Process was Like

Jacob got his application in in September as soon as he got back to school, beating the large number of students who leave it to the last minute. His A-Levels wer in Maths (A*), chemistry (A*) and biology (A).

Applying for university was a lot trickier than I had initially thought it would be. There are deadlines to meet and I was pretty scared I would lose out on my course choice, so I decided to start my UCAS application as early as I possibly could. The first step in the whole process was to sign up to UCAS and select the relevant study year. This generated a username, password and I.D. that was specific to me. I would now be able to save and edit information about myself.

As soon as I was given this information, I started filing out all that I could. There are 6 different sections to fill out. I got this from my UCAS adviser. This allows your school/college to be able to view your information and add references for you.

The second and most important step was researching the course I wanted to study, and the university I wanted to attend. If I got either of these details wrong, it would mean either the next few years would have been spent in regret, or I would have to start all over again.

The course I finally decided on was medicine. Doing a course such as this has an earlier deadline than others. Also applying to Oxbridge carries a much earlier deadline. This made me very nervous. I couldn't picture doing any other course and I didn't want to lose out.

Having had already filled out my details and choices, I began to work on the only thing that would set me apart from my peers - my personal statement. With my personal statement my mind was completely blank. I really wanted to shine. If my personal statement was unique and eye-catching I would have a better chance of securing a place in the course I wanted.

I started brainstorming about why I was so passionate about studying the course I had chosen. I also enlisted the help of my family and friends. I asked each of them what makes me unique and good for this course. This was insightful as they mentioned things I never would have thought of. I made sure to also include my voluntary and paid work experience. I spoke of the lessons and skills I had learnt through my various experiences, and how these would help me to be the ideal student.

I wrote several drafts of my personal statement until I was content with what I had written. Again I asked friends, family and a few tutors to read through this. It was good to receive their positive comments along with constructive criticism. With my personal statement uploaded and all the other sections filled and checked, all I had to do was pay for my application. My reference was one of my tutors who would fill out a reference when prompted by UCAS. All that was left to do now was hope for the best!

References

Your admission tutor is going to see three things: your predictive grade, your personal statement, and your reference. Each of these is equally important to ensure that you get to the right course. But how you get a reference and how do you know what goes into it?

The reference is a vitally important part of your application. You get to control what goes into your personal statement but not what goes into your reference, and sometimes you might not even see it before it gets sent off.

If you are at school or college, they already have this set up. All you need to do is fill in all of the other sections online, including the pay-and-send, and then the next step will be left up to the person writing your reference. Schools have extensive systems in place for writing UCAS references and teachers are very experienced at doing this. This can be your tutor or one of your teachers, as they have access to the UCAS system as well. They can pop in your reference and then click send, and it will go off straight away.

If you're not currently in school, then you have two choices. You can either ask your old school to do one for you, or you can ask an employer to write one for you. If you were to get your old school to write one for you, you need to talk to somebody there and get them to agree to write the reference for you. Once they've accepted, you need to ask for the school 'buzzword' and make sure you write it down accurately. When you log into UCAS, you can then add the school to the section to write your references. You'll need to ask a registered school to write your reference, then go into options on UCAS and type in the 'buzzword'. Then you need to wait for the college or school to accept you before they write your reference. Once they've submitted it, it goes off just the same.

If you've been out of education for a while, then an employer is going to be the best person to write your reference for you. The first step, again, is to check that the employer or person you're working for is happy to write a reference for you. You can then get into the UCAS system, add their details under referee, and get UCAS to send them an email. They'll be sent an email, and they can log in to that website and write your reference for you there. You'll know when they've done that because the reference section on the UCAS application form will have a nice little red tick next to it. UCAS will email you when this is all complete. Do not get your friends, relatives, or partners to do it, because UCAS won't accept this.

Any reference that is written for you should talk about how suited you are academically for the course that you're going to do. It should include any work experience or skills, anything you've got that is relevant to the course that you're going to do, or any transferable skills that you've acquired. Any predicted grades that you've got for classes that you're sitting should also be included. If you manage your reference carefully, there's no reason it should hold you back.

Sarah's Story - The Application Process

Sarah had a great attitude to her personal statement and sensibly started planning it and adding to her skill set early on.

My personal experience of the application process was fairly straightforward, as I'd known what I wanted to study for a while up until that point. I ended up submitting mine very early, in October, and going into interviews starting November, even though the pharmacy UCAS submission deadline was January. What I'd wish I'd done differently is speaking to the teachers writing my references and predicted grades, as my college tutors didn't know about any of my extracurricular activities or volunteering and therefore didn't have the chance to mention them, or let them influence their reference for me. If you speak to the teacher (or manager, or colleague) writing your reference and make sure they know you're a great student, it will reflect in whatever they write about you.

At the end of the day, the application is your chance to really sell yourself to admissions boards. Universities want to know what will make you the right candidate for their course, and too many students fall into the trap of simply talking about their academic achievements – which is important, but it isn't the only thing you should be talking about. Don't be afraid to talk a little bit about your hobbies as well. Any interest in things like books, music concerts, art and other culture is something to be shown off. In my personal statement I talked most about studying and appreciating Art, and whilst this doesn't sound related to Pharmacy as a subject, I used it to show that I was well-rounded and spent my time pursuing something cultural, and as an added bonus it's interesting to talk about.

By the time I came to write my application, I had spent the summer of year 12 volunteering for Oxfam and working part-time in a restaurant, and whilst this was good experience to put on my CV for the sake of employment, I mainly did it knowing I'd be writing my application in September. When writing my statement, I talked about this in depth and made sure to relate it back to why it made me a better candidate – charity volunteering especially pushed the idea that I am conscientious and empathetic, and my work experience shows responsibility and resilience. Work experience was an easy way to set myself apart from other candidates because a lot of applicants go into university having only ever been in education.

How to Get a Good UCAS Reference

You are in control of your personal statement, but you are not in control of your reference. That being said, you *can* influence what goes into it and make sure it shows you off in the best possible light.

As we discussed earlier, your admissions tutor's going to pay attention to your predicted grades, your personal statement, and your reference. You know your predicted grades and you have a lot of influence over these because they're dependent on how hard you work. Your personal statement, you write that yourself. But somebody else writes your reference, and this is a critical thing that admissions tutors pay attention to. If they see something they don't like in your reference, no matter how good your personal statement is, you are going to end up straight in the 'no' pile.

Firstly, give the person writing your reference a lot of notice. It will generally be one of your teachers or one of your tutors from school, and teachers are busy people. If you don't give them a lot of notice, or if you expect them to write it overnight or in a short period of time, chances are it's not going to be very good. Make sure you give your teachers a lot of notice so that they have time to get the information they need.

While one person's probably going to be writing it, they're going to ask for input from all of your subject teachers. Go talk to your subject teachers, especially the subject teacher who teaches the course that you want to study. Explain to them why you love the course, why you want to do it at university, what sort of things you've been doing outside of school that will help you be good at this course at university. Perhaps show them your personal statement and ask for input on it. This will give your subject teachers lots and lots to write about. They can then pass this on to a tutor who's probably going to be writing it. Then that one person who's writing it can collate all of the information from the other teachers. But if your teachers don't know the stuff that you're putting into your personal statement, it'll be very hard for them to write it in your reference.

Talk to the person writing your reference, have a sit down with them, and show them your personal statement. This may not be one of your subject teachers; it may just be your form tutor or head of year, both of whom you may only see infrequently. It might be the head of sixth form, or it may be a professional person in school who writes the references, but make sure they know about you. Make sure they know about you outside of school, all the extracurriculars you do, all the skills that you've got from other things, why you have a passion for this subject, and so on. The more they know about you, the easier it is going to be for them to write a good reference.

The reference is going to be the right place for the school to discuss any exceptional circumstances that may have had an impact on your performance. Any family issues, any health issues, anything that's affected you which may have had an influence on your grades, either positively or negatively. Talk to the person who's writing your reference about this.

Chances are you're never going to see your reference. You do have the right to know if you want to, but most of the time they just submit it and send it off. Teachers don't write bad things in references, but sometimes the absence of certain things is more telling for admissions tutors. Teachers write stuff that we have backed up by evidence, so the more good evidence you can give us, the more good things we have to write.

And then, lastly, don't hassle your teachers about your reference. Teachers and tutors are incredibly busy people. We have a billion things to do, and if we have one student who's hassling and nagging us, it doesn't necessarily inspire us towards writing that reference for them. We know what the deadlines are—your head of the sixth form is nagging us by email every day, so it is definitely on our to-do list!

Make sure you talk to the people involved, make sure you tell them what you're good at, make sure you give them the information to write for your reference. Hopefully your reference will work together with your personal statement, and the admissions tutor will see what an amazing student you are!

Do GCSE Results Matter?

The journey to the university of your choice starts a lot earlier than you might expect. And some of you are going to be very surprised to find that your GCSE results might stop you from getting into the university you want.

In the majority of cases, once you have the qualification and moved to the next step, the previous qualification doesn't matter anymore. For the majority of you, your GCSEs will only be important in determining what A-Level course you get onto, or what A-Level college you get into. But for some of you, your GCSE results are going to be a vitally important part of determining whether or not you get into universities that you want. As a very basic rule, you have to have a good grade in your GCSE English and your GCSE Maths, typically at least a four or a five. This may vary depending on the university, but some places are going to go even further than that and require a seven, eight, or nine across five different GCSEs. Some might require eights and nines in a specified set of GCSEs, or eights and nines in ten or eleven GCSEs. Some places, while not explicitly saying that GCSEs are essential, might still make them a big part of determining who they invite for an interview and who they reject.

This is because your GCSE results are the only official results you have by the time that you apply. Because the government has removed AS exams, you're going to have your GCSE results and your predicted grades when you apply. Your predicted grades might be right, or they might be completely wrong, so your GCSE results are really the best indication of how you're going to do at A-Level. The universities might think that GCSEs are a good indication of what you're going to do at university, but some others might say that they're *not* a good indication and not look at them at all. Some universities are also going to require a particular set of GCSE subjects, and may require you to take a catch-up course in your first year if you don't have all the subjects. For example, some universities like it if you have a language GCSE, and if you don't have that, they want you to do a language module in your first year.

Having said all of that, a weak set of GCSE results is not disastrous. A robust set of predicted grades, a reliable reference, and a strong personal statement are going to look good. And in some cases, they will outweigh an unfortunate set of GCSE results.

Mo's Story - Things I Wish I Knew before University

Mo did A-Levels in History (B), maths (C), and biology (D)

Many people are in the same boat as I was a few years ago. I was the only one out of my group of friends who went to Aston. Therefore, I was petrified about walking in and feeling overlooked. Little did I know that I had nothing to be anxious about! Because I wasn't the only person by myself; everyone would be the same. From the first lecture you're in, everyone around you will be trying to make friends, so make sure you're doing the same and moving out of your safe zone. Everyone wants to meet new people and make new friends, so ensure you say hi and move on to know everyone you meet!

You don't need to join every group or club at the Freshers' Fair. Universities frequently have a Freshers' event where you get so bombarded with societies and night clubs that you often decide to join three sports activities groups, a film world, a games modern culture, and loads more. Don't feel pressured to become listed on societies you haven't any involvement in. Think about your passions and what you would like to try, and don't be afraid to provide it a chance!

Remember the students you meet in your first few lectures, be sure to inquire further what events they're going to and try to hang around with them. Know which are best for you to attend, and check up on others if they are attending. That's very important if you are communicating as you will not continually be on campus to meet new people. Try to attend as many events as possible and develop your contacts.

Budgeting is the main element to success on campus. It will definitely have to be a major part of your student life. The coffees you're buying each morning before your 9 am lecture really accumulate, so make an effort to resist enticement. Bring a treat from home or a travel mug with a hot drink; this will minimize you from buying out every time. Get yourself a notepad and devote it to finances; split up your bills and exactly how much everything costs. This will highlight how much you will need to save for bills on a monthly basis and exactly how much you can devote to yourself. Don't go crazy!

Reading lists or library? You might have found out about the feared long reading lists for which you have to buy every book. This is not always the situation. Don't buy every book before you begin university as your library might have all you need! Some literature you'll need during your colleges years, whereas some you're better off just loaning.

The library is going to be where you may spend most of your time over summer and winter, so make use of it correctly. My university has an excellent library with every publication on my reading list. Take a look before spending unneeded levels of money on books for your course. Also understand how to work with the library systems, such as finding online publications, because these come in handy!

Add everyone on Facebook. Whether you prefer Facebook or not, it's fairly useful if you are at university. Add your coursemates along with people you met in freshers' week, this way you'll keep in mind who they are and can probably bump into them on campus. Facebook is the most readily useful as it pertains to group work. You don't want to start looking for them one by one, so adding everyone in your group on Facebook will help you have group chats and plan *conferences. Societies also use Facebook as a means of getting in touch with everyone so ensure you sign up for all the groupings and remain updated.*

Socialize with people on campus. Having friends on campus makes life so much easier! Whether you're returning from a particular date, late dinner, library session or maybe want to settle before your 9 am lecture. It is also simply perfect for those long spaces in-between lectures, and you will have a fresh destination to revise!

Networking is so important as students. It could impact job opportunities when you have graduated, and it can benefit massively in obtaining a great final quality! When opportunities to meet important professional people happen, do not miss them because you never know when that interconnection might come in very useful. Remember to expose yourself and make an optimistic, lasting impression.

With campus opportunities, get involved! Through the University Student Union, learn to be a Student Ambassador. There are also several paid jobs on campus that you can try. It certainly is good to earn some money to take care of yourself with, and it'll look amazing on your CV! Don't only give attention to the paid assignments, however, but look at the voluntary ones, too. As long as you're on campus, you may as well help build your CV at the same time.

The first year will count. During the first 12 months, there are always some students that come to classes with a mindset that generally does not help get to the final level. First year is extremely important in providing you with various tools to help you through your university years.

You don't have to surpass the college student stereotype. Some students, including myself, love making a to-do list, getting things done and fulfilling ourselves with a good movie and cup of tea. Don't let the scholar stereotype pressure you into performing a certain way at the university. You will discover a wide variety of types of students who I'm sure you can have a movie and PJs nights with.

Freshers' flu is not really a myth. I laughed when confronted with folks who explained about Freshers' Flu. Surely I, with my brilliant disease fighting capability, wouldn't be pulled down with a cold? I was wrong, and also have stayed wrong every September since. Freshers' Flu is real; you'll get it, and so will everyone around you, including your tutors. Prepare yourself!

Additional Entry Requirements

As well as A-Levels, some university have specified additional entry requirements. Specifics for medicine and Oxbridge are listed in those sections of the book. This is mainly due to the decrease in students sitting for AS-Level exams, which means that the only formal exam results on your UCAS application form are your GCSE results, which may not be in the subject you are applying for and not all universities think these are representative of how you will do at university.

While not a replacement for A-Levels, a good grade in the following exams may compensate for a poor performance in GCSEs and may be reflected in an unconditional or reduced offer.

Thinking Skills Assessment. The University of Oxford, University of Cambridge, and UCL (University College London) all use the TSA for a range of different courses. This takes place at the end of October. For Section One, you have 90 minutes to answer 50 multiple choice questions. This is a skills test, not a knowledge test, so you're going to be tested on your ability to use numerical and spatial reasoning, your ability to solve problems, and your critical thinking skills using everyday language. Scores for each question are scaled based on difficulty, and your final score for Section One will be out of 100. The University of Cambridge and UCL only require candidates to sit Section One, but the University of Oxford also requires Section Two. Section Two is a 30-minute essay writing task to demonstrate good use of English and ability to communicate. The marks are passed on to the universities to which you have applied, and these will be released in mid-January. While there is no specific content you can study for this test, as with any exam you can prepare by looking at past papers, which are freely available on the assessment website. The test is taken in school and your exams officer needs to register you for the test.

Law - Bristol, Durham, Glasgow, King's College London, Nottingham, Oxford, SOAS and UCL all require the National Admissions Test for Law (LNAT).

University admissions tutors know that not everyone has the opportunity to study Law at A-Level, so they need an alternative way of determining who would make a good lawyer. The LNAT doesn't test subject knowledge, so you don't need to have studied Law to get a good grade. Instead, the LNAT tests the skills that lawyers need, such as comprehension; interpretation; analysis; synthesis; induction and deduction; and other verbal reasoning skills that are essential for a successful career in law. The LNAT will not be the only factor that admission tutors take into account, but it will play a big part alongside your personal statement, predicted grades, and references. Each university will place a different amount of importance on the results.

The LNAT needs to be sat the year you are applying to university and you can only sit it once per admission round. It is a computer-based test, and must be sat at an authorised test centre; you cannot take this within school.

The test is 2 hours and 15 minutes and has two sections. For Section A, you get 95 minutes to answer 42 multiple chose questions. You will be shown 12 paragraphs and then will need to answer 3 or 4 questions on each. For Section B, you will get 40 minutes to write an essay on a given topic. In Section B, you will need to show that you can use the English language well. The results are sent out twice a year, with the first results sent out in mid-February, meaning you cannot use the results to help determine where you apply via UCAS.

There is no content that you need to study, but you can help yourself prepare for the test by looking at the past papers which are available for free on the LANT website, lnat.ac.uk

Maths – The University of Oxford and Imperial College both require the Mathematics Admissions Test (MAT). The University of Cambridge and University of Warwick require the Sixth Term Examination Paper in Mathematics (STEP). Durham University and Lancaster University require the Test of Mathematics for University Admission; this test is also advised to be taken by applicants to the University of Warwick, University of Sheffield, University of Southampton and London School of Economics and Political Science.

The MAT is sat at the end of October after the deadline for Oxford applications, so you can use the results to determine if you should apply to Oxford or not. This is administered by the Cambridge Assessment Admissions Testing Service—but don't get confused, because it is still needed even for Oxford and Imperial. This is a subject-based test, and it is best that you let your teacher know you are planning on taking it so they can ensure that you learn all the content in year 12. You don't need to have taken Further Maths at A-Level to be able to understand the content on this test. Both Oxford and Imperial have an extensive collection of past papers and worked solutions to help you prepare for this test, so you should take advantage of the resources that both universities offer.

The test is 2 hours and 30 minutes long. No calculators or formula sheets are allowed, and it is taken within school under exam conditions. You will need to get your school exams officer to register you for the test. You don't get sent your results; these are sent directly to the university, but you can request them for the university.

Test of Mathematics for University Admission is spread across two 75-minute papers which are taken consecutively. Paper

One is thinking and Paper Two is reasoning; for both of these papers you are not allowed any calculators. The test is taken at the end of October and the results released to you a month later. The results are not automatically sent to universities, but you can select which universities you want to share the results with via the results website. This test is sat within schools and you need to get your exams officer to register you for it. The content is going to be based on what you are studying, and there are lots of free practice papers available on the testing services website.

STEP, or the Sixth Term Examination Paper in Mathematics, has three papers but not all are required by every university. The papers you are required to take will depend on what A-Levels you are taking. Each paper is 3 hours long and has 13 questions (8 pure, 3 mechanics and 2 stats). It is suggested that you pick 6 questions and answer them, but you can attempt as many questions as you like. Only the six highest scores will be used. Paper 1 and 2 are based on A-Levels Maths content, while Paper 3 is based on A-Level Further Maths. These exams are sat at the same time as A-Level exams in June, and results are released at the same time as A-Level results. This means that your offer may be combination of A-Level results and STEP results. The STEP exam will be sat in school and your exams officer needs to register you. The University of Cambridge has a very extensive range of free preparation material available on their website.

Interviews

Some universities are going to send out offers without interviews. Some universities are just going to expect you to turn up for an open day, but some universities are going to want to interview you, and there are two different types of interview.

Some universities are going to do "soft interviews", where they're 99% per cent decided to accept you. They just want to interview you to make sure that you're right for them. On the other hand, some universities are going to do full-on interviews, where they're properly going to be assessing you and taking what you say into account when they decide to give you an offer. The problem is, you've got no way of telling you which type of interview it is!

I'm afraid there's no way to know whether you've been invited to a soft interview, or if your interview will be decisive in your acceptance to the university. You have to be prepared for any interview you get invited to. You can expect to be asked questions about your personal statement, so it is a good idea to print this off and re-read it. For some of you it may have been a really long time ago when you submitted the application form, and you might have forgotten a few of the things on there. The interviewer can pick up on anything you've said on your personal statement and ask you to expand on it, so make sure you haven't forgotten anything. Make sure that you remember what you've said. Can you reflect on anything? Can you draw anything out? Maybe make a few rough little notes. This is a reason why it's really important not to lie on your personal statement, because you might get found out at interview.

There are loads of common questions that they can ask you about your personal statement, about your subjects, about your work experience, about anything you've done. I've listed some of these later in this section. For the common questions, like with your personal statement, it's a really good idea to go through and make a few key points on each topic, just so that you have it fresh in your mind and so that you're not stumbling too much during the interview. Don't try and write long answers or memorize them beforehand, because it's going to seem false and you might trip over yourself if they ask the question a slightly different way to how you're expecting.

You may not have ever had an interview before, so you can ask your teacher to give you a mock interview to help you get used to how intimidating it can be. You could be facing a panel of interviewers where one person will ask the questions, and one person will stay silent, staring at you the entire time, trying to psych you out. Then there might be one person being really bubbly and happy and enthusiastic about everything you say. You may get feedback, or you may not get any feedback.

At some universities, you might have a one-on-one interview, or you might have a series of short interviews where you go around talking to lots of different people. These all can be quite intimidating. You might be asked to solve some problems in the interview, or you might be asked your opinion on current affairs. They might give you some scenarios and ask how you'd react.

A really common question is, "Tell us something you're interested in..." Now, hopefully you've found a passion or something you're interested in, but if you haven't done that already, please look at the section on personal statements found in this book. It's going to be exactly the same advice for how to show passion for your subject in your interview.

It is essential that you do research into the university, the course, the lecturers, the modules, the units, and the assessment style at the university, so that when you go for your interview it's clear that you know what you're talking about. They might ask you which part of the course you're looking forward to most, or what you think about the coursework element—if you can't answer these questions, it's going to show that you're not prepared for the interview. Spend some time doing your research, and work out some questions that you can ask at interview as well—remember, this is a two-way thing. You are interviewing them just as much as they are interviewing you. They may give you an offer, but you have to decide whether to accept that offer or not. Be as prepared as you can for this interview.

You might want to consider staying overnight before your interviews so that you don't have a long drive or a long train journey. There are loads of cheap student accommodation that you can find. Get up early, and remember to eat breakfast. I know you're going to be nervous, and maybe you won't feel like eating, but it is going to be really important. Your interview packet may tell you to turn up at a certain time, but then there might be a tour or a talk before you actually get around to the interview; it may be while before you get a chance to eat any actual food, so please have breakfast. Do everything you can to avoid rushing around and avoid stress on the morning of the interview. Have your outfit picked out and ready. Have how you're going to get to the university sorted. Buy your tickets in advance. Have your timetables ready, so you know exactly what to do. Have a look at a map of the university so you know where you're going. Have contact numbers for the interviewers, so you can notify them if you're going to be late for any reason. Prepare as much as you can so that you're not stressing on the day of the interview.

Be yourself in the interview. Remember, they want to admit *you*, not the person that you think they are looking for. You are a unique, brilliant, amazing individual, and they want you at their university. You've gotten this far. You've impressed them with your personal statement, your references, and your predicted grades. Remember this when you get there. You shouldn't think, "Oh, I'm not sure about this, I'm not sure that I'm good enough." You *are* good enough—you just need to let that shine through. Remember, you are worth a lot of money to the university. They are trying to attract you as much as you are trying to impress them. So this interview is much more of a two-way process than it might seem from the start. They want you to come there, but they also want to make sure that you are going to be the right person for this offer. So ask questions about how things work, about what support you'll be getting, about what lectures you'll be taking, about how much contact time there is, about how many tutorials there will be, or how much time you will actually be expected to devote to individual study, lectures, or potential labs.

Neesha's Story - The Interview Process

Neesha has two Advanced GNVQ's

Although some courses might offer you places straight away after reading your personal statement, my chosen course had an intensive interview process. My application was the first point of contact with admissions boards, but the interview was my first direct contact with my future tutors and the university campus.

One thing that I learned from experience was that interviews aren't the time for humility – you want to prove that you're the best candidate for the position, and with some universities receiving 35 applications for every available place, you need to do what you can to set yourself apart from the rest.

It helps to know a little bit about what you're applying for. I didn't have any related work experience so I had to prepare myself to answer questions in a specific way that related my experience back to the subject. During my interview I was asked about previous experience, my hobbies, and a little bit of background knowledge about what I already knew about the course. Interviewers don't expect you to have a wealth of knowledge already, but they like seeing that you've done a little bit of background reading beforehand. During my interviews I was asked questions such as, "What are five different methods of administering drugs," and, "Can you name five non-steroidal anti-inflammatory drugs?" If I had gotten these questions wrong, I don't think I would have been turned down, but having researched the topic and being able to give an answer, I felt much more confident about the rest of the interview and it definitely showed.

The last thing I would say is that by the time you get to interviews, you've got a very good chance of getting in. By the time I reached the interview stage, at least one person had already looked through my application and decided that I would be a good fit based on my grades and my personal statement. I definitely let this give me a much-needed confidence boost. The interview stage for me was about having a conversation with recruiters, letting them see my personality and whether it fit the course, seeing if I would be good to work with. My advice is to relax and be confident, and let them see you for who you are as a candidate.

Interview Questions

Think about each of the following questions. Write a few short bullet points for each. Don't write out long answers and memorize them exactly, because this will seem false and you may get flustered if they ask the questions slightly differently.

General Interview Questions

- Why did you decide to study (the subject you've applied for)?
- Why have you chosen to apply to this university?
- Which module on this course are you looking forward to most?
- Why should you get a place here?
- Why did you take ...... for A-Level?
- What have you enjoyed most about your A-Levels?
- What have you enjoyed least about your A-Levels?
- What would you change about your A-Levels?
- What have you enjoyed most about school?
- What have you enjoyed least about school?
- What would you change about your school?
- Do you think your grades are a good reflection of you as a student?
- What have you read about (the subject you've applied for)?
- What are the current trends in (the subject you've applied for)?
- Why is (the subject you've applied for) important?
- How Is (the subject you've applied for) relevant to everyday life?
- What are you interested in?

- What have you done outside of your A-Level studies to develop your subject knowledge?
- What are your strengths?
- What are your weaknesses?
- What are you proud of?
- What mistakes have you made?
- How do you deal with stressful situations?
- How do you react under pressure?
- What makes a good student?
- What work experience / volunteering / part-time work have you done?
- What skills did you gain from your work experience / volunteering / part-time work?
- What are your long-term career plans?
- How did you decide on this career path?
- What are your long term goals?
- What are your short-term goals?
- How are you going to achieve your goals?
- Where do you see yourself in five years' time?
- Where do you see yourself in ten years' time?
- How much do you expect to be earning in five years' time?
- How does this degree help you achieve your gaols?
- What motivates you?
- What makes you happy?
- What does success in life mean to you?
- What are the most important rewards in life?
- What advantage has doing ...... extracurricular given you?
- Can you give an example of where you have worked well in a team?
- Do you work best on your own or as part of a team?
- Can you give an example of when have helped another person?

- When have you shown leadership skills?
- What five words best describe you?
- How would your teachers describe you?
- Why did / didn't you take a gap year?
- Tell me about your EPQ / extended project?
- What was the last book you read?
- What was the last film you saw?
- What is your favourite book?
- What is your favourite film?
- How do you choose the books you read?
- Who inspires you most?
- Who has influenced you most?
- Which historical figure would you most like to meet?
- What is the most interesting place you've visited?
- Where would you like to visit?
- What has been your most interesting experience to date?
- What are your opinions on tuition fees?
- What advantage has the DoE given you?
- How you got any questions?

'Outside the Box' Questions

These are not 'trick' questions. Most of the time there are no right answers and no wrong answers; the interviewers just want to see how you approach answering the question and how you solve the problem.

Gap Year Questions

- Why did you decide to take a gap year?
- What did you do on your gap year?
- How was your gap year arranged?
- How did you decide what to do on your gap year?
- What impact has your gap year had on you?
- How have you grown as a person during your gap year?
- Did your gap year help with your future career plans?
- Did taking a gap year put you at a disadvantage?
- What was the best part of your gap year?
- What was the worst part of your gap year?

Katrina's Story – Interviews for Art Students

Katrina has A-levels in Art (A), geography (C) and drama (C)

There are lots of different styles of interview for university applicants. For art students, however, all of these include a portfolio review which is done either whilst the interview is happening, or without you present before the interview takes place. The main topics of discussion were: what I think the course was; what I was hoping to get out of it; what my practice is; and what I hope to end up doing with it after my studies are finished.

Out of the four interviews I did, the one for the illustration course at Falmouth was the most stressful. It was completely different to any of the others I had done, in that it had a sort of speed dating feel to it and was a lot more commercial. There were six potential students (including me) and five interviewers sat at tables. We had to go to each of them in turn as they all looked through our portfolios and interviewed us. I personally found the more informal, conversational interviews to be much easier and enjoyable. Having the personal conversations (i.e., where I come from, what I enjoy doing in my free time) just put me more at ease and helped me learn about the interviewer just as much as they were learning about me.

I think the interview that I felt the most nervous for was my first one, purely for the fact that I had never actually done anything like it before. To any students getting ready to go through this now, remember there is no use in stressing about the interviews, just believe in yourself and what you know you can do. The university needs you as much as you need it. But that being said, don't try and blag your way through it. Do your research on the courses and universities you are interested in. True passion and drive cannot be faked.

Art and Design Questions

- What is the most important piece you have created?
- Which piece in your portfolio are you most proud of?
- Which exhibition have you seen that has had an impact on you?

English Interview Questions

- What text did you study at A-Level?
- Which was the best book you studied for your A-Levels?
- What have you read outside the text you needed to read for your A-Levels?
- What makes a book 'good'?
- Should older books that offend modern ideals still be studied in schools?
- What is literature?
- Are film adaptations of books ever any good?
- What is the ideal length of a book?
- Why are so many series written in trilogies?
- How long is a story?

Engineering Interview Questions

- What has been engineering's most important contribution to society?
- How dangerous are mistakes?
- How would you explain force?
- What is the difference between engineering and physics?

Teaching Interview Questions

- Which of your teachers influenced you most and why?
- How important is classroom environment to student learning?
- How disruptive is low-level misbehaviour?
- What is your opinion on OFSTED?
- What have you chosen this year group?

Your Offer

How to Decide between Offers

When you get all of your offers in, you need to make some decisions. You need to pick a firm choice, and you need to pick an insurance choice. But how do you make the right decision?

You should wait until you have all of your offers in. I know this can be really, really hard. In my case, my dream university didn't send me an offer until the end of March when my first offers were coming in before Christmas. Some of the courses send out offers really quickly, whereas others take a bit more time over their decisions. Your friends may already have all of their offers in before you even get any through!

As I have said many times before, I think you should go to the place where you are going to be happiest, and hopefully, you've got an offer through from them and that can be your firm choice. But if you haven't gotten that offer, or if you're wondering how to decide on your insurance choices, then there are a quite a few things you need to take into account.

First, you need to make sure your insurance choice has lower grades than your firm choice. This is because your insurance choice is where you're going to go if you don't get the grades for your firm choice. I don't mean just one grade below in one subject; it's generally a good idea to go at least one grade below in all subjects. That way it can be a proper safety net if your exam results aren't exactly what you need. You could decide to take the risk and put down an insurance choice that is only just below your firm choice, but you're going to have to acknowledge that this is a risk.

If you have no one particular university in mind, or if you're not sure what to pick as your insurance choices, then there are quite a few different factors you can take into account when making your decision. The first thing would be your grades. Are there two courses where you'd be equally happy on either, but one has quite high grades and one has grades which are a bit more attainable? If you went for the one that has the higher grades, would you be spending next few months really stressed and trying to push yourself a little bit too hard? Maybe if you went for the one that had lower grades, you could relax a little bit and not be quite so stressed over the exam periods, slightly surer that you would actually get those grades.

If you can afford it and have the time, you can go and visit your choices. This could just be for a day trip, and you could just go and do all the touristy things. Go and spend some time in the city or just hang out at the university. This may give you a particular inclination towards a given university, or it may completely put you off the place.

You could be really brave and call the universities you are choosing between. Most universities have students' unions that are really enthusiastic and want to share their enthusiasm with loads of other people. If you don't want to call them up, universities these days have a big presence on social media, and all of them are going to have Twitter accounts, Instagram accounts (which are usually managed by students), or volunteers who are there to answer your questions. There are also loads of student vloggers that you can catch on YouTube, and many of them will be studying your course or studying at the university you're looking at (I've made a list of vloggers in a previous section).

You can spend some time delving deep into the course units and the modules. You might have done this when you were applying for courses, but that was probably a few months ago now, and you might have forgotten. So spend a bit of extra time and look in detail at exactly what each course entails. Does one course stand out a little bit more to you? Does one course have something you're not sure about? Look at how they assess—is one course really exam-based, and the other really coursework-based? Ask yourself which style of assessment is going to suit you best.

And then lastly, before you actually fill in UCAS Track, you should make a firm decision, and then sleep on it. If you're still happy with your decision when you wake up in the morning, you can be fairly sure that you've made the right choice. If in the morning you're still unsure, and you're not very confident with the decision, make a different choice and sleep on it again. This is probably the biggest decision you've made in your life thus far, so give it the time it needs. There's no need to rush!

Don't forget that you can decline all of your offers if you change your mind, or if none of the offers are what you really want. If you're not confident that you're going to be happy in these courses, or confident that you're going to be happy at this university, then you can decline all of the offers. You can apply through Clearing, or you can take a gap year, or you can just start again next year and apply fresh with your results already in hand. You have lots of options, but even if you make the wrong decision, it is not the end of the world.

10 Worst Ways to Pick between University Offers

I have talked a lot about how to pick between your offers, but here are 10, terrible ways to pick between your offers.

1. Do not accept an offer just because it is an unconditional offer. Unconditional offers are given out by universities to tempt you in, to try and encourage you to go there—but if you're not confident that you're going to be happy there, do not accept it just because it's an unconditional offer.

2. Do not follow your boyfriend or your girlfriend. This is a bad idea! You are a different person than them, and you may not be happy at the same university as them. If your relationship is meant to be, it will last long distance.

3. Do not go somewhere just because your parents went there. I have seen this so many times before, with friends, with colleagues, with people I've met in my career. You are not your parents, so do not feel pressured by them to follow the family tradition or the family history.

4. Do not go somewhere just because somebody famous is there. Don't go to a university because there's a famous lecturer, or because there's a famous person enrolled as a student. As an undergraduate, you will probably never see the famous lecturers. If there is an academic who you are desperate to work with, your best chance to work with them is as a postgraduate. As an undergraduate, you're probably not going to see them.

5. Do not pick somewhere based on the weather, because weather is changeable. I know that up north sometimes it can be a bit cold and rainy, but that doesn't mean you're not going to have an absolutely fantastic time. Down south is generally sunnier, but not always, so don't pick a university based on what you think the weather's going to be like.

6. Do not believe the advertising. Universities want you to go there, so they pay a lot of money for advertising, and they pay a lot of money to try and entice you to come. Do not believe the advertising, do not believe the hype. Do your own research.

7. Do not pick a university based upon its position in a league table. League tables are constantly changing, and it doesn't necessarily tell you whether the course is going to be suited to you, or what type of course is going to be best for you. Whether it's part of the Russell Group, or not part of the Russell Group; whether it's a Red Brick university, or not a Red Brick university; these are all just labels.

8. Do not pick a university just for the nightlife. Yes, your social life is important, but you can always take a train to a big city to get your nightlife. The most important thing is you being happy with your university and with your course. Don't just pick somewhere because it has a good club scene.

9. By no means should you go completely random and pull something out of a hat. This is so bad, just don't do it.

10. Do not go to university because you can't think of anything better to do. University is expensive, university is time consuming, and university is a lot of work. If you can't think of anything better to do, then maybe try a gap year and think about what you actually want to do.

This is a big, big decision. Do not feel rushed into it. Do not feel pressured to make a decision that somebody else wants you to make. You need to make the right decision that is best for you, not what is best for other people. This is a really stressful time, but it's also a really exciting time for you.

What to Do if You Don't Get any Offers – UCAS Extra

If you don't end up with any offers from universities, don't panic—you have a chance to put an extra choice on. If you've been rejected from all of your five choices, or if you only applied to one and you got rejected, then you can have another go. But the process is slightly different.

This second chance happens after the UCAS deadline has passed, so we have from mid-February until mid-July to get this sorted out. You need to look through the UCAS website and find courses that have spaces available on them. Then you need to contact the university directly, and see if they'll consider you for a place. You can then go and add your next choice onto your UCAS Track. Then we just need to wait for the university's decision. Now, the university may reject you. It may ignore you. If it ignores you for three weeks, then you can go through the process again and pick another course. They may offer you a place and you accept it, in which case, brilliant. Or they might offer you a place, and you might have changed your mind, in which case you can reject it and pick another course. And we can keep picking courses and keep picking courses until you find one that suits you.

If you are in this position, and there aren't courses coming up that you think are going to be a good fit for you, then you can consider taking a gap year and applying straight away in September with your A-Level grades already in hand. This can reduce your stress levels, because so much depends on what happens on results day in August. If you apply next year with your results already sorted, then you might get an unconditional offer. You can also tailor which university is your priority based on your grades.

Suzanne's Story – What Is It Really Like at Uni?

A day in my life as a university student is comparatively different to my days spent as a college student. I was never one for an early morning start.

Now I live by the saying, "The early bird catches the worm." Since joining the local gym near my university, I wake up at 6.30am and head out for a one-hour gym session. With all the endorphins produced whilst working out, I feel ready to conquer the day ahead. I head straight back to the house to grab a shower. I usually then arrive at the university cafe by 8am. The food selection for breakfast never fails to disappoint.

I have a two-hour lecture which begins at 9am. Today's lecture is all about Pharmacology. This is one of my favourite modules this year, so I'm definitely looking forward to this lecture. The next two hours are spent studying and discussing a variety of medicines and their side effects on the human body. Once the lecture is over, me and my friends decide to take a trip to the university shop to pick up some snacks.

It's now approaching midday and next on the agenda is the university library. This building has become a second home to me! I have a meeting with my classmates to complete some group work for another module. We spend at least an hour comparing and completing our assignments. We're all done by 1pm and we grab some well-deserved lunch.

I work part-time at a nearby clothing shop 3 days a week, between 2pm and 5pm. This job allows me to have an extra bit of cash towards the weekends. Once my shift is complete it takes me 20 minutes to walk back home. I'm a big lover of music, so I pop on my headphones and off I head.

I'm back at home by 5.20pm. My housemates and I have set a rota with everyone alternating between cooking and cleaning daily. We also do a big clean together on Saturday morning, leaving the rest of the weekend for our enjoyment. This system really works. I arrive home to the smell of a freshly made meal as it's my housemates turn to cook today. We finish up on our food and I help another housemate to clean up.

It's now 6.30pm and I chill out with my housemates, catching up on our days activities. At around 7pm I take a cup of tea up with me to my room. I'll spend a couple of hours going through my lecture notes, writing them all up in a neat manner. I love doing this, as it means that I can get a head start on exam revision. The rest of the evening is all mine. I usually watch a movie on Netflix and catch up on social media. The day has been full of hard but rewarding work. Off to bed now so I can do this all again the next morning!

Unconditional Offers

Unconditional offers are a double-edged sword. If you get an unconditional offer, it can be really flattering because the university is telling you that they *really* want you to come to the university. It's their way of saying that your interview, your personal statement, and your admissions test were all so amazing that it doesn't matter what A-Level results you get, they still want you to come. But so often I see students accept unconditional offers, and then relax a little too much; some of them barely scrape by with three Ds when they should be on for three As.

There are a few ways that you can get an unconditional offer, and the stats from UCAS show that unconditional offers are on a massive increase. Whereas previously they used to be very rare, now each university is giving out five to ten, whereas before you wouldn't see any. If you have shown in your interview that you have an overwhelming passion for this subject—that you live and breathe this subject, that you've put the effort in, that you've gone over and above your A-Level studies to do extra independent research—then the person interviewing you is generally going to be really impressed by this. This is how I got my unconditional offer at university, and I was told in the interview that they were going to send me an unconditional offer.

Because so few students sit AS exams anymore, pre-interview assessments, tests, and written work are really on the rise. You may be asked to take a test or exam, or you may be asked to submit written work, or you may be asked to submit a portfolio or a couple of audition pieces, and based on the strength of these, you may get an unconditional offer. If your test results or your portfolio was truly outstanding, this can heavily influence the university's decision to accept you no matter what you get in your A-Levels. You are also more likely to get an unconditional offer if you have your grades already. For example, if you've taken a gap year after school, then you already know what your A-Level results are before applying to university. We don't have to wait and find out what your grades are, so in that circumstance, universities may give you an unconditional offer.

While it's great that you're not stressed about your exams anymore, it is important to take your A-Levels seriously. Your A-Level results stay with you, and you're going to be writing them on your CV for the rest of your life. And if for any reason you decide to change courses or change careers later on, having poor A-Levels will make this more difficult for you.

It's also important to realize that just because you've relaxed because you've got this unconditional offer, that does not mean your teachers are going to relax. Your teachers will know if you've accepted the unconditional offer, and we will know that you are going to be relaxing. However, your exam results are going to be a reflection of your teacher, and a reflection of your school. Your teachers are still going hassle you to do the work, and they might even be hassling you a bit more because they know you've relaxed a little bit. Don't expect your teachers to think that your unconditional offer is a fantastic thing; they're actually going to be slightly worried, because we've seen what could happen.

Remember, if you get an unconditional offer, this is the university enticing you, trying to get you to come to them. You don't have to accept it. If you don't think you're going to be happy there, if you don't think it's an exact right fit there, then don't fall for it.

My Story – How I Got an Unconditional Offer

Some lucky people are getting unconditional offers, just as I did years and years and years ago. I didn't take it up, though, because I changed my mind. I didn't want to go there, but how did I get this fabled, amazing, unconditional offer? Your personal statement gets you an interview and your interview gets you the place. Now, unconditional offers are very, very rarely given out, but they are given to people who show passion for the subject that they are applying for.

So, in my interview (and this was quite a few years ago), I'd already decided that I didn't want to stay in London for university, and the only reason I want to the interview was I fancied a day off school. I went along to the interview so relaxed, because if they gave me an offer, then they gave me an offer; if they didn't, then they didn't. On the train on the way in, I picked up a New Scientist and the main article that week was about heat shock proteins.

The interview started off with a fairly like standard question, "Tell me something you've read recently that interested you." And I went blah, blah, blah, blah, blah, blah, blah, blah, heat shock proteins, and literally the guy couldn't get a word in edgeways for about 15 minutes because I was just going off about how interesting I thought heat shock proteins were. Now, you've probably never heard of heat shock proteins, and that's absolutely fine because they're not part of the A-Level course. Because I could talk for so long and so passionately about something that hadn't come up in my A-Level course, the guy just sat there and then said I've got no other questions for you. I mean, don't go on for much longer than

15 minutes, because the person interviewing you will probably get bored! But you need to be able to talk passionately and confidently about a small, unusual subject, because that in essence is what becoming a student is.

A-Levels give you a very broad introduction to things. But to get that unconditional offer, you have to show that you are well on your way to becoming an expert in something. Now, you don't have to pick a different thing for every university, just pick something and become interested in it. If you're not entirely sure what you're interested in, that's fine. You need to show passion for your subject; you need to show that you are the most committed and enthusiastic person they're ever, ever met, and they can't afford not to have you at university. I didn't take up my unconditional offer because I didn't want to stay in London; I wanted to go to Bath, which is the best university in the world. So just get out there and get reading and get researching!

How UCAS Points Work

You are going to need a certain number of UCAS tariff points to get into university, but what are they? How do you get them? What can you do with them?

You must have heard of UCAS points when you were looking through the prospectus, seeing what courses you want to apply for. Some of them are going to talk about grades, some of them are going to talk about points, and some of them are going to talk about a combination of the two.

You can get UCAS points from a range of different things. You can get them through A-Levels, AS-Levels, the Extended Project Qualification, Scottish Highers, Scottish Advanced Highers, Scottish Baccalaureate, International Baccalaureate, Cambridge International Pre-U Diploma, Cambridge Technicals, or the Welsh Baccalaureate International Diploma. I'm not going to go into every single one here, because the UCAS guide on this is 170 pages long. It is thoroughly comprehensive. The reason they've moved towards points instead of grades is to level the playing field for people that are coming in who haven't done A-Levels, or who are coming through a somewhat non-traditional route. This makes it easy for universities to see and compare somebody who has A-Levels, somebody who has NVQs, and somebody who has an International Baccalaureate.

Your offer might say you need 112 points. It might mean you need 112 points from three A-Levels, or it might say you need 112 points from at least two A-Levels. You need to be careful that you understand the specifics when you're applying to a course. The point system cannot be played, simply as that. You can't just do seven AS-Levels, get your 112 points, and think that you managed to get around not doing full A-Levels. It doesn't work like that. AS-Levels you only get about 40% of the points that you get for a whole A-Level.

A-Levels and Highers

Grade	A-Level	AS-Level	EPQ	Advanced Highers	Highers
A*	56		28		
A	48	20	24	56	33
B	40	16	20	48	27
C	32	12	16	40	21
D	24	10	12	32	15
E	10	6	8		

International Baccalaureate - IBO Certificate

Grade	Higher Level	Grade	Standard Level	Grade	Extended Essay
H7	56	S7	28	A	12
H6	48	S6	24	B	10
H5	32	S5	16	C	8
H4	24	S4	12	D	6
H3	12	S3	6	E	4
H2	0	S2	0		
H1	0	S1	0		

AP (Advanced Placement) Exams

Grade	Points
5	28
4	24
3	20
2	16
1	12

Gaokao

Grade	Points
Top tier	64
Second tier	48
Third tier	40

The UCAS guide covers GNVQs, all kinds of baccalaureates, YMCA qualifications, and loads and loads of other qualifications you wouldn't necessarily have thought of.

What to Do After You Have Accepted Your Offer

The UCAS process is an incredibly long one, and I'm afraid it doesn't stop after you've accepted your offers. Once you've made your decision, but before you actually know your A-Level results, you still have more decisions to make. You still have more forms to fill in, and you still have more things to do.

There are two important things that everybody needs to take into consideration. First, you need to apply for your student finance. If you want your student finance to be in place by the time you start university, this needs to be done by the end of May. Before you can apply for your student finance, you need to have made the decision and accepted a firm place. This is what you will put in on your student finance form.

Second, you need to think about your accommodation while at university. You need to think about the location of the accommodation; whether it's going to be catered or self-catered; whether you're going to have en-suites or whether you're going to have a shared bathroom; whether it's going to be a small flat with maybe only a couple of bedrooms, or whether it's going to be a big house. There were 13 people in the house that I lived in at university. You need to think about whether it's going to be for term-time only, or whether you can stay there and leave your stuff over the holidays. This way, even though you're paying for the time in the accommodation that you're not actually using, you don't have to move out and move back in again over Christmas, Easter, and potentially even reading week.

If there are any additional things that you are going to need at university, now is also the time to apply for them. Make sure that you've got everything in place. That way when you turn up for Freshers' Week in September or October, you are ready and raring to go—and you're not held back by having to fill in loads of forms, or waiting for a support cheque to come through, or waiting for accommodation allowance to be put in place.

If you're an international student, you will also need to get on with applying for visas.

Well done on accepting your place! Good luck with your exams that are coming up soon, but I'm afraid we still have loads and loads of things to do.

Results day

Preparing for Results Day

On A-Level results day, you're going to need to have two plans in place: one where things don't go as expected and you need to apply through Clearing; and a second where things go better than you're expecting, and you need to apply for an Adjustment place.

Spend time on the UCAS Clearing website and find places that will be available to you if you don't get the grades and want to apply through Clearing; do the same in case you get better than expected grades and want to apply through Adjustment.

You're eligible for Clearing if you didn't get any offers or if your university place isn't confirmed. The most likely reason your place won't be confirmed is if you didn't get the grades you needed. You need to have a plan in place for this before results day, because things are going to happen fast after this.

Places are going to be given away quickly, and you will not have time to do the planning on results day. You have to do it now.

You've got to be realistic. You're not going to be able to get a medicine place through Clearing because the grades are very high, so if you're not getting your grades for your firm choice, then it's unlikely you're going to be able to apply for medicine somewhere else. But have a look through and see if there's anything that catches your fancy because, things are going to move really, really quickly on results day. You need to get started as soon as you can.

What Happens on Results Day

On results day, it's likely you'll be tired from a sleepless night and things are going to happen very quickly.

In an ideal situation, you'll get exactly the grade you need to get into your first choice and you can go and celebrate with your friends.

The UCAS website will update at 8am, and any conditional offers you hold will change to 'firm' or you'll see that you have been rejected.

The UCAS website will tell you whether you've gotten into university or not, and your A-Level results will show your grades. There is the chance that if you don't exactly get your A-Level results, you might still get into university.

However, if you check the UCAS website before you go to school, you can see whether you've got into university or not irrespective of what your A-Level results are. It is possible to not get the grades you need and still get your place at university, this decision is completely at the discretion of the individual universities.

Schools will generally open early to give you your results, and they know UCAS track updates at 8am and they want to give you as much time as possible to apply via Clearing if needed.

You'll need to start acting immediately if you want to apply for an Adjustment place or if you need to apply via Clearing.

Applications via Adjustment

An Adjustment place is a place that you apply for when you get better than expected A-Level results.

To qualify to use an Adjustment place, you need to have met and exceeded your results. Say your offer was for an A,B,B with an A in Chemistry, and you got an A,A,B, but your B was in Chemistry. You may have exceeded your results—you got two As and a B, which is better than the A and two Bs they asked for—but you didn't get that A in chemistry, so you haven't met your offer even though you've exceeded it. You not only need to get better grades, but you need to meet and exceed any individual conditions placed within you offer. I know that sounds a bit weird, but you have to exceed your targets if you're going to qualify to apply for an Adjustment place.

You do not have a lot of time to do this. You have five 24-hour periods from the time that your offer turns to an unconditional firm offer. That might not be on results day; it might be the day after, or there might be some confusion and it might be a couple of days later. You cannot rely on there being any good Adjustment places because loads of places are full and universities want full courses. They're not going to save places just in case someone better turns up on UCAS results day. You need to be looking through the UCAS website and seeing if there are any places that you might want to apply through Adjustment.

You should have some ideas already mapped out, but you cannot rely on there being any decent places this year just because last year some spaces came available through Clearing. Even though universities want to fill all their places, some people will unfortunately not have gotten the grades that they want, and those places will then be available to other people—people such as you, who have got better-than-expected results and applied for Adjustment. Your original offer—the one that has turned from a conditional firm into an unconditional firm—is safe while you look around. They're not going to take that away from you just because you're doing inquiries about Adjustment places. It is only gone once you have confirmed your new place. So, be really certain that you want to change your place, because once you've confirmed your new place, your old place is gone.

The first thing you need to do is find the course you want, call up the university, and make it really clear to them you're looking for an Adjustment place. Give them your UCAS ID so they can log onto the system and find you. Tell them you are just looking around, that you just want information. You can call more than one place, but make it really clear to them that you haven't made up your mind yet. Once you have made up your mind (and remember, things are going to go really quickly, so spaces will fill up fast), call the university back and verbally confirm that you'd like the Adjustment place. They will then put it all through the UCAS system and it will change on the UCAS website for you. Only do this once you are very, very, very certain you want to change places.

This is an excellent situation to be in. It can be quite a stressful situation because you have to work quickly, but hopefully, some of you will get excellent new places from this.

Mason's Story – Results Day and Adjustment

I can't deny how nervous I was for results day. This was possibly one of the biggest days of my life. In comparison to receiving my GCSE results, this was an entirely different experience. We had been told by our college tutor that on the morning of results day, we would be able to check our offers. This would be on the UCAS website under tracking. If our results were good, our offers would show up as unconditional offers. It may also show the offers as conditional or no offers at all, dependant on our results.

The first thing I literally did after waking up was attempt to log on and check my offers. The server however was far too busy and the offers weren't loading. My mum had to drag me away from the laptop as I was obsessively pressing the refresh button. She told me to relax and that I would know my results shortly after arriving at college. So we made our way to college. I spotted my friends who had eagerly been waiting for me. Everyone was so nervous. You could feel the trepidation in the air.

We made our way to queue, and it was beyond busy. My stomach was in knots as I was handed my envelope. I couldn't open it immediately; I needed a quiet place where I could open it. Peeling back that envelope is probably one the most nerve-racking things I have done so far. I couldn't believe my results—they were so much better than I had expected or even wished for!

After phoning my family I went straight to my favourite tutor. She had always told me that she believed I could get better results than I was predicted. She immediately told me to check my UCAS (I had forgotten all about the offers by this point). I had unconditional offers! My tutor knew from our previous discussions that ideally I wanted to study a different course. Because I anticipated I wouldn't get the results I needed for that course, I settled for a similar course. She told me immediately to register for Adjustment on the UCAS website and to speak to our college UCAS adviser.

With Adjustment, I would be able to apply for a different course or even a different university whilst holding onto to my unconditional offer. This can only be done within five days. On the adviser's advice, and not wanting to let this amazing opportunity pass, I rang the university to ask if they still had places available on the course that ideally I had wanted to study. They told me they did and talked me through the process. I could be notified at any time. The suspense was still killing me as I went out with my friends to celebrate. Luckily, it was only a few hours when I received an email telling me something had changed on my offers page. I checked and I had been accepted. I couldn't believe it! Now I could finally relax!

Applications via Clearing

As soon as you find out that you haven't got a place at university, you need to start the Clearing process immediately. Universities do not want empty places; they don't like empty seats in lecture theatres, and they do not wish to have empty spaces on courses. They want them full, so they're going to be filling up their places as quickly as they can. They are not going to wait a week for you to decide and hold that place for you. They are going to be filling up quickly, which is why you need to have a plan in place before results day.

Now, one of the things you need to think about is whether the course you have applied for maybe has slightly too high requirements. Or maybe think about a different course; is there a slightly different course that has loads of space on it, just because it's a little bit non-traditional?

For example, I did Biochemistry with a year in industry, but maybe straight Biochemistry would have had lower requirements. One of my friends did Biochemistry with a year abroad, and they all had different entry requirements.

Electrical Engineering is quite hard to get onto, but one of my friends did Electrical Engineering with Psychology. It wasn't a very common course, but there were loads and loads of places left on it because people didn't think of combining the two courses. This is something you really should consider when looking for Clearing places, because you might be able to still go to your dream university. You could do a course that is 90% the course that you wanted, but maybe you just have to add Psychology or French or a year in industry onto the end of it.

Consider different locations and universities. You might have time to visit these, or you might not—because like I said, things happen very, very quickly after results day. Fortunately, YouTube is a fantastic thing for visiting places. You don't actually have to go to them, but if you can find time to see them in person, it is really worth it.

UCAS will list all the clearing vacancies on their website. Once you've had a look through the website, call up the university and talk to them. They're going to need your UCAS ID so that they can log onto the system and see your results and everything about you.

Get informal offers. Now, make sure the universities are very, very clear that these are just informal offers. You can get as many of these as you like, but don't take too long about it because these places are not going to hang around.

Once you have made your decision, and are confident that you're happy with your choice, you can add it to the UCAS website. The university will take over from there, and they will confirm it.

If they don't confirm it after a certain length of time, then you can add another one, but you can only add one at a time.

Helena's Story - What I Wish I Knew When I Was Applying

Some things aren't known until time goes on. One may make mistakes unknowingly and keep on regretting the past mistakes. While celebrating another year older, I have come to understand some lessons that I never knew before. Below are some lesson I wish I knew when I was young:

1. Stop worrying how other people think of you.
Whenever I made any decision or did anything during my young age, I was so worried about how other people perceived me or reacted to my actions. It's clear to me that if you keep on seeking people's validation, approval or respect, then you will never accomplish your goals. Even though every person has his/her own opinions, people's opinions are based more on their perceptions than actually anything you do. It's always good to rely on your own assessment rather than seeking other people's feedback.

2. Today is what is important
Always learn to appreciate and enjoy every moment that you get today, just because there is no guarantee for tomorrow. Do what you have done today and don't excuse yourself by saying you'll do tomorrow. Always know that tomorrow is determined by what we do today, and today's actions and decisions are the foundations of our future.

3. Believe in yourself
Always know that whenever you have confidence in your abilities, value, and contribution to society, then everyone will trust you. Have some faith in your intrinsic worth. Sometimes

we have something to offer, but the problem is that sometimes we may never know what it is. Sometimes we feel like we can't succeed just because we can't tackle a particular task, but we don't have to be able to see the end zone. This does not mean it will not happen; it's just a matter of time.

4. Money isn't the most important thing in life
Like any other young person, I grew up knowing that money is an essential thing in our lives. Once you don't have money, you feel unwanted, and you think that you belong to the low class. Even though we use the money to settle our bills, at the end, money isn't the goal. Getting a good job that will always keep you happy is a more motivating goal. Always learn that money can't buy happiness, and it does not insulate your pains and suffering. Money is just a currency that allows us to have something to eat, something to wear, and to live.

5. Life is not a race
Life is not about competing with your friends. Every person has his/her own unique goals to accomplish, and there is no need to hurry to get to your destination. Some people might think that you are lost just because you don't walk their way, without knowing that we all have different paths to reach our destinations.

6. Always see good in everything
Learn to stay positive. Celebrate with your friends at all the beautiful moments. Instead of criticizing others, give an encouragement reason for them to live.

Your Options if You Don't Get a Place

If you don't get any offers for a place at university, or if you didn't get the grades on results day that you need to take up your place at university, then you have lots and lots of options. Do not despair, it is not the end!

You can apply through Clearing. If you didn't get any offers, you're at a slight advantage with Clearing because you can plan ahead, but if you do have an offer and on results day you find you don't get the grades, you're going to need to have a plan in place in advance. You cannot leave Clearing until results day. Have a look at the UCAS Clearing website and see what courses and universities are available there.

Maybe you have your dream university in place and you just need to change your course ever so slightly. Would adding on a year in placement, or adding on a second subject like a language, change the grade boundaries ever so slightly? Even if they don't change the grade boundaries, they might still have places, and they might still accept you if they're under-subscribed for a certain year.

If you have a dream course in mind, could you change your university and go further away, or a bit closer to home? Can you change the type of university from a city to a campus? Ideally, you will have looked around at all of these places before you apply, but things can happen very quickly in Clearing, so that isn't always going to be the case. Use the internet, it's a fantastic place. There are so many people student vloggers on YouTube (see list on page 210, so you can actually get a feel for what the universities are like without having to visit.

Another option is to wait, and this is going to be a hard one. If there's nothing that catches your eye on Clearing, you can reapply next year. Get your application in as soon as it opens in September, so that you are right there at the beginning, at the top of the pile. You'll have your grades already sorted, so you won't have the stress of waiting around. Start planning now, and get your application in as soon as it opens. You can take this as kind of like an enforced gap year, and use this time to really, really bump up your personal statement and your CV and make it look amazing. And I don't just mean by going to work in the local supermarket or going to work in the local pub. You're going to need to get some fantastic work experience on there, some fantastic volunteering. Because you won't have school or exams to distract you, you can really focus on working out exactly what you want to do and exactly how you're going to get the experience to show that you're going to be amazing for this particular degree.

You also have the option of re-sitting year thirteen—or re-sitting year twelve and year thirteen—so that you can try and improve your grades. Now, some of you are going to be July and August birthdays, which means you are nearly a whole year younger than some of the other people on your year—this also means on results day, you may not even be legally allowed to celebrate with a drink in a pub! For some of you, this is going to be a big, big difference, and for those of you who maybe struggled a little bit, re-sitting year thirteen could be a really sensible and viable option for you. This will give you the opportunity to really think about what you want to do at university, really improve on your A-Level grades, and boost your personal statement.

You can think about whether you actually want to go to university at all. University isn't right for everybody. Maybe going out and getting a job straight away would be a better option. Maybe getting an apprenticeship or a degree apprenticeship course would also be something that might suit you a little bit better. Do not despair, everything is not lost. You have lots and lots of options!

Gap Years

If you are feeling burnt out after years in the school system, you can take a gap year between the end of school and the start of university. If you're going to go down this route and take a gap year, I'm afraid it can't just be sitting around playing computer games, hanging out with your friends, and working in the local supermarket. You have to have a plan, otherwise this gap is going to look weird on your CV, and it's going to be hard to explain to universities when it comes time to apply. This time can be put to such fantastic use.

You can go abroad and travel on an epic journey. You will be the envy of all of your friends who are back at home studying, especially when they see your Facebook and Instagram and see all the amazing places that you are visiting. (Although, making other people jealous shouldn't be a reason for you to go traveling!) You can go and teach English, or art, or drama, or music to under-privileged children in countries around the world where they don't have as many opportunities as we do. You can go work in hospitals or orphanages, or you can go and dig wells for communities. You can do things that can have a long-term, lasting impact on all the people that you're going to spend a year helping.

You can work in an animal sanctuary, or you could find an ecological conservation project that you're really passionate about. Maybe this links in with your degree, or maybe this links in with your long-term career goals. Maybe it doesn't, but then you could find a project where you can give back to the community while you're taking a year off.

If you want to stay local, then you can go work in a care home, or you can work on a community project, or you could pick a cause that you're passionate about and spend a year trying to make it better. Doing petitions, sorting out things in the local park, talking to the council, talking to the local community, trying to fix whatever projects—whatever thing that you decided needs fixing.

If you wanted to stay at home, you could be entrepreneurial. You could spend the year setting up a small business, and this has loads of advantages. It's going to give you loads of skills for when you get to university. You could be making money, and this could be a long-term thing that could keep you sorted out money-wise while you're at university.

You could go away from home and do a big working project. You could go work on a farm, you could go abroad and do fruit picking, or you could do a really interesting internship somewhere. This gives you the opportunity to learn skills related to the career that you potentially want to be following after university. If you're going to live abroad, you should immerse yourself in that culture. It maybe something completely different to what you're used to—or it may be somewhere that speaks English, but somewhere that needs an au-pair. Either way, you can go properly get into the culture, and learn the traditions and customs of your host country.

The advantage of taking a gap year is the massive wealth of experience you're going to come away with. You're going to come away with new skills, and you'll be able to get on with people that you didn't necessarily think that you'd get on with. You could be earning money while you're doing this. You've got the chance to be refreshed after years and years churning your way through the exam factory that is our school system. You're going to come out of this a little bit more mature, a little bit more independent than you were before. And you'll have time to reflect on what you're about to do next. Is university really what you want to be doing? You've got the opportunity to undertake a massive challenge, something that you'll really, really be proud of. Something that you can take and give back to the world, give back to communities that are less fortunate than us. Sometimes we take what we have for granted. We don't realize how access to clean running water, and access to electricity is actually a privilege that so many people in the world don't have. You have the opportunity to spend a year doing a little bit towards fixing these problems.

However, as brilliant as I think gap years are, there are a few disadvantages to them. If you don't plan them well, it can just be a massive waste of time. You may have all these grand plans to go off and save the world, but if you don't actually get around to doing it, then you're just sitting at home for a year, which is a dull waste of time.

If you go on an epic journey that will make everyone jealous, then that is going to be really expensive. You might have to work and save up for this. You might have to take a loan out from your parents, or from a bank, which you'll have to pay back, and that's a lot of money.

While you are off doing amazing, fantastic things, you may decide that you don't want to go back to university. Now, some of you may see this as an advantage, and some of you may see this as a disadvantage, but this could be a massive interruption in your life plan. Then the shock of going back into the school system—into the university system, into the exam system—might be a bit hard for you to get used to.

Then while you're off having amazing fun on all of your adventures, you may forget everything you have learnt at A-Level. So when you start in your first year at university, there are going to be people who have only been a few weeks out of A-Levels, and you may find yourself at a little bit of a disadvantage. Now if you decide to take a gap year, you're going to have to expect to talk about it in interviews and explain why you took it. Please make sure you have a proper plan in place for this. And if you do go off on a gap year, I'm very, very jealous!

Deferred Entry

If you want to take a gap year but still apply to university at the same as everyone else, then you can defer your entry. To apply for deferred entry is really easy: you just tick a little box on the UCAS application. But before you do that, make sure you check that the courses you're applying for actually accept students who have deferred entry. Some competitive subjects, some universities, and some courses don't like students who have deferred entry. They want students who come straight from school, so there's no gap in their studying. Before you apply for a course and deferred entry, make sure that they are going to accept you.

You're going to need to explain your decision to defer on your personal statement. You'll need to explain why you decided to take a gap year, and why you decided to defer your entry. If you can't come up with a good reason, or if you can't explain it well enough in your personal statement, then you're going to be in a little bit of a tricky situation. You're going to need to have plans (or at least an idea of plans) in place. You can't just turn up at the interview and say, "I'm going to play computer games for a year." Because, unless you're applying for computer games design, they won't see the advantage. You have to have a plan; you have to do something productive, something useful, something good with this year.

If you want to defer your entry after you've already confirmed your spot, then contact the university directly and see if they will allow you to make the change. If you've applied for deferred entry but then don't want to take that up anymore, this a little bit of a trickier situation, because the university might not have places for you straight away. If they've allocated your place for a year later, there might not be space for you to start this year.

If you want to take a gap year, the advantages of deferring entry are that you're going through the process with all of your friends at the same time. You're applying at the same time, getting offers at the same time, you have the whole experience on results' day and the anxiety about what is going to happen. And when it comes to teachers writing your references, you're much fresher in their minds as opposed to having to remember you a year later. Applying at the same time and deferring entry is going to be a much easier application process.

Your other option is taking a gap year and then applying a year later so you have your grades in hand. Now, you can go through the process with your peers, writing your personal statement, but don't actually apply. Leave your application till September and get it in right when the UCAS applications open. Because you're already applying with your grades, you can pick and choose your universities a little bit better because you know whether you're going to meet the grade requirements or not. And because you've done this, the universities might give you an unconditional offer. You might also have firm plans in place, because you've had more time to work out what you're doing on your gap year. When you apply for the UCAS deadline in January, you may not know what you're doing over the summer. But if you leave it for a year and apply when the next round of applications open in September, you might have got your gap year plans already sorted out so you can better answer questions in your personal statement and in an interview as to why you're taking a gap year and what you're going to get out of it.

If you're going to take a gap year, you've got two choices: You can apply with everyone else and defer your entry, or you can get your results and then apply and take your gap year later, knowing that you've got a place waiting for you when you come back. The downside of this is that you might be invited to interview while you're planning on trekking a rainforest or relaxing on a beach.

Gap years are fantastic, amazing things, but only if you use them properly.

What If You Make a Mistake and End Up at the Wrong University?

If you think you've picked the wrong university, then all is not lost. It happens. A lot. You have made a really big decision. Potentially the first big decision you've ever had to make by yourself. You've potentially moved really far away from home to study a subject that you've not studied before. You may have made the wrong the decision, and you need to know that **it's going to be okay.**

There are lots of things we can do in this circumstance. First thing you need to think about is: why do you actually think you've made the wrong decision? Is it something that we can fix easily, or is it a big thing?

Is it your accommodation that's making you unhappy? Are you a quiet person who has found themselves in a party household with roommates who are up all night? Are you in a flat with roommates that steal your food from the fridge and you're just not happy there? Could you potentially get in your own place? Obviously, it's going to be more expensive, but could applying for a switch in accommodation or getting your own place make you a lot happier? Would that solve the problem?

Or is it the course that you're not quite happy with? The majority of similar courses actually have the same first year, so you can make a slight switch in direction and still be prepared. Or you might have to catch up one more year, or you might maybe need to add on a language or a year abroad—or take one of those options off. Could a slight switch in course correct the problem?

But if those aren't the problem, and you really feel that you have made a mistake, there are two things you can do.

You can try and transfer universities. This is going to work fairly early on in the course, generally in the first few weeks of the first year if you just want to have a direct transfer. It's probably only going to work if you're going to transfer to similar course where you're not going to be too far behind. In this case, just call up the university you want, see if they've got spaces, and if they have, then they will talk you though the process of switching universities. If you want to switch universities between years, then this is going to be done via UCAS.

If you can't find a university transfer, or you're a little bit later down the line and you've realized you're just not happy where you are, then you can leave and start again. You can take a gap year. Maybe you'd be better off getting a job, or maybe you'd be better off going into an apprenticeship. Maybe you want to travel further away from home, or maybe you want to stay closer to home. And then you're going to just apply through UCAS like we did the first time—this time with your grades in hand, so you're likely to be able to target where you apply better. In your personal statement and your interviews, you can explain why your first course didn't work for you.

So if you have made a mistake, if you have gone to the wrong university or ended up in the wrong place, it's okay. Everyone makes mistakes. If we didn't make mistakes, we wouldn't be human. But this is ultimately fixable. You have loads and loads of options. So please, please don't worry too much. There are lots and lots of things you can do.

Glossary and Acronyms

A-Level – An A-Level is an advanced level qualification that is subject-based. A-Level is also referred to as the General Certificate of Education (GCE) and also works as a qualification for leaving school that is offered by U.K.-based educational bodies. The educational authorities of British Crown dependencies also award students the A-Level when they complete their secondary and pre-university education.

BMAT (Biomedical Aptitude Test) – BMAT is an established test of admission that is used globally by leading universities. The BMAT test is given so that students with the right skills and success aptitudes are selected for courses that are challenging within the dental, biomedical and challenging medical course. BMAT tests skills that include problem-solving, critical thinking, communication, application of scientific knowledge, and data analysis.

BTEC (Business and Technology Education Council) – This qualification has a number of different levels and can be equivalent to GCSE's or A-Levels but are more vocational in nature. These can be studies alongside GCSE or A-Level qualifications. They are more practical in nature and tend to cover subjects that are not traditionally taught at GCSE or A-Level

COPA (Cambridge Online Preliminary Application) – COPA is an application that allows individuals to collect useful data that may not have been part of UCAS applications. With the COPA application, one would make arrangements for their overseas interviews and any engaged organ trials. When completing COPA applications, they should be in addition to the UCAS applications. In the case of Cambridge University, the COPA applications must be received together with the UCAS one for an application to be valid.

Erasmus (European Region Action Scheme for the Mobility of University Students) – Erasmus is a program that works as a students' exchange in the European Union that was developed in 1987. The Erasmus program works with other independent but registered ones, and they are incorporated into the Socrates II program. The Erasmus program combines schemes for education, training and youth and sports.

GAMSAT (Graduate Medical School Admissions Test) – GAMSAT refers to a test that assists in the selection of students for graduate entry medicine. The test was developed by the Australian Council for Educational Research and also selects students for the dentistry and health science programs.

GCSE (General Certificate of Secondary Education) – GCSE is known as an academic qualification that is taken by students in the Wales, England and Northern Ireland countries. The qualifications for GCSE are based on particular subjects and they stand alone but within a suite of qualifications. GCSE sets qualifications that must be accepted as records of achievements by sixteen years. The GCSE examinations are taken within a period of two or three academic years.

HAT (History Aptitude Test) – HAT is known as a standardized test that acts as part of the Oxford University admission process. The HAT is only relevant for undergraduates who are making applications to read History or any subject that relates to History. An example of HAT tests includes the situations of students who intend to study subjects like English with History. The test is undertaken in a two-hour period and other universities are increasingly showing interest in them.

HIS (Immigration Healthcare Surcharge) – HIS is a service that focuses on dealing with the problems of medical tourism that involve the NHS in England. For someone to qualify the NHS free care, they have to be ordinary residents of the U.K., and a number of vulnerable groups are excluded from the free healthcare. The service is given under extensive guidance and all NHS organizations should follow the rules especially when checking eligibility.

IELTS (International English Language Testing System) – IELTS is a test that is an international standardization of proficiency in the English language. IELTS is compulsory for non-native language speakers of English and is jointly managed by the Cambridge English Language Assessment, British Council, and IDP: IELTS Australia. Since its establishment in 1989, IELTS has been accepted by many academic institutions in the United States, Australia, Canada, the U.K., and New Zealand.

LNAT (National Admissions Test for Law) – LNAT refers to an aptitude test of law admissions in the United Kingdom. LNAT was adopted in 2004 by law programs in eight U.K.-based universities as a requirement of admission for all people making applications from home. The test is often undertaken in two sections that take 135 minutes to be completed. When sitting the LNAT test, an individual is often allotted forty minutes to complete the required essay and a subsequent ninety-five minutes to answer the multiple choice questions that are forty-two in number. Both the essay and questions aim at testing the reading comprehension and skills of logical reasoning.

MAT (Mathematics Admissions Test (MAT) – MAT is an A-Level exam that is undertaken by mathematics students. Any student who wants to study mathematics at the University of Oxford must undertake the MAT test either in their schools or any local test centres. Once a student is interested in the test, they must register with their test centres through the Admissions Testing Service Website and have their tests via the Entries Extranet.

MLAT (Modern Languages Admissions Tests) – MLAT is an entry for particular undergraduate courses that focus on linguistics, modern languages, and related joint schools. The only known institution that uses the test is the University of Oxford and most of the U.K. candidates are requested to take the test particularly when interested in full-time education. The tests can be undertaken at the students' colleges and schools for students whereas individuals that don't attend schools can find a test centre and have their examinations.

MOOC (Massive Open Online Courses) – MOOCs are online courses that operate with the aim of achieving unlimited open access and participation by use of the web. MOOCs provide problem sets, readings, traditional course materials, and interactive user forums. The MOOC provisions work with an aim of supporting community interactions among students, teaching assistants, and professors.

NHS (National Health Service) – NHS refers to public health services in the U.K., including England, Scotland,

Wales, and Northern Ireland, among other nations. NHS was founded and works with principles of comprehensive services, universality, and freeness at the point of delivery. The health service systems operate independently and are politically accountable to their respective governments.

NSAA (Natural Science Admissions Assessment) – NSAA is an assessment that acts as a preparation course for all students who are seeking expert guidance on natural science course. NSAA is given based on the area of test and students undertaking their different A-Levels are given two-and-a-half hours every Sunday to engage in the tests. In the NSAA examination, the Mathematics section is compulsory.

NVQ (National Vocational Qualification) – is a qualification that can be gained while working. This allows students to gain more experience and on the job training. There are few or no exams with assessment done while working.

OLAT (Oriental Languages Admissions Test) – The OLAT is defined as a test that is paper-based and is designed to provide an assessment of the ability of candidates in analysing how languages work. The test is taken in thirty minutes for University of Oxford students and its joint schools and does not depend on students' knowledge of any language.

Oxbridge – Oxbridge refers to the portmanteau of Cambridge and Oxford. Oxbridge mixes the two universities because they are the oldest, most prestigious and most highly ranked universities within the educational facilities of the U.K. The term Oxbridge focuses on defining the two universities collectively against other British universities based on their characteristics and superiority of intellectual and social statuses.

PAT (Physics Aptitude Test) – PAT is an aptitude test that is mandatory for everyone who makes applications to study Physics and Philosophy of Physics at the University of Oxford. The test has no exceptions because every intending student has to go through it. In the past, PAT was given in multiple choice, but recently it is more exposed and students must indicate their work and how they reach their answers.

PPE (Philosophy, Politics, and Economics) – PPE refers to an interdisciplinary degree for both undergraduates and postgraduates. PPE combines study from the three disciplines of economics, politics, and philosophy. PPE was first offered at the University of Oxford as a degree course in the 1920s and it has produced notable graduates, including the Nobel Peace Prize winner Christopher Hitchens.

SAQ (Supplementary Application Questionnaire) – SAQ is an application that is submitted by undergraduate applicants of the University of Cambridge once they have submitted their UCAS applications. SAQ is made available to ensure that the university has complete and consistent data about the engaged applicants. SAQ is also important to assist in collecting information that may not be part of the UCAS applications.

SELT (Secure English Language Test) – SELT is a test that is approved by the U.K. visas and immigration. The test is approved for purposes of visa, and individuals planning to undergo it have to visit the Trinity College London. Two major types of SELT that are available for candidates include the graded examinations in spoken English and Integrated Skills in English.

TB (Tuberculosis) – Tuberculosis an infectious disease caused by the bacterium *Mycobacterium tuberculosis*. Tuberculosis is known to affect the lungs but can also cause harm to other parts of the human body depending on the region that is affected. Tuberculosis is majorly spread through the air in coughs, spits, sneezes, and speaks.

TEF (Teaching Excellence Framework) – TEF is a system that assists in the assessment of the quality of teaching within England-based universities. The TEF system is also found in some universities within Scotland and Wales. The TEF framework was introduced with the intention of providing a resource for students so that they can judge the teaching quality in universities and be part of increasing teaching excellence importance.

TSA (Thinking Skills Assessment) – TSA is an assessment that measures personal ability in critical thinking and skills that relate to problem-solving. The skills examined by TSA are presumed to be essential for success in every part of higher education. The University of Cambridge, the University of Oxford, and University College London are known to be the best and oldest institutions that offer the TSA assessments.

UCAS (Universities and Colleges Admissions Service) – UCAS is an organization that is based in the U.K. with a major role in operating all procedures of application in British universities. The organization operates as an independent charity that is funded by the fees charged to applicants and engaged universities. All services provided by UCAS come in online application portals, search tools, and directed advice.

UKCAT (U.K. Clinical Aptitude Test) – UKCAT is known as a test that is applied in the process of selection by the consortium of U.K. University Medical and Dental Schools. UKCAT is run by the UKCAT consortium and gives tests that are designed to offer information about candidates and their cognitive abilities. The tests take place using four reasoning tests that include the professional behaviour situational judgment test testing attitudes.

Printed in Germany
by Amazon Distribution
GmbH, Leipzig